# LAST STAND IN SINGAPORE

# LAST STAND IN SINGAPORE

The story of 488 Squadron RNZAF

Graham Clayton

*Ka ngarue ratau*
*We shake them*

RANDOM HOUSE
NEW ZEALAND

*This narrative is dedicated to a group of young New Zealand men that volunteered to serve their country in its time of need. They came from all walks of life and backgrounds for a common purpose — to stop the invaders from the east. Some died in that cause and many, many more suffered in mind and body for the rest of their lives.*
*Their story needs to be told.*

For more information about our titles go to www.randomhouse.co.nz

A catalogue record for this book is available from the National Library of New Zealand.

A RANDOM HOUSE BOOK
published by
Random House New Zealand
18 Poland Road, Glenfield, Auckland, New Zealand

Random House International
Random House
20 Vauxhall Bridge Road
London, SW1V 2SA
United Kingdom

Random House Australia Pty Ltd
Level 3, 100 Pacific Highway
North Sydney 2060, Australia

Random House South Africa Pty Ltd
Isle of Houghton
Corner Boundary Road and Carse O'Gowrie
Houghton 2198, South Africa

Random House Publishers India Private Ltd
301 World Trade Tower, Hotel Intercontinental Grand Complex
Barakhamba Lane, New Delhi 110 001, India

First published 2008

© 2008 Graham Clayton
The moral rights of the author have been asserted.

All photographs courtesy of Bert Clayton except where stated otherwise.
Front cover: A rare photo of an almost complete squadron of Brewster Buffaloes over the coast of Malaya.
Back cover: Air crew sheltering under the wing of a Buffalo (p.102).

ISBN 978 1 86979 033 2

This book is copyright. Except for the purposes of fair reviewing no part of this publication may be reproduced or transmitted in any form or by any means, electronic or mechanical, including photocopying, recording or any information storage and retrieval system, without permission in writing from the publisher.

Design: Sarah Elworthy
Printed in China by Everbest Printing Co Ltd

# Contents

| | | |
|---|---|---|
| Preamble | | 6 |
| Preface | | 9 |
| Acknowledgements | | 12 |
| Introduction | | 15 |
| 1 | To Singapore — the journey begins<br>*488 Squadron travels to its new posting* | 25 |
| 2 | An introduction to the East<br>*New experiences, sights and sounds* | 35 |
| 3 | The struggle to become operational<br>*Bad aircraft, no spares, limited training* | 51 |
| 4 | The arrival of the storm<br>*The Japanese invasion* | 73 |
| 5 | The beginning of the end<br>*A defensive collapse — too little, too late* | 103 |
| 6 | The end draws near<br>*Obliteration of the airfields and aircraft, evacuating to Sumatra* | 143 |
| 7 | Flight from the storm<br>*An ignominious departure, evacuation on the* Empire Star *and escape from the Japanese* | 173 |
| 8 | In the eye of the storm<br>*Arrival in Batavia and setting up for a second line of defence* | 207 |
| 9 | Of those that were left behind<br>*The final stand — six brave men POWs in Java* | 219 |
| 10 | Into calmer waters<br>*Escape again, reaching the relative safety of Australia* | 237 |
| 11 | Safe but still far from home<br>*A journey across the outback* | 243 |
| 12 | The aftermath<br>*Questions needing answers* | 249 |
| Appendix 1: 488 Squadron Personnel | | 266 |
| Notes | | 271 |
| Bibliography | | 272 |
| Index | | 274 |

# Preamble

Of all the characters that figure in any narrative, there is always one who will stand out because of his or her personality. 488 Squadron had such a character. His name was John R Hutcheson, born in Wellington, New Zealand. He was posted to 488 Squadron as a flight lieutenant after early war service with the RAF in the United Kingdom. Known to all and sundry as 'Hutch', he personified the typical Kiwi attributes of that time: bravery and a stoical outlook on life. His attitude was to 'give it a go'. He suffered hardship with humour and this endeared him not only to his commanding officer but to fellow 488 Squadron aircrew members and the groundcrew that served with him. He was to become a Flight Commander of B Flight of 488 Squadron during the Singapore and Batavia campaigns.

Hutch's nephew, Mike Hutcheson, kindly gave the author access to the diary notes and flying logbook that Hutch compiled during his time in the Far East, and the content of these notes figures significantly throughout the following narrative. I thought it fitting that the introduction that Hutch wrote all those years ago be printed here as a posthumous preamble to this narrative, as a tribute to his contribution to the defence of New Zealand at a critical time in our history. He survived the war after being shot down on many occasions before finally crash-landing in the jungle of Sumatra. He suffered continuing bouts of malaria in later years as a result of those experiences but died peacefully at home in 1984. He is remembered fondly by the surviving members of his squadron. For many years after the war his printing business in Tory Street, Wellington became a focal point for many of the ex-488 Squadron. In his own words:

> Many people to whom I have spoken have laid the blame for the loss of Malaya and the Netherlands East Indies on Britain. This is not just. To obtain a reasonable perspective of the Malayan Campaign one must realise that Great Britain had been through Dunkirk, the Battle of Britain, and a heavy reverse in the Middle East. All the equipment and men that had been lost had to be made good. At this time, the amount of Lend Lease aid that was being made available to Britain was of no account. Much of the equipment received by Britain was obsolete and only accepted to keep faith with the American

The inimitable Flight Lieutenant John Hutcheson 'Hutch' whose spirit said it all, seated in his Brewster Buffalo fighter aircraft at Kallang, Singapore in late November 1941.
*Ministry of Information, Singapore*

*manufacturers after the fall of France, which had placed the original contracts. I myself saw cases and cases of American aircraft that were destined to remain crated. They were of no operational use, for their day was already past. Therefore Britain herself had to supply all the needed equipment, or a very big proportion of it. She had to rearm herself against a possible German attack and to re-equip the Middle East forces.*

*Imagine how badly off we would now be had we lost the Middle East instead of Malaya. Possibly had we diverted sufficient equipment to Malaya to hold it, the Japanese would not have attacked, which would mean that the entry of America, at that stage anyway, would have been very problematical. To make Singapore strong enough to make it obvious to the Japanese that it would be a very tough nut would have required that equipment and men intended for the Middle East should be diverted with a consequent weakening of Egypt and the whole Middle East. Remember also that war was very real in the Middle East but only a threat so far as the Far East was concerned. There was always* the chance that it might be avoided. Sir Robert Brooke-Popham has often been criticised because he said that Singapore could withstand any assault. What else could he say? 'Come and attack us, Japan'? We could only offer feeble resistance. Certainly it was a bluff, but he had no choice.

Still, this is not a political argument. It is the story of Singapore as I, a fighter pilot, saw it. Certainly there was much that could be criticised, and many who did not do what they should have done, or did it badly. Generally, though, there is good reason to doubt that even if everyone had done their very best possible we could have held out much longer.

This is mainly the story of No. 488 (NZ) Fighter Squadron, a squadron with no experience and little training which was called upon to face up to odds greater than could reasonably have been expected. None of the pilots, with the exception of the commanding officer and his two flight commanders, had any experience of war. The rest of the pilots came straight from flying training schools in New Zealand, and against the standards of today had very few hours. Few if any of them had done more than twenty hours on Brewster Buffaloes at the outbreak of the Pacific War. Yet, in very inferior aircraft and with practically no training, they stood up without complaint to the best the Japanese could send.

Of the groundcrew personnel I cannot say enough. The social rules of the Far East debarred them from much of the society that they were accustomed to, for non-commissioned ranks rated equal with the native populace. They were not permitted to frequent the places that we commissioned officers could, and even we were not welcome. Before the war, to them (the local European population) service personnel were a 'dull and unnecessary bore'.

Our groundcrews worked terrific hours, had little sleep and bad food. Yet never once did they let us down. With inferior aircraft, hardly any tools, and only a will to fight, they backed us up to the hilt. They were the heroes. We could fight back. They could only repair and adjust. When the war came their way they could only cower in the slit trenches and pray. They placed more faith in slit trenches than prayer.

*John R Hutcheson DFC,*
*Flight Lieutenant, Flight Commander, B Flight*
*488 Squadron, Singapore, Java and Sumatra 1941–42*

# Preface

The mere mention of Singapore in historical terms raises visions of rubber tree plantations, and typically English people sitting in the cool of the evening on the verandas of their bungalows, sipping gin and tonics and being waited on by local servants. Thanks to the writings of the prolific English author Somerset Maugham, this picture epitomises the 'pukka sahib' mentality of the then ruling class in colonial Singapore early in the twentieth century. Pukka sahib ('true gentleman') referred to the attitude affected by many British administrators of being aloof, impartial but superior beings. This was the vision painted by Somerset Maugham, Joseph Conrad and fellow authors during that period and reinforced by many books and Hollywood movies. It was in fact a very accurate picture.

In the modern era, Singapore has had three very definite historical periods and the Second World War was the crucial element that changed the way of life for the island, the surrounding region and the whole of South East Asia generally. In fact, the way of life for both New Zealand and Australia was for a time very seriously threatened. We did not suffer the degradation that invasion and conquest produces but our place in the world and the attitude of a good number of our citizenry was changed forever by the effect these events had on those caught up in the conflict.

Singapore had been controlled at times in the seventeenth and eighteenth centuries by the Dutch and Portuguese until Sir Thomas Raffles stepped ashore in 1819. He recognised the island's strategic location in the Far East (as the British then referred to all lands on the Asian continent east of India) and signed a treaty with Sultan Hussein Shah on behalf of the British East India Company to develop Singapore as a British trading post and settlement. The island was ruled as a British crown colony from 1867. Thus, depending on which end of the social system you were born into, the island of Singapore and the mainland of Malaya enjoyed, or suffered, many years of colonial rule.

The onset of war ended that phase in its modern history. The British surrender to the Japanese forces on 15 February 1942 effectively demolished the colonial era in Singapore and in the Far East generally. Over 100,000 British military, and many thousands more of its civilian population, mostly

Chinese, were subjected by the Japanese occupiers to enforced labour and slavery. The local people saw their former ruling classes subjected to humiliation and degradation by their captors. There was no going back.

The indigenous population of this growing trading nation had three years of being controlled by another colonial power, the empire of Japan. When the Japanese were finally beaten in 1945 the British took back their territories. However, the locals did not welcome back their old masters with any enthusiasm, despite the terrible treatment meted out to them by the Japanese. Instead they seized the opportunity to make a bid for some independence. Despite the collapse of the Japanese Empire in South East Asia, the island of Singapore would never again revert to its days of colonial grandeur. Slowly, through the 1950s and 1960s, it began to find its own way in the world. Stirred initially by communist insurgents, ironically trained and funded by the British to fight the Japanese behind the lines, the political scene gradually moved towards a new independence from Britain. It became a self-governing state within the British Commonwealth in 1959. In 1963 it declared independence from Britain unilaterally before joining Malaya, Sabah and Sarawak to form Malaysia, but less than two years later split from the federation to become the independent Republic of Singapore on 9 August 1965. Its economy and standard of living have grown impressively since then. Today, the legacy of British control can be found in Singapore's laws and system of government, and in the colonial-era architecture, but the personnel, personalities and colonial systems that for a long time wielded power over the region are long gone.

Mention Singapore in the company of older people with a military background and you get a very sharp reaction. Whether they are army, navy or air force, they all remember the treatment given to those unfortunate enough to be captured by the Japanese Army. The trauma and pain of those experiences can be understood by anyone interested in researching or reading of the dreadful ordeals suffered by our imprisoned countrymen and -women in South East Asia during the Second World War.

Singapore, we must never forget, was the stepping-off point for the death camps in Thailand and Sumatra, and the port of embarkation for many thousands transported to the slave camps in Japan.

When 488 Squadron arrived in October 1941, the colonial era was still extant. The island's political and social systems supported colonial rule, and the New Zealanders encountered a mind-set that was to eventually cause them considerable distress. The class distinction particularly impacted on these men, and the pompous, racist attitude of the local expatriate community and the British military high command, without a doubt, caused the eventual collapse of the island's defences. A different attitude would have given a completely different outcome. Singapore was effectively given away to the invaders with tragic consequences for many of our young men far from home. They took no comfort from the fact that while England referred to this area as the Far East, the Australian and New Zealand people at that time worried about events unfolding just to the north.

I pondered long and hard why these young men of New Zealand, not only in the air force but also servicemen in the military generally, bothered risking their lives to fight for Great Britain. It is simplistic to suggest that they were motivated by loyalty to the Crown or some other factor. The ultimate truth remains that if Britain had been conquered by the Japanese, or for that matter the Germans, New Zealand, being part of the British Empire in those days, could potentially have fallen to the conquering powers. No invasion would have been necessary as New Zealand and Australia were territories of Great Britain and, unpopular though the decision may have been, could be pressured into surrender under the terms imposed by the invaders. On that basis, for those young men, the decision to be part of that defence was logical and simple. Through the changing circumstances of time, it is probably less easy for us in this day and age to comprehend their reasons for doing what they did.

The story of these brave young men is largely untold and this narrative will seek to put that right. Most of the ex-488 Squadron members that I interviewed had never discussed their experiences with family or friends and, to a man, downplayed their part in these events. They felt they were only doing a job at that time and only in very recent years, probably in the reflective times of old age, felt the need to talk about their experiences, and I am proud to have been the catalyst for that.

My story does not seek to answer any of the questions raised by this debacle as that has been well covered by others more skilled than myself, but it looks at the effect on just one of the many groups of young men that were involved in this conflict. I hope I do them justice.

# Acknowledgements

The author wishes to acknowledge the assistance of many people who contributed in some way to my project, helped with research and allowed access to documents, diaries and treasured family photograph albums. The list will never be complete:

Bee Dawson, Royal New Zealand Air Force Social Historian, who provided many pages of information and photographs, including transcripts of interviews she had carried out during her own research into RNZAF activities from the war years. It was her support and hard work on my behalf that ensured that this narrative saw the light of day and reached the people it was intended for.

Jane Provan, Research Curator at the Air Force Museum in Christchurch, New Zealand. Patient provider of information on archival material held on squadron activities.

Victoria Garrington, who was Jane Provan's successor at the RNZAF Museum.

Mike Hutcheson, nephew of Flight Lieutenant John Hutcheson, who kindly allowed me access to John's private diary notes and his pilot's logbook.

John King, editor of *Sport Flying Magazine*, with his many contacts who assisted with this research and his interest and support in the project. It was John's serialisation of John Hutcheson's diary that allowed me access to much valued material.

Ruth Adcock, widow of 'Johnny' Adcock, a member of 488 Squadron whose initial information set me on the right path in the early days of my research.

Hugh 'Red' Nelson, Clem Randall and Ted West, former members of 488 Squadron, for their interest and support in giving answers to the many questions asked of them.

Mona Randall, for her expertise in proofreading and the many hours she spent in editing the draft manuscript.

Stu Smart, ex-488 Squadron, for access to his personal photographs and general information on squadron activities.

Jim 'Paddy' Cromie, ex-RAF who was seconded to 488 Squadron, for his interest, support and provision of personal memoirs and photographs.

Max Boyd, ex-488 Squadron, for access to his personal diary kept throughout the squadron's time in the Far East. Max kept a comprehensive record on a daily basis.

Don Layton, whose response to my request for information on 488 Squadron led to contacts that proved invaluable in the construction of this story.

Barbara Kuhn, widow of Eddie Kuhn, who gave me access to Eddie's accounts of his experiences in prisoner of war camps in Java, Singapore and Japan. She also became the link to Eddie's comrade-in-arms, Jim MacIntosh, who shared the horror of the camps with Eddie.

P Joan MacIntosh, widow of Jim MacIntosh, for her support, and kind permission to use extracts from Jim's diary accounts of his experiences in Singapore and Java and subsequent imprisonment by the Japanese.

Rohan Greenland, fellow researcher in Australia, who shared his knowledge of the events leading to the death of Captain TKW Atkinson RN, the Singapore Harbour Master during the escapes by sea from Singapore.

Allan Jones, author of *The Suez Maru Atrocity*, who provided valuable information on the 'Hell Ships' and death camps of Sumatra and Java and the tragedy that faced the six pilots from 488 Squadron captured by the Japanese in Java.

Harry 'Bunt' Pettit and his wife Betty, for their ongoing support and kind permission to use data, diary notes and photographs collected by Bunt during his imprisonment in the death camps of Java.

I wish to record my appreciation of the historical and technical input by both David Duxbury and Robin Klitscher, and for their critique of my draft manuscript. And finally, my appreciation for the support and encouragement from Sam Hill and Margaret Sinclair of Random House New Zealand.

This narrative has been compiled by a very enthusiastic amateur with apologies for any indiscretions in advance. The author makes no apology for the use of material from many sources that add to the telling of this story. There has been no intention to infringe copyright. Where sources are identified, the quotations used are fully acknowledged and listed in the Notes and Bibliography.

Any opinions advanced are personal and as a good amount of material is sourced from anecdotal information, the passage of time may have dimmed its accuracy somewhat. If nothing else, any interest or indeed controversy raised by the publication of this narrative can only help to publicise a relatively unknown chapter in New Zealand's military aviation history. Hopefully, this will restore some dignity and a nation's heartfelt thanks to those young men that were part of New Zealand's effort to stem the tide of Japanese imperialism that very nearly reached our shores during the time of the Second World War.

Many of the photographs were scanned from precious family albums that were showing the ravages of time. They are no less priceless for the wear and tear of the passing years and provide important links to those surviving members of the squadron struggling with failing memories to make the connection with events from all those years ago.

Some of you reading this publication may have access to further information to add to the narrative and the author welcomes any contributions that build on what is known about 488 Squadron's time in the Far East. I make no claim that this is the complete story.

# Introduction

The Otahuhu Passenger Transport bus pulled into the kerb at Wyndham Street in Auckland City to pick up a solitary figure standing very forlornly with a small kitbag at his feet. It was late in the day on 31 March 1942. The man in a faded, battered khaki uniform, showing him to be an air force serviceman, stepped onto the bottom step. He looked tired and somewhat emaciated with skin the colour of burnished teak, as only could happen by being exposed to the tropical sun for some time. He asked for a ticket to his home in Otahuhu and offered an Australian 10-shilling note to the driver. 'Sorry mate,' said the driver, 'we don't take Aussie money.' The serviceman protested that he had no other, having just arrived by ship from Australia after escaping from the Japanese in Singapore. The driver just shook his head and as the serviceman turned to get back off the bus, a passenger got up and paid the fare. One would have wished that bus driver a very uncomfortable ride for the rest of that journey.[1]

That serviceman was my father, Albert Lionel Mark Clayton, and such was his hero's return to his home and safety. He walked from the Rutland Street Army Drill Hall after disembarking at the Auckland wharves, to catch the Otahuhu bus at the Wyndham Street stop. His air force squadron, having arrived back in Auckland, had paraded at the Drill Hall and the personnel were dismissed to return to their homes. Like most of his squadron, his one burning desire was to return to the safety and security of his home and catch up with a life seriously threatened over the past months. He walked out of that drill hall to find the Otahuhu bus and had a reasonable expectation that he would be treated better for defending his country from the ravages of the Japanese Army.

The following narrative is an account of the saga of 488 Squadron's operations in the Far East and the experiences at that time, through the eyes of one of its personnel, my father, Albert Clayton, known to his family and friends as Bert. He is an unassuming man and like many of his fellow servicemen speaks little of the deprivation and ordeals that he encountered during his time overseas during the Second World War. Up till very recent times the only knowledge our family had was from accounts related by my late mother Phyllis. It was said that on the night of his return from

My father, Bert Clayton, after enlistment in July 1939.

Singapore, he sat down with his parents, his younger brother Trevor and his fiancée Phyllis Graham to tell them of the events that led to his escape from death at the hands of the Japanese. He said at the time that he would speak only that one time of his experiences and thereafter never discuss the subject again, such was the trauma for him.

After the death of my mother in 1990, Bert embarked on what can only be described as a crusade to compile the family genealogy. Now into his late 80s, he is computer literate and corresponds with fellow genealogy enthusiasts all round the world. He and my mother were inseparable and her passing left a terrible void in his life. His new interest helped fill that void and his little flat at Mt Albert in Auckland has become a veritable repository for family history, not only his but of many other family members. At some stage in this process he found time to record his life's story and each of his children received a copy. It was constructed around his other passion, photography. It is a monumental work with every page telling its own tale.

On the face of it, Bert lived a very ordinary life. Like many other young men of his generation he enlisted at the start of the war. He joined the Royal New Zealand Air Force shortly before the outbreak of the Second World War, on 18 July 1939. Bert applied for aircrew training but pressure from his then fiancée, Phyllis Graham, and his family gave him second thoughts. Eventually, the RNZAF decided that he would be better covering a shortage of skilled groundcrew so the decision was made for him and, as later events proved, this was a very good conclusion. After his initial training in New Zealand he was posted with the newly formed No. 488 Fighter Squadron to Singapore. This was set up as a squadron under the control of the Royal Air Force of Great Britain but using New Zealand personnel. It was in fact the very first New Zealand based fighter squadron.

At that point his life story became very interesting. I got the feeling on reading his memoirs that he had downplayed his experiences during the time spent in Singapore. Significant events had taken place at that time. I undertook some further research on Singapore over the period that Bert was posted there and the intrigue deepened. The Japanese invaded just a month after his arrival and he and his squadron became embroiled in the debacle that had huge consequences for the Western world and for some time threatened the existence of lives in the whole of South East Asia, extending southwards to both Australia and New Zealand.

In just 70 days, General Yamashita of the Japanese Imperial Army led his invading forces down the Malayan Peninsula and forced the surrender of Singapore on 15 February 1942. He had allowed himself 100 days to complete the task. For the Allies and the Western world it was the most catastrophic loss in the Second World

War. The garrison at Singapore surrendered and well over 100,000 Allied military personnel became prisoners of war and many thousands of civilians became internees. The results of that surrender, and the events leading up to the capitulation, had a profound effect on the lives of countless thousands of people, and my father, Bert Clayton, was just one of them.

Bert survived his wartime experiences and continued as a career serviceman, serving for 24 years in the Royal New Zealand Air Force. Later in his career he was posted back to Singapore and our family lived there for almost three years from 1955 to 1958. It was an intriguing part of my life and the mystique of the East was further enhanced with the knowledge that, just a few years before, significant events had occurred around where we were living and my father had been part of that scene. He alluded to incidents that had taken place during his earlier time on the island but, as I recall, details regarding his involvement were very sketchy. Anything he spoke of generally referred to experiences relating to others. His personal reminiscences were non-existent and that encouraged me to find out more.

For most of our stay we lived within a stone's throw of the notorious Changi Prison and the evidence of earlier traumatic times could still be seen all around us. The Selarang Barracks, where the bulk of the prisoners of war were held, was just down the road and the beach-front at Changi where civilians were machine-gunned to death in their hundreds was within walking distance of our home. Terrible atrocities were carried out by the Japanese, and the scars, both on the landscape and in the minds of the people, were still very much in evidence. Bunkers on the Selarang side of Changi Airfield were still being excavated during our stay there. I recall watching these being worked on while passing by on my bicycle one day. Human remains had been unearthed and were being laid out on canvas sheets just below where I was standing. We also visited the area where Chinese civilians were massacred by the Japanese Army at Siglap. Research I have done in recent months has revealed a startling connection with 488 Squadron, the atrocities at Siglap and the area where 488 Squadron were billeted.

The military were still a big part of Singapore life in the fifties but the emphasis had changed to a fight against the communist influence in the area and some of the servicemen that served in Singapore fighting the Japanese were now back fighting a new enemy. These were still very unstable times even 10 years after the end of the war with Japan. The communists had infiltrated the jungles of northern Malaya using the skills they had been taught by the British during the Japanese occupation just a decade before. The communist influence and propaganda had permeated the local universities and colleges, so life in Singapore during our stay still had an element of danger due to the unrest in the community.

Singapore was on the verge of moving on from the British colonial regime that had ruled since the early nineteenth century and the communists were looking for a share of the action. In the days leading to our return to New Zealand, the city had taken on the appearance of those wartime years, with riots in the streets and burning buildings. Many died, including looters that were shot in Tampines village just a couple of kilometres from our home. Our next-door neighbours, living in the end house on the street, had an army machine-gun post set up in their front bedroom in case of trouble. Fortunately for us the weapons were not needed. Our school was close to Changi village and we were taken there and back in a wire mesh-covered army lorry with a Sikh army bodyguard in the back with us.

I decided to investigate the wartime period in Bert Clayton's life, and as the research developed, Bert recalled events, some of which answered questions he himself had pondered over the years. He survived these experiences, partly through luck and fortuitous circumstances, but also due to his bravery, and the dedicated efforts of others who had been largely unknown to him for all these years. We made contact with as many of his old squadron mates as we could find, by advertising in RSA magazines and posting contacts on websites. This led to reunions with mates he had not spoken to since the war years.

When the depleted and demoralised 488 Squadron finally returned to New Zealand in March 1942 many of the personnel were posted to other squadrons at home and overseas. This led to almost total lack of contact between its members in subsequent years. 488 Squadron was reconstituted and reformed with new members in the UK on 25 June 1942 at Church Fenton Air Station and served with distinction fighting against the Germans.

My research started with the internet. The word 'Singapore' opened a Pandora's box of information, considerable controversy and a large number of reference points for future use. The fall of Singapore had huge implications for life in South East Asia and the South Pacific. The changes wrought by the Japanese conquest changed forever the concept of colonialism and the Western world's hold over its territories around the world. The Japanese seized on the concept of 'Asia for the Asians' in an attempt to garner support for their expansionist policies in Asia and the Pacific. They damn near succeeded. For a long time our way of life in New Zealand was at great risk.

Bert and his squadron were an integral part of the defence of Singapore Island, and the subsequent collapse of those defences into annihilation and defeat was totally out of their control. His squadron contributed in no small way by slowing and delaying the enemy advance which had been emboldened by a string of successful skirmishes. It has been said that this delaying action caused the Japanese to reconsider their attack on Australia and New Zealand. It gave the Allied forces time to regroup and, with American help, form a considerable naval force which was able to stem the advance and change the Japanese plans of conquest.

The intrigue and drama of those times is the subject of much discussion even today, despite being some 65 years after the event. Many of those mates that served with Bert have passed on now and my contact with the remaining families revealed a common theme. Those young men who escaped with their lives from that island never quite recovered from the stigma that the defeat and surrender produced. They always felt they had been deserted in their time of greatest need by those they were trying to help. To a man, they understated their experiences. Most families reported that very little detail or information was disclosed or discussed by the returned men. They carried considerable bitterness right into old age. They were resentful that after their return to safety in New Zealand and the hell they had been through, the air force high command saw fit to break up their squadron and disperse the men throughout other squadrons. There may have been very good logistical reasons for this action, but at a time when they were psychologically most vulnerable they lost the support of those who had shared the trauma with them. Little wonder that many of the spouses of these men reported their husbands having nightmares, in some cases up until the day they died.

They effectively escaped Singapore and then Java (in the Dutch East Indies, present-day Indonesia) by the skin of their teeth, managing to leave by the last large ships that departed both islands before their capitulation. There was much speculation that those who escaped in the final hours before the capitulation of Singapore actually deserted. That theme found considerable support after the war, particularly among the thousands who were trapped on the island and eventually captured by the Japanese to face humiliation, deprivation and death in the prison camps of South East Asia. Clearly the stigma of desertion was also a factor in the bitterness that these 488 Squadron survivors felt. They had escaped in controversial circumstances while countless thousands of others had not been so fortunate.

The aircrew, who fought against impossible odds, rightly gained a lot of publicity and this must have given those who survived something to cling to in later years. Not so for the groundcrew. They were merely pawns in the wider machinations of the bureaucratic disaster that unfolded. They were very much aware of their own value and the need to be part of the defence of their own homes to the south. They were cruelly denied the opportunity to regroup until the very last moment. They watched their own aircrew flying away to safety and had to suffer the ignominy of watching groundcrews from other squadrons being repatriated to service their own aircraft and support their own aircrew. There was the inescapable realisation that those replacements were being favoured by the British authorities, while they were to be sacrificed so that those that were substituted for them could escape the approaching conflagration.

The vehicle for the salvation of 488 Squadron was the merchant navy ship, the MV *Empire Star*. The saga of the *Empire Star* has been the subject of much discussion in books and documents since, and the ship is linked forever with the fall of Singapore and the ultimate collapse of Western rule in the Far East. That link with 488 Squadron and its New Zealand personnel is explored in this story.

It should be noted here that 488 Squadron was to all intents and purposes a New Zealand air force squadron, although its official designation was 488 (NZ) Squadron, Royal Air Force. When the squadron was first formed at

Rongotai, Wellington, in September 1941, New Zealand still considered itself part of the British Empire, and its citizens simultaneously British and New Zealanders. Contemporary documents list the squadron that way. The squadron was under the control of the British military at all times during its existence, even though the vast majority of its personnel were New Zealand born. This distinction will become more important as this narrative is told.

Later historians have used the designation RNZAF instead of RAF, and while generally accepted in principle, this is not strictly correct. Proof of this is found when trying to access official 488 Squadron histories. These are available only from British Defence archives in England; very little official data on the squadron can be found in New Zealand Defence Force archives.

A decision was made with this narrative to use place names current at the time that events took place but reference to the maps and illustrations that occur through the various chapters should allow the reader to identify the modern-day equivalents of those places.

This, then, is the story of 488 Squadron and specifically of one of its groundcrew members, Bert Clayton. It describes the events that led to an escape from the Japanese invasion of South East Asia in 1941 and the subsequent shambles that was the defence of Singapore. It tells of the final journey and death of a squadron.

Bert Clayton receiving his service medal in 1957.

Keppel Harbour and the city of Singapore in 1941.

one

# To Singapore — the journey begins

### 488 SQUADRON TRAVELS TO ITS NEW POSTING

On 11 September 1941, at just 23 years of age, Bert Clayton boarded the SS *Tasman* at the Wellington wharves with fellow members of No. 488 Squadron (NZ) of the Royal Air Force. The squadron had earlier assembled at Rongotai Aerodrome in Wellington. The groundcrew was made up of specialist technical people handpicked from all over New Zealand. The aircrew, by contrast, were almost straight out of training school.

The ship left at 4pm for the long sea voyage to Singapore. Other than a few senior officers none of the air force personnel had any idea of their destination. Sea voyages at that time were fraught with danger due to the ever-present menace of submarines and German surface raiders, who had sunk numerous ships in the waters of the South Pacific. Security was tight to prevent ship movements being relayed to the enemy by fifth-columnists or spies. The war with Germany had been under way since late in 1939, and although Japan had yet to enter the fray, wartime conditions were imposed. The *Tasman* headed out past Barrett's Reef and through the Wellington Heads, followed the coastline northwards until clear of the northern tip of the South Island and set a northwesterly course for Sydney. The aircrew and officers were allocated cabins but Bert and his fellow groundcrew slept on mattresses on deck, albeit under temporary covers. The weather was bad and the sea rough. Bert stood against the stern rail of the ship and watched the coastline of New Zealand being swallowed up in the darkness as the ship powered away into the night. He thought sadly of those he had left behind, his family and his beloved fiancée Phyllis Graham. He wondered if he would ever see her again. He was heading off into the unknown for the very first time in his life.

The rolling of the ship and the fact that their accommodation was right next to the cooking galley caused discomfort that continued for the four days it took to reach Sydney. The food served up was oily and almost inedible. The impact of smells coupled with the badly cooked food and the gut-wrenching motion of a ship in heavy seas meant that little food was eaten during the voyage, and it was with some relief that the coast of Australia was reached and the calm of the inner harbour settled their gastric juices. Bert recalls the imposing sight of the Sydney Harbour Bridge highlighted by the afternoon sun.

The squadron enjoyed Sydney for eight days. They were given a relatively free rein and spent time sightseeing, taking in most of the attractions and scenic parts of the

Final view of New Zealand from the departing SS *Tasman* at Wellington Heads.
*Collection of Stu Smart*

The main contingent of 488 Squadron on board the SS *Tasman* on the way to Singapore in September 1941. Bert Clayton is third from left in the very back row.
*Official RNZAF Photograph*

largest Australian city. What food they had on the boat seemed to cause an outbreak of diarrhoea among many of the airmen and that took the gloss off the first couple of days.

On 23 September the *Tasman* left Sydney Harbour heading out into the Tasman Sea towards the Pacific to an unknown destination. Some of the squadron were left behind due to overcrowding on the ship and followed on later in the month. On board were 96 officers and airmen. After a few days' sailing they were told that their next port of call would be Port Moresby in New Guinea. By that time they had the food situation sorted out, by complaining to the senior officer on board, Flying Officer Ernie de Suza, whom Bert had worked under at Hobsonville Air Base. The weather was much calmer and conditions improved markedly.

The ship arrived at Port Moresby in the early morning hours and anchored offshore. There was limited deep water in the port so the airmen travelled by barge into the wharf area. Temperatures were well into the 30s but summer kit had been issued so they were better equipped to deal with the heat. They spent just the one day in Port Moresby, having managed to get a good feed of steak and chips and peas. Bert and his mates met up with an Aussie air force serviceman who took them into a local café, and Bert reckoned it was his best meal since leaving New Zealand. Later that evening they left Port Moresby and sailed through the Torres Strait, passing close to Thursday Island and into the Arafura Sea. The water was as smooth as glass, with not a breath of wind. The only sounds were the throb of the engines and the sound of the bows cutting through the ocean. Bert saw his first tropical sunset that night.

It was to be the calm before the storm. The *Tasman* continued through the Timor Sea and on to the port of Surabaya on the northern coast in the east of the island of Java. This stop was to put ashore a party of oil engineers who had travelled from New Zealand. One of them had given a lecture on board ship about oil exploration in Taranaki. He indicated that oil had been found and the wells had been sealed for later uncapping. This was, of course, in 1941.

On board lectures were held and gave some clues as to the ultimate destination of 488 Squadron. Much information was given on an aircraft known as the Brewster Buffalo, so the more astute guessed that

First tropical sunset in the Torres Strait.

the airfields of Singapore would be the squadron's target. Shipboard life was relaxing and quite boring, the quiet times being enlivened only by organised games and competitions. The airmen were restricted to their section of the ship; the ship was also carrying a complement of civilians.

When the equator was reached the uninitiated were introduced to the Crossing the Line ceremony, a tradition celebrated on board all ships crossing the equator. Those who had never crossed the line were plastered in flour and water and unceremoniously dunked in a large tank of water set up on the deck.

Singapore Island was reached on 10 October 1941. The ship berthed alongside the wharves at Keppel Harbour, and following a medical inspection the squadron members disembarked and were trucked the few kilometres around the coast to Kallang Airport, which was to be their base for the duration of the Far East campaign. It was the main airport on the island and when built just a few years before, in 1937, was credited with being the finest in the Empire — it was soon to be known as Japan's

Kallang Airfield in early 1941.

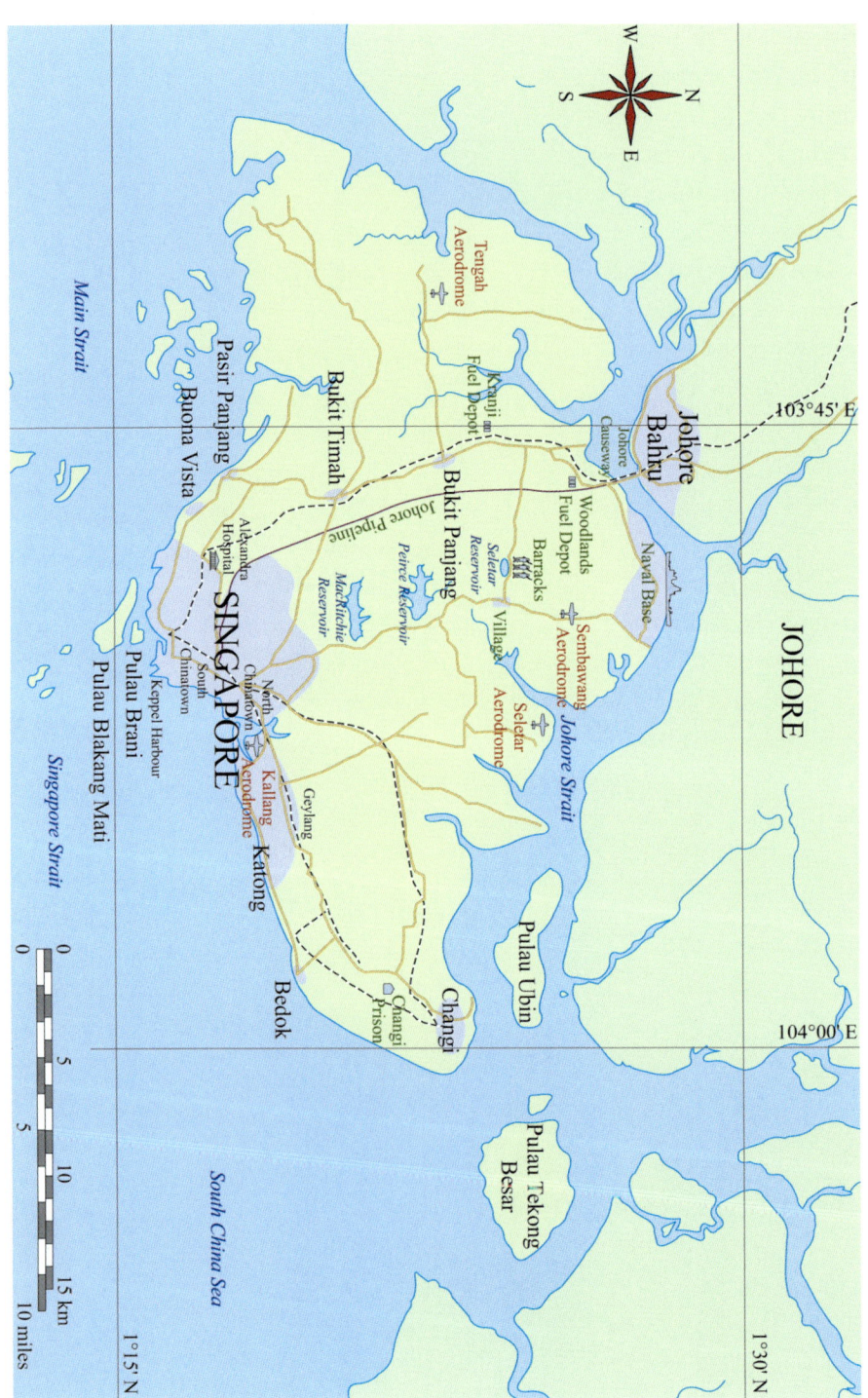

finest target. It was a circular area built on reclaimed swampland of roughly 1500 m diameter, slightly domed in the centre to facilitate drainage; it was unique in that it was built using coolie (local unskilled Chinese) labour. Two hundred thousand tonnes of earth a month was cut and transported from hills over 6 km away. Its use as a military airfield was limited as it had no natural protection and was totally vulnerable to attack from the air. On the seaward section of the perimeter was a slipway for the flying boats of Imperial Airways. There were three other military airfields in use at the time on the island, Tengah, Seletar and Sembawang, scattered around an island of only 580 sq km (an area that has since grown through reclamation to over 700 sq km).

Recently opened following years of construction on the northern shores of the island at Sembawang was the new British naval base. This had cost England in excess of £60 million to construct but had over 30 sq km of deep-water anchorage, huge oil-storage capacity and an enormous floating dock. The British Government had approached Australia and New Zealand to contribute support costs to the project as early as the 1920s. After the opening of the naval base, Singapore became known as 'Fortress Singapore'. This name was

Opposite: Singapore Island showing the airfields in use in 1941.

## Singapore

*The island of Singapore, measuring just 42 km by 23 km, is located between the Indian Ocean and the South China Sea and is situated at the convergence of some of the world's major sea-lanes. It is separated from Indonesia to the south — at the time, a major Dutch colony known as the East Indies — by the Singapore Straits and from mainland Malaysia to the north by the Straits of Johore (a causeway spans the straits to link the island with the Malayan Peninsula). Singapore Island is composed of a granite core with Bukit Timah at 166 m being the highest point.*

*The island lies 137 km north of the equator. Its climate is uniformly hot with high humidity and abundant rainfall throughout the year.*

further enhanced when the navy put in place batteries of 15-inch guns with a range of over 30 km around the southern coast, supposedly to protect the island from a seaborne attack.

Although October was in the cooler time of the year the heat practically bowled the new arrivals over. Not the cooling breezes of a moving ship at sea! Most of the half million population in 1941 were centred on the port area. The main bulk of the island was covered in regenerated jungle interspersed with rubber tree plantations. The island was a Crown colony administered by the British and one of the principal trading ports of the world for the export of tin and rubber.

Prior to the outbreak of the war, Malaya and Singapore combined had a population of 5.5 million. Europeans totalled just over 28,000 and surprisingly there was a resident Japanese population of 8000. Singapore alone had a civilian population of 500,000, 75 per cent being Chinese and 8000 European. With the huge influx of military the island became known irreverently by local Europeans as the island of 'Chinks, drinks and stinks'. To others it was known as 'a first-class place for second-rate people' in reference to the local European population, or the 'pukka sahibs' as Bert referred to them.

A walk down any of the narrow city streets meant the senses were assailed by the sounds and smells of the East. Rickshaws plied for hire in the sweltering heat, the aroma of exotic spices masked the stink of dreadful sanitation, and the babble of many languages and dialects was foreign to the English-speaking ear. Chinese, for instance, consisted of Hokkien, Hakka, Cantonese, Teochew and Straits-born Peranakan; each group also had their own political parties and belonged to their own kongsi, or clan organisations, often operating as secret societies.

The ethnic groups were divided into kampongs or

villages. The Europeans lived to the northeast of the government offices or in the spacious western garden suburbs. The Chinese community lived mainly around the mouth of the Singapore River, with Indians in Kampong Kapor and Serangoon Road, Muslims in the Arab Street area, Tamil Muslims in Market Street and Malays on the northern fringes of the city.

Rigid social segregation was enforced among the European community. The expatriate elite, a few thousand planters, bankers, shipping executives and civil servants, lived a life of leisure playing tennis, cricket or bridge, dancing, or drinking at the Raffles Hotel and the Tanglin Club, both of which reluctantly admitted military officers but were off limits to other ranks. Any non-European was forbidden, even if moneyed or titled.

The harbour and its port facilities, if not the largest in the world, were certainly among the busiest. The Singapore Roads, as they were known, held lines of ships awaiting access to the port facilities. These were the days before container ships and most of the unloading and loading was done using coolie labour. Along the harbour frontage and up either side of the Singapore River were large, ramshackle storage buildings known as godowns, many constructed in the late 1800s. All around the harbour small sampans plied their trade, each propelled by a Chinese standing up in the craft moving it along in a series of zigzags using a large single-sweep oar. The sampans on the Singapore River held several generations of families who were born, lived and died on them, and hardly ever stepped onto dry land. It was a very interesting and intriguing place.

Early-morning tropical humidity in the jungle fringes around Kallang.

two

# An introduction to the East

### NEW EXPERIENCES, SIGHTS AND SOUNDS

The new commanding officer of 488 Squadron stood on the dock with a small group of servicemen and watched the SS *Tasman* arrive in Keppel Harbour. He was New Zealand-born Squadron Leader Wilf G Clouston DFC of the Royal Air Force, who had seen service in England with No. 258 Squadron. He had been dispatched to the Far East to take charge of the inaugural New Zealand fighter squadron and had arrived on 19 September 1941.

Clouston had been flying for the RAF since arriving in England in 1936 and had won the DFC for his exploits during the Battle of Britain. He was described by one of his ex-258 Squadron members as 'a fierce dark man with a formidable personality, a name to conjure with in flying history'. His successor at 258 Squadron, Squadron Leader Jock Thompson, was said to have had to face an 'intensely difficult task ahead, taking over from a legend'. Such was the reputation that Wilf Clouston enjoyed among his peers during his time in the UK.

Clouston had filled in time until 29 September 1941 when he alone formed the official reception committee for his two new flight commanders, who arrived on board the flying boat *Corsair* from the UK. They were Flight Lieutenants John N 'Mac' Mackenzie DFC and John R Hutcheson,

Squadron Leader Wilf Clouston DFC.

The Brewster Buffalo — 'a nice old gentlemen's aeroplane'.

also both New Zealand born. (John Noble Mackenzie was the grandson of a former prime minister of New Zealand, Sir Thomas Mackenzie. He left New Zealand for the UK in 1937 to join the RAF and had an impressive record during the Battle of Britain before joining 488 Squadron in Singapore.) Clouston had been Hutcheson's commanding officer in the UK. After seeing them through Customs he took them to the mess and shouted them some of the local brew. 488 Squadron was now three strong.

The two new flight commanders shared an adventurous journey out to the Far East. They should have arrived by sea but instead made a series of hops from the other side of the world. They began by ship to Freetown in Sierra Leone, ferried Hurricane aircraft to Cairo in Egypt, then carried on to Karachi in Pakistan by an Imperial Airways flight and then another flying boat to Singapore. They must have been more than ready for that beer. Hutcheson was to remark much later that he wished they had stayed in Cairo.

The next day, both Mackenzie and Hutcheson introduced themselves to the Brewster Buffalo single-seat fighter aircraft and the phrase 'a nice old gentlemen's aeroplane' was born. The pair were absent for each of the next few days familiarising themselves with the idiosyncrasies of the Buffalo, courtesy of No. 67 Squadron of the Royal Air Force — this squadron had a pilot strength comprised of more than 90 per cent RNZAF personnel. These were the aircraft that 488 Squadron would eventually inherit after 67 Squadron left for a new posting in Burma.

They both had a close shave on 3 October when Mackenzie hit the back of Hutcheson's tailplane during a tight manoeuvre. I guess Mackenzie would have been buying the beer that night. It was reported that Mac thought it very funny but Hutch's comments were not reported. On 4 October Wilf Clouston joined them and the three caused havoc among the Chinese coolies working on Kluang Aerodrome on the mainland of Malaya, north of Johore, by carrying out very low level mock bombing attacks. The coolies were clearly not amused so the trio returned to Kallang without landing at Kluang.

On 5 October the strength of 488 Squadron increased by another three, an advance groundcrew party consisting of Leading Aircraftmen Ken Burnell, Ray Gillatt and Eric Hooper. They were all on the wharf again five days later to welcome the Dutch troopship the SS *Tasman*. The

The original 488 air crew (from left): John Hutcheson, Bunt Pettit, Tony Cox (bending over), Terry Honan, Grahame White, Jack Meharry, Frank Johnstone, Vern Meaclem, Eddie Kuhn, Perce Killick, Jack Burton, Deryck Charters, Don Clow, Jack Godsiff (front left, kneeling) and Peter Gifford (front, kneeling).

squadron was now almost a reality. 488 (NZ) Squadron Royal Air Force was officially designated and formed six days later on 11 October 1941.

The aircrew, who had received only basic training in New Zealand on Harvards, were sent north on 12 October to Kluang, in Johore on the Malayan mainland, for a conversion course on Brewster Buffaloes. The pilots were reported as not being particularly thrilled with Kluang. They had travelled over the causeway at Johore by rail in decrepit railway carriages hauled by tiny steam-engined locomotives with shrill, piercing whistles. They had left Singapore station at 12 noon, arriving hot, tired and hungry at 8pm after many stops on the way where, according to Jim MacIntosh, they were harassed constantly by locals selling all sorts of commodities.

Mackenzie provided those at Kluang with some light relief when he and Hutcheson tried to make a sneaky, surprise visit on 13 October and, much to everyone's amusement, Mackenzie arrived with his undercarriage warning horn blowing at full pitch and making a terrible racket. A faulty lead was the cause.

The final batch of two sergeant pilots and nine airmen arrived in Singapore the same day on the SS *Boutkae*.

Front door of Hut Seven, Bert Clayton's first home in Singapore.

They had been left behind in Sydney due to overcrowding on the *Tasman*. The newly formed squadron consisted of 12 officers and 143 men, nearly all of whom were New Zealand born despite 488 being set up as an RAF squadron.

Bert and his mates initially found the accommodation at Kallang a bit daunting. The barracks were single-storey, timber-framed and weatherboarded huts on concrete floors with attap or palm leaf roofs. Beds were spaced down either side of the room and privacy was non-existent. The barracks were a good 20 minutes' march from their work area on the opposite side of the airfield so getting there and back was a real effort in the tropical conditions. They were positioned on the seaward side of the airfield, completely open and exposed with no natural cover to protect them from the elements. The sun beat down mercilessly, although some relief was gained when the work areas were reached, due to their open-ended construction that allowed the sea breezes to waft through. A line of slowly rotating fans attempted to cool the barracks. Everyone slept under mosquito netting as the tropical night air brought out stinging, crawling and biting creatures and insects that most New Zealanders had never seen before.

Clem Randall found the accommodation good but was disgusted with the mess facilities for the airmen. The food was, in his words, 'inadequate and couldn't even

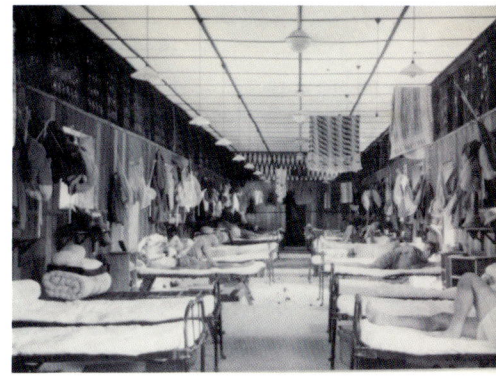

The interior of Hut Seven — Ray Stephenson looking slightly disturbed.

An introduction to the East 39

## ✈ Coping with the conditions

The weather played a big part in the lives of these men. There were no great temperature changes between seasons. The most marked was the start of the monsoon season and the heavy, though isolated, downpours, when rain would descend in huge quantities. It was possible, however, to simply cross to the other side of the road to avoid the rain as there was insignificant wind at any time of the year and the rain was mostly vertical. Most of the residences and other buildings had no guttering or spouting systems as these would have been unable to cope with the volume of water. All stormwater was carried away by concrete run-offs to deep concrete monsoon drains which ran down both sides of most urban roads. There was also a weather phenomenon known as a sumatra, which arrived moments before a tropical downpour. This was a barrier of air pressure which preceded the rain and was a timely signal to take cover. The majority of evenings saw the spectacle of sheet lightning which flashed continuously, without the accompanying thunder, and would last through the early evening.

The high humidity took its toll on equipment and body alike. Shoes, leather goods generally and most clothes in a very short time hosted mould. After some time in the Tropics most of the 488 Squadron boys adapted to the conditions. The worst toll was on the

> body, which was used to changing seasons in New Zealand but did not adapt well to constant heat and that scourge of the Tropics known as 'prickly heat' which was roundly cursed by all and sundry. Constant showering to nullify the heat brought its own problems, bacterial infection of the feet with tinea or athlete's foot being particularly prevalent. Mosquito-borne fevers such as dengue and malaria were not uncommon but most health problems were kept in check with regular medication. The heat also caused the notorious Dhobi Itch, a rash that targeted the crotch or groin. The cure was to apply Menthol Violet paint to the infected areas and this, according to Bernard Grindrod, made the communal showers look like something out of Disneyland.[1] In time, though, physical injury resulting from the conditions of warfare tended to render sickness and disease more and more insignificant.

be classed as of a very low quality. The half-full bucket of tepid greasy liquid in which to rinse your cutlery was a shocker.' Needless to say, very early in their stay they kicked up merry hell for better facilities. They were appalled to find that the RAF airmen were happy to accept these conditions. The New Zealand boys had considerable support from their senior non-commissioned officers (NCOs) and officers and in a very short time things did improve. What rankled was the canteen next door to their mess run by the NAAFI (Navy Army Air Force Institute) where you could go for the best of meals, provided you were prepared to pay for the privilege. This was operated at a profit, but the same organisation ran their Airmen's

Mess. Later in the campaign when their mess was blown to pieces in a bombing raid, the airmen took great pleasure in ordering the NAAFI staff out of the place and taking over their own catering until a new mess was established a couple of kilometres away.

The nightlife was centred on Lavender Street in the city or the Worlds: Happy World, Great World and New World entertainment parks. Happy World was an establishment on the outskirts of the airfield perimeter and, although set up initially as an entertainment centre for all ages, was quickly changed to cater for the large number of military prior to the start of the war. The site consisted of roughly built dance halls with open verandas facing the street where what were known as 'Taxi girls' posed and paraded. Servicemen would be persuaded to purchase tickets for drinks and dance partners and choose girls from those displayed on the verandas. It would appear that these establishments were reasonably tightly controlled but an adjacent establishment catered for what my now elderly confidants called 'the naughty bits'. Happy World was, unfortunately, in a line with the main hangars on the airfield and suffered bomb damage in the very first air raid on Kallang. It was eventually destroyed during a later raid.

The work programme was relatively easy at first, as the squadron under training was working to what Bert called pukka sahib rules. The colonial mentality of the British Empire was endemic to Singapore and this was reflected in the military serving on the island. The British High Command had control and the Kiwi work ethic was to be sternly tested. At the start the work hours were laughable, for example 7.30am to 12.30pm, home for a two-hour lunch and then most afternoons off. Every Wednesday was a half-day holiday or sports day and no work was allowed on Sundays.

Uniform was another matter. Tropical kit was expected at all times: shorts, shirt, pith helmet, socks and shoes. The socks and shoes were taken off at the slightest opportunity and replaced with sandals or flip-flops (jandals). Barefoot was a no-no as the notorious tropical hookworm parasite was very prevalent. Socks were never left lying on the floor overnight as they became host to a plethora of biting creatures.

There were some hilarious events, particularly when a new uniform issue was made shortly after arrival. Someone in the central stores must have had an exaggerated concept of the size of the average New Zealander, as the clothing was more suitable for a legion of giants.

Bernard Grindrod remembers well the day of the clothing issue. The airmen swapped gear among themselves to make the situation even more ridiculous and organised a clothing parade outside the RAF Commander's Office on the station parade ground. Squadron Leader Clouston went along with the farce and

Top: Tropical Issue! Bert Dunn, 'Squeak' Herbert and 'Fitz' Fitzgerald.

Centre: First uniform issue: George Clancy in front, Jim Boddy at rear.

Below: Hut boy shining shoes.

An introduction to the East   43

ordered all the officers to parade also for a mock inspection. It was a riot with much hilarity, but the point was made and better gear was issued from that day on.

The pukka sahib influence surrounded the men. There were numerous native civilian workers employed by the British military. Each barrack had its designated 'hut boy' who kept the place clean, shone the regulation shoes daily and lowered the mosquito netting over the beds at night. Each barrack also had its 'sew-sew' girl; in Bert's she was elderly and looked after uniform repairs. Bert recalls that the workers were badly treated by the British and paid a pittance. The Kiwis looked after them and in return got considerable loyalty. There was a group of hired girls who carried out repairs to the huts and did most of the manual work. The camp security was carried out by Sikh Indian army troops. They were all tall, well educated and spoke good English. They carried out guard duties within the camp but also protected the perimeters of the airfield and Bert recalls being greatly reassured by their presence.

The settling-in period involved some recreational activities and the squadron

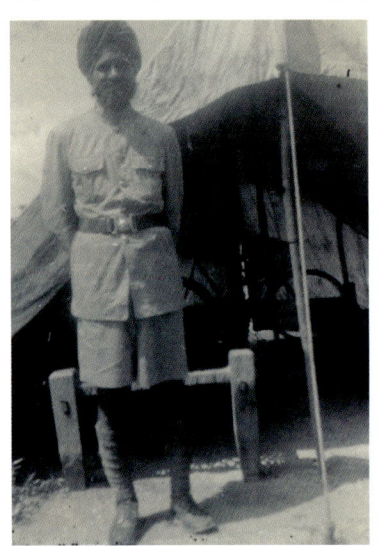

Top: Work girl.

Centre: Sew-sew girl.

Below: One of the Sikh airfield guards.

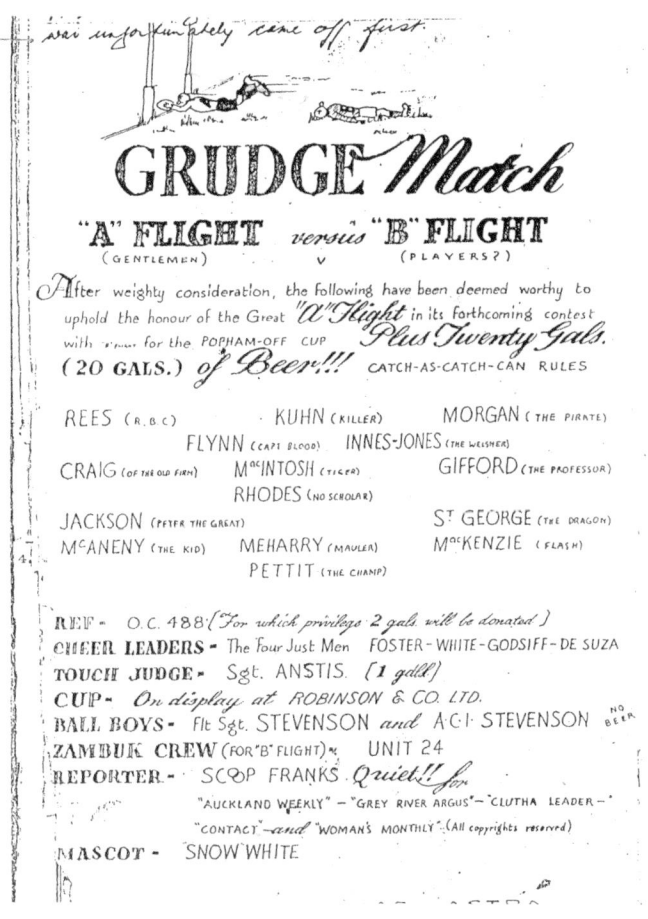

Rugby match poster played in the days leading up to the Japanese invasion.
*Collection of Barbara Kuhn*

members were surprised to find that despite the tropical conditions rugby was part of that scene. Some members of the newly arrived squadron took part in a challenge match between Kallang and Seletar just four days after their arrival in Singapore, winning the match 9–0. The team then went on to greater heights, winning all its matches. Members included Flight Sergeant John Rees, Sergeants Jack Meharry, Eddie Kuhn and Ian Montgomerie, Leading Aircraftman Jim Boddy, and Pilot Officers Noel Sharp and Jack McAneny.

Bert got regular mail from home, with Phyllis writing almost every week. The mail arrived by flying boat from

Australia twice a week. It landed on the seaward side of Kallang at the old Imperial Airways slipway. After seeing its arrival the 488 boys always knew that about four hours later the mail would turn up at their Kallang base. Bert got food parcels from Phyl's family regularly and also from the Otahuhu Methodist Church. He remembers still the thrill of receiving mail and the importance of it to the morale of his squadron.

Food generally, after the bad start when they first arrived, was plentiful and good value, the mess being just across from their barracks. On the end of the mess was the NAAFI, run along the lines of the YMCA where the airmen could get drinks, cigarettes and the little things that make life comfortable, although at a cost. The NAAFI was run by the British but staffed by the local Chinese or Malays.

The Tropics turned on constant surprises, things quite unlike those found at home, with tropical storms, the constant lightning at night, and the myriad of creeping, crawling and biting insects. The jungle fringed the inland perimeters of the airfield and this proximity allowed the young Kiwi boys visions of another terrifying world: snakes, bats and even the odd crocodile. Even the tiniest of insects had a bite or sting that could cripple a donkey. One species of red ant had the sting of a wasp; just standing still for a moment would allow dozens of them to swarm over the lower limbs. Periodically, soldier ants would go on the march, always at night, in columns tens of metres long and a hand span wide. Stand on one of those at your peril. There were giant frogs up to 20 cm long, scorpions, centipedes and huge spiders which lived on cockroaches. Very tame lizards called chit chats lived on the ceilings and kept the mosquitoes at bay. Fireflies were caught and kept in jars.

Out of the camp the men encountered a world totally

unlike anything in New Zealand. Primitive villages were close by in the jungle clearings with filthy and run-down huts and shelters. An excursion into the city did not improve the perception of the living conditions. The centre of the city was bisected by the Singapore River, fetid, black and slow flowing. The streets were dirty and the smells impacted on the senses continually. The Kallang River flowed into the Singapore River and passed close by the air base, its twists and turns preventing a fast outflow of water that might have cleared its pollution more readily. Both banks of the two rivers were home to numerous godowns or warehouses that stored all kinds of exotic foods, spices and vast stacks of rubber sheeting. Many of the buildings dated back to before the turn of the century. The godowns were serviced by lighters which transferred the produce out to and from the rows of shipping at anchor in the Singapore Roads or outer harbour. The godowns were surrounded by acres of run-down shanty housing where countless workers lived in the most primitive of conditions.

The areas around the British accommodation and clubs were in marked contrast to those inhabited by the locals. The British colonial attitude with its class distinction was like something out of a period drama. It affected recreational activities, particularly for the enlisted men. If you were a commissioned officer, this gave you entry to most of the private clubs in Singapore. Not so for the other ranks. There was a concession for them to use the Singapore Swimming Club pools but they were banned from using any of the other facilities. There was, however, a club set up by local expatriate Australian and New Zealand women, mostly wives of civilian businessmen. They called it the ANZAC Club and it was well patronised by the Kiwi groundcrew based at Kallang. They were very thankful for its existence and it was one of the very few facilities that they were allowed access to.

Unlike the RAF squadrons, the New Zealand squadron enjoyed a good working relationship between officers and enlisted men. All were on a first-name basis. Fraternisation was frowned upon between ranks in the RAF system, and the Kiwis had difficulty with this. There was a marked difference, almost a form of demarcation, between the air force squadrons in Singapore at that time. The New Zealanders felt more at home with their fellow 'colonials' the Australians but seemed to have great difficulty in establishing any sort of rapport with their Royal Air Force counterparts. Less than a month later a number of RAF groundcrew joined 488 Squadron and from all accounts these men fitted in well with the Kiwi ethos,

The ANZAC Club.
Collection of Jim Cromie

but it must have been a real culture shock for them. The biggest problem seemed to be the relationship with the RAF commissioned ranks who imposed a culture of class distinction which had long disappeared from the psyche of the New Zealand people.

Bert and some of his groundcrew mates following a visit to the ANZAC Club: Reg Hall, Bernie [?], Bert Clayton, Nobby Hall, George Clancy, Bert Dunn and Bob Friend.

Flight Lieutenant John Hutcheson.
*Air Force Museum, Christchurch.*

three

# The struggle to become operational

### BAD AIRCRAFT, NO SPARES, LIMITED TRAINING

Shortly after 488 Squadron's arrival the first of their combat aircraft were handed over. These were Brewster Buffaloes, one of the most unlikely fighter combat aircraft of all time. Although the squadron inherited 21 aircraft, not one of them was serviceable. No. 67 Squadron of the Royal Air Force at Seletar left them behind after they departed for Burma. More amazing was that these aircraft had no tools or spare parts; the only equipment found abandoned with the aircraft were six trestles, six chocks, one broken ladder and six oil-draining drums.

Work started in earnest to try to get the aircraft airworthy but the frustration must have been enormous. Working hours were restricted and most of the off-work hours were spent scrounging and stealing gear as only Kiwis can. Stripping some of the more damaged aircraft for parts effectively solved that problem and these planes became known as 'Christmas Trees'. The resourcefulness of the Kiwis was severely tested, but later observers noted that this scenario was repeated time and again throughout most theatres of war where the RNZAF squadrons were set up. The Buffaloes had originally been crated out from the US to Singapore and assembled at Seletar Air Base earlier in the year. Most of the work was done by local labour.

Of the 21 Brewster Buffaloes that the Squadron inherited, not one of them was serviceable. Kiwi ingenuity helped get the planes airworthy.

488 Squadron shared Kallang with RAF No. 243 Squadron and a Netherlands East Indies Brewster Squadron, so it wasn't long after the arrival of 488 that those squadrons found some of their stocks and supplies diminishing. Although 243 was a RAF squadron, most of its aircrew were Kiwis who had been posted there before the formation of 488 Squadron. There was tremendous competition between the three squadrons, with 488 becoming proud of consistently being first in the air when the scramble call was made, in fact one day getting all 16 available aircraft in the air in less than six minutes. It was found later that Pilot Officer Jack McAneny and Sergeant Jim MacIntosh had taken off without ammunition, and despite some hilarity at the time it was deemed to be quite a serious matter.

One of Bert Clayton's colleagues, Leading Aircraftman Max Boyd, talked about refitting the squadron's Buffaloes with armour plate. He remembered working at the time alongside the only proper air raid shelter at Kallang, which was almost at sea level and built over a reclaimed swamp. Because of this, the shelter was almost always full of water and therefore useless if its protection was required. The groundcrews worked flat out for three days trying to get all the armour plate fitted. Max Boyd remembered that the plate had arrived with all the bolted connection holes drilled in the wrong place. The hardened steel could not be redrilled and considerable improvisation was needed, some being fitted literally using the proverbial Kiwi No. 8 fencing wire.

As the aircraft were made airworthy the aircrew ventured out on what were effectively test flights. This early training was not helped by the complete absence of radio gear. The only means of communication was by hand signals or wing wagging, both of which required careful judgement as they had to pull alongside one another to communicate.

The Brewster Buffaloes really were a sorry saga. Two international publications list them as the worst fighter aircraft in the Second World War. The Buffalo story goes back to 1932 when an aeronautical engineer by the name of James Work bought the aircraft division of Brewster and Co. in the United States. The US Navy was looking for a carrier-based fighter-bomber. There was competition from the Grumman Wildcat but the Buffalo won out due to its better handling and the fact that many of its systems were hydraulically controlled, particularly the undercarriage. Amazingly, the Wildcat still had a manual winding system for its undercarriage. Brewster got the contract and an order from the US Navy for 54 aircraft.

When war broke out with Germany in 1939 the United States was still neutral and the Brewster factory were exporting their aircraft to Finland. When Finland was overrun by the Russians, the US pushed sales to other European countries, including France, but of course the German invasion beat the delivery to both Belgium and France by a wide margin. Britain took over the Buffaloes and assigned them to 71 Squadron of the Royal Air Force.

The model sold to Britain was the modified Model 339E and they were used as trainers, due mainly to the

## Brewster Buffalo — the 'world's worst fighter aircraft'

The 339E was a variant of the early F2A-2 models designed for carrier use for the US Navy. They were powered by a Wright R-1820-G105 Cyclone engine that developed 1100 hp. The British specification increased the weight by 6500 pounds, almost 1000 pounds heavier than the standard F2A-2. The top speed was lowered to 528 kph and the rate of climb lowered to only 2600 feet per minute. The increased weight raised the wing loading, and reduced overall manoeuvrability. One of the modifications was a change to the fuel line pressurisation system, as fuel starvation became a problem above 18,000 feet. The Curtiss Electric cuffed propeller was replaced with a 10 foot 1 inch Hamilton Standard propeller and the small retractable naval-type tail wheel was replaced by a larger fixed tail wheel.

The Cyclone engine installed in the Buffalo Mk1 had been selected as there were sufficient numbers of engines available to meet the first British contract. Unfortunately, insufficient numbers of these engines were available for the second contract supply and Brewster was forced to purchase used Cyclone engines from commercial airlines which had been using them to power their Douglas DC-3 airliners. Used engines were returned to Wright, which reconditioned them to the G105 standards.

The Buffaloes did have some good characteristics but

*also considerable deficiencies. There were officially 27 modifications that had to be made to make them battle-worthy. One of the major problems was faulty interrupter gear. This was the device that timed the firing of the guns through the arc of the rotating propeller without shooting it to pieces. The Buffalo had four Colt Browning .50-calibre machine-guns as its armament. Two were mounted behind the engine and one in each wing. They packed a punch. That is, when they decided to fire. The downside was that they were too heavy, which affected the manoeuvrability and rate of climb of the aircraft. When lighter .303 machine-guns were fitted and the amount of ammunition carried reduced, things improved.*

*The fuel load was also reduced to try to improve their competitiveness but this had the effect of limiting the time they could spend in action. It was a constant battle to see which ran out first, the ammunition or the fuel. Mostly, the fuel lasted longer as much frustration was reported by many of the aircrew over getting into a good attack position, waiting until the last second before squeezing the fire button and having either nothing happen or, if you were lucky, a very short burst then nothing. Some aircrew were so frustrated that for a split second they considered ramming the target aircraft!*

*The Buffalo's (reduced) top speed of 528 kph was seldom reached. It had an operating range of 1400 km, which was exceptional.*

The Brewster Buffalo fighter.

fact that they had no armour plate and not enough guns. Worse, the fuel tanks were in the wings and a single bullet hole meant a total rebuild. Britain ordered more Buffaloes built to new specifications and these acquisitions were sent to the Far East to bolster the defence of Malaya and Singapore. Despite the British Air Ministry declaring the Brewster Buffalo fighter unsuitable for RAF use, just a few months later they placed an order through the British Purchasing Commission for 170 Model 339Es. At this stage they were then deemed suitable for use in the Far East.

Despite the criticism levelled at the Buffalo, both Mackenzie and Hutcheson had earlier described them as 'nice old gentlemen's aeroplanes' so clearly some of the aircrew found them okay to fly. The consensus opinion was that they were not the most accommodating aircraft. Most of the aircrew had experience on Harvards but these Buffalo beasts were something else. They had an extremely high landing speed due to their brick-like aerodynamics and once on the ground the pilot had very limited forward vision because of the large radial engine. The comment was often made that on a cross-wind approach they would line up for the end of the strip and on turning into the wind on final approach would lose sight completely of the runway. Taxiing was fraught with danger and generally carried out in a series

Prop replacement: Stu Smart facing camera.

Open-air repairs, showing the lack of suitable equipment. 'Spike' Appleby, George Clancy and Stu Smart replacing an airscrew after an 'oil gulp'.
*Collection of Stu Smart*

of zigzags with the pilot either standing in the cockpit or leaning out either side of the aircraft and there were many accidents or near misses on the ground. They were not sleek with their fat little bodies and stubby wings. The propeller appeared ludicrously small for such a heavy-looking aircraft.

The commanding officer of 488 Squadron, Wilf Clouston, reported his concerns about the ability of the Buffalo to do the job, being particularly critical of its manoeuvrability and poor armaments. But he did concede that he considered the technical staff provided by

*Service completed: 'Hopper' Mant and Dan Weckesser. Collection of Stu Smart*

the RNZAF for Singapore were of a very high standard:

> *They were handpicked men and their selection was subsequently justified by their skill in servicing the Buffaloes despite the appallingly poor facilities at Kallang. The groundcrew made a name for themselves in Singapore second to none, they showed so much initiative, and if they couldn't get spare parts then they went round to where the spare parts were and simply 'took' them.*

The squadron seemed to possess that great Kiwi work ethic in which there was no demarcation between sections or rank. When one man finished his work, he helped others until that work was finished also. This attitude came to the fore when things got really tough over the coming weeks.

Much work was required to set up 488 Squadron as an operational unit. Clouston harangued the British High Command for additional groundcrew. He had been ordered by RAF operations to get his squadron operational in the shortest possible time and his persistent pressure paid off when extra ground staff were posted to the squadron from other units. Once airworthiness was established in the aircraft, the groundcrew were instructed to look at protection of firstly the parked aircraft then the

Above: A rare picture of an almost complete squadron of Buffaloes over the coast of Malaya.

Left: Des Hargreaves digs his foxhole.
*Collection of Stu Smart*

Left: Robbie Nixon takes over.
*Collection of Jim Cromie*

The struggle to become operational

Robbie Nixon, Clem Randall, Archie Service (later killed). In front, Des Hargreaves and Harry O'May.
*Collection of Stu Smart*

servicing areas and finally their own safety. Sandbagged embankments were built to shelter parked aircraft in what were known as dispersal areas. Commanding Officer Wilf Clouston warned them that their survival might ultimately depend on digging into the ground. At his insistence, slit trenches or foxholes were dug. Two-man foxholes were dug close to the accommodation and larger trenches closer to the work areas. In the end they were to save many lives.

Clem Randall remembers the foxhole digging clearly. Getting below ground level was imperative and he and others actually dug long open trenches alongside pathways so that anyone caught out while running for shelter could

British Bofors anti-aircraft gun emplacement at Kallang – one of the very few.

60  Last Stand in Singapore

at least dive off the path into the trenches to get below ground level.

Bert was not impressed with the overall airfield protection. The perimeter was guarded by units of the Indian Army, Sikhs and Jind regiments. The Gurkhas were mostly on night patrol and there were countless stories of men being suddenly confronted by Gurkha soldiers seemingly rising out of the ground in the darkness to challenge those late home to barracks. (Some 2000 Gurkha troops, known as the Gurkha Guard Company, were seconded to the Singapore Police. They were from the 2nd Battalion King Edward VII's Own Gurkha Rifles, one of five battalions serving in Malaya at that time.)

The airfield anti-aircraft defence was left to an apparently poorly trained group of British and Indian gunners using Bofors anti-aircraft guns and twin .303 machine-guns. Clem was also critical of the gun crews as he does not recall a single instance of those around Kallang hitting any Japanese aircraft despite mass formations arriving overhead.

The gunners seemed to Bert to be slow on the uptake, except for one occasion when a more alert Indian gunner spotted a Japanese aircraft latching on to the end of a flight returning to Kallang. When the guns suddenly opened up Bert's first impression was that they were trying to shoot down their own aircraft. It was obviously a common enough event in the Far East as the Japanese Zero[1] from a distance had a similar profile to the Buffalo and would fly in astern, unseen by the others. As the aircraft in front of him slowed speed to land, he would open up, a very cunning trick but foiled this time! Unfortunately, the shooting was bad and this Japanese opportunist escaped unharmed, no doubt to try the trick some other day.

Once they had serviceable aircraft, the groundcrew established a regular routine, set up maintenance

Top: Bert Clayton: mail from home has interrupted digging of foxhole!

Above: Col Cameron in hole with Nobby Hall behind it, trying out their temporary homes.

programmes and slowly built a supply of spare parts to try to keep the aircraft flying. The aircrews spent many hours familiarising themselves with the idiosyncrasies of the Brewster Buffalo. The training gradually intensified and eventually the groundcrew became focused on airfield defence. This meant protection for the aircraft as well as the personnel that serviced and flew them.

These early stages in Singapore were hampered by a total lack of communications equipment. There was no means of exchanging information between aircraft in the air other than visual signals. Apart from the interminably bad weather, by far the biggest impediment was the bureaucracy that controlled the island. In spite of the threat of war, the British High Command carried on peacetime activities, routines and red tape that today seem incredible. Wednesdays were compulsory half-holidays and no work was permitted on Sundays. Even on full working days flying was permitted only between eight o'clock in the morning and three in the afternoon. This was a squadron that started with no serviceable aircraft, no spare parts and no tools desperately trying to establish itself on an operational footing.

When aircraft were eventually rendered serviceable they were mishandled by inexperienced pilots resulting in far more wear and tear than would normally be expected. The man who bore the brunt of all these reverses was the senior technical NCO, Flight Sergeant WA (Andy) Chandler, who was later decorated for his exploits.

All those when asked which of the personnel of the squadron stood out, responded: Andy Chandler. He was liked and respected because he was a superb organiser and looked after his men and equipment. If there was a job to be done he did it. He was well supported by Sergeant Stan Guiniven, a quiet, modest man by all accounts, and they simply got on with the work. They had a task to do

Flight Sergeant Andy Chandler BEM pictured some years after the Singapore debacle while serving in the Pacific with the rank of Flight Lieutenant.
*RNZAF Official*

Buffalo at Kallang with Reg Hall and Jim Boddy.

Gordon Sigley on the left.
*Collection of Stu Smart*

and it was largely through their efforts that 488 Squadron had probably the highest proportion of serviceable aircraft available at any time. They were good leaders and by setting targets and encouraging a good work ethic they motivated the men under them to carry out their allotted tasks efficiently and conscientiously.

Squadron Leader Clouston was angry about the lack of spares available and commented that, despite the start of the war and with the Japanese breathing down their necks, vital parts were withheld from them by the Stores

Depot at Seletar Air Base on the grounds that they were war reserves. In the end Chandler found a way around this problem by turning up at the stores with a bunch of groundcrew and helping himself. On many occasions Chandler was also known to have headed into the city to purchase tools, paying for them with air force IOUs and getting away with it every time. The commanding officer who took over from Clouston, Squadron Leader John Mackenzie, commented after the war that both Chandler and Flying Officer Cecil Franks (the squadron equipment officer) picked up gear from everywhere. No questions were asked but he remembered one occasion when they were short of a truck and after discussing this with Cecil Franks the latter turned up driving a truck, followed almost as quickly by an irate Chinaman looking for his vehicle! In this manner 488 Squadron slowly built up equipment that was to stand them in good stead during the coming weeks.

There were many accidents that resulted in loss of life during this trying period. 488 Squadron lost 12 aircraft and 2 pilots before any enemy aircraft were shot down.

Bert remembers one day in particular that had the groundcrew almost tearing their hair out. A flight of 488 Squadron had left earlier in the day with some Dutch East Indies air force Buffaloes that had flown in from Batavia (modern-day Jakarta). The Dutch pilots had plenty of experience with this type of aircraft and the flight was part of a training exercise. While the group was away, Kallang experienced a heavy tropical downpour. Bert reckoned the water was 6 inches deep on the runway. The 488 boys landed first and ground looped five of their aircraft onto their noses (or the nose hit the deck and they bounced back). Not good news for the propeller on the front, as the blades got bent back around the engine cowling. Fortunately, no one was hurt but quite severe damage was done to each of the five aircraft. There were no problems for the Dutch fliers as they had the experience and landed all their aircraft safely and the right way up.

The accident situation was not helped by the lack of training. On 19 October when eight of the aircrew returned from Kluang and the so-called training course it was found that they had only been trained on Wirraways (Australian-produced training aircraft) and had yet to fly a Buffalo. The following day they were up in the patched-up Buffaloes and the realities of operational flying were really brought home to them. Each pilot went solo, which, after the paucity of training they had received, must have been a traumatic experience both for them and the watching groundcrew. On 20 October, the next batch, Noel Sharp, Len Farr, Jack McAneny, Grahame 'Snow' White, Pete Gifford and Harry 'Bunt' Pettit all went solo on a Buffalo for the first time. No incidents were reported, although there were several go rounds or bounced landings.

The learning continued. On 21 October, Pilot Officer Len Farr hit one of the airfield boundary lights during a landing, followed the next day by Pilot Officer Noel Sharp who landed too fast and ground looped his aircraft, causing damage to the wingtip and tailplane. It was not necessarily his fault as another aircraft cut in on him during his final approach. Len Farr initially reported to great amusement that he had struck or been struck by a beer bottle that shattered his cabin floor Perspex panel. Over the next couple of days Len Farr, Sergeant Eddie Kuhn, Sergeant Jack Meharry and Sergeant Terry Honan all had their share of prangs. The repair areas must have resembled hospital waiting rooms as the frustrated groundcrews worked to get the planes airworthy again. Despite these accidents, the morale of the squadron was high. Clem Randall confirmed that when one of the groundcrew had finished his work he went and helped out

Sergeant Jack Meharry.
*Air Force Museum, Christchurch*

others who were still trying to get aircraft serviceable.

The airfield at Kallang was the main civilian airport on Singapore Island and was under mixed control at the time before eventually being taken over by RAF operations control. Prior to the military takeover the air force commanders were being constantly warned by the civilian authorities that they would be charged for any damage to the airfield facilities. The threat seemed to have made no difference to Len Farr as he made use of the fence instead of his brakes and bust a wing. Jack Meharry had a rough ride on 28 October with his first solo and wrote off his aircraft, fortunately without injury to himself. The following day it was Terry Honan's turn to be embarrassed, with a very heavy landing that caused considerable damage.

November brought a change in the weather and rainy, squally monsoon conditions disrupted the training programme. On the first day of the month Peter Gifford gave everyone a severe fright when, during poor visibility, he landed downwind and luckily got away with it. The accident rate worsened with the weather and the squadron diary lists a series of mishaps. Pilot Officer Grahame White volunteered to assist the island's anti-aircraft defences by providing himself and his aircraft as a live target on 6 November. It was a brave effort at the time as he was relying on the ack-ack gunners to have correctly set their fuses to some 9000 feet below his altitude. He would have been a bit more relaxed had he known then that later events showed the gunners to have an appalling record of accuracy, which benefited the Japanese greatly as the war progressed.

The shared airfield situation caused a tragic incident when one of the 243 Squadron Buffaloes landed on top of an unsighted Tiger Moth biplane from the civilian flying school. The Buffalo was hardly damaged but both occupants of the Tiger Moth were killed.

Pilot Officer Tony Cox wrote off his Buffalo on 11 November when he stalled during landing with a damaged propeller. He had earlier damaged the propeller with a classic case of low flying when he struck the water in the Straits of Johore and later left his aircraft in a heap on the airfield at Seletar. (Clem Randall recalls that the propeller tips were bent forward, indicating that Cox was under full power when he struck the water, no doubt with his heart in his mouth at that time and fighting to pull his aircraft up clear of the water.) His engine had failed when he limped in sounding like a chaff cutter on his final approach. Terry Honan busted a tail wheel off during a heavier than allowable landing. Two days later, Pilot Officer Jack Godsiff actually left his tail wheel behind on the boundary fence at Kallang and after following sign language from his fellow pilots had to make a tail-down landing, also at Seletar.

Flight Lieutenant John Hutcheson had his share of scrapes. On 14 November he attempted a belly landing with his undercarriage retracted, damaging the Buffalo extensively, but he was unhurt, despite the aircraft hitting a concrete parapet and eventually ending up in a concrete drain. When the station medical officer arrived in a great hurry with bandages he did not appreciate the choice language being used by Hutch and ended up using them to cover his own ears. Hutch could have said he was just practising, as late in January he had to do another belly landing, but this time he was badly shot up and barely escaped with his life. The groundcrew were pleased that he escaped unharmed on both occasions but were generally peed off with the state in which he returned the aircraft to them.

Another near miss was reported on 19 November when a section that was formation flying almost hit the hangar, giving everyone watching a severe fright. The flying practice continued and the skill level did increase markedly, much to the relief and surprise of the groundcrews.

The squadron had a formal visit from Sir Robert Brooke-Popham, the Air Chief Marshal, on 19 November, and the reason for their being in Singapore was clearly spelt out to them. His message was brought home to them the following day when they had their first verification that the Japanese had an interest in the Far East.

That morning, 20 November, three Buffaloes from 243 Squadron were sent up to the Thai border to investigate some strange reconnaissance aircraft seen prowling around in the area. The date and time of this event coincide with the memoirs of Masanobu Tsuji, a staff officer to the Japanese General, Tomoyuki Yamashita, who was responsible for planning the attack on Malaya and Singapore. Tsuji had flown south from a base in French Indochina (comprising modern-day Vietnam, Cambodia and Laos) with the sole purpose of investigating the airfields in northern Malaya. The information he took back was vital for the Japanese planning. Diary notes from

Kallang at this time express the tension and expectation that the war with the Japanese was imminent.

The difficulty with communications was really brought home with Pilot Officer Noel Sharp having to buzz the airfield control tower to alert them to a potential problem he had noticed with Hutch's aircraft. The port wing cover had come adrift and he was concerned that Hutch would have some difficulty in landing. They had radio-telephone (RT) sets installed in each aircraft for air-to-air contact only and the next day, 21 November, tests were carried out but with limited success. Communication was still a very hit-and-miss affair.

The accident rate increased a few days later on 24 November when Sergeant Eddie Kuhn hit the wind tee on his landing approach and stalled into the ground. He was unhurt but his aircraft was written off. The subsequent conversation with his flight commander Mac Mackenzie was reported as very one-sided where every second word was 'bloody'. Eddie Kuhn was reportedly rendered speechless by Mackenzie's tirade. A 243 Squadron aircraft suffered engine failure on 25 November and ended up in the Kallang River at Geylang. Unfortunately for the pilot, the river was one of the most polluted on the island, serving as a drain for sewage, slops, trash, dead dogs and the odd corpse. He was uninjured but it was said that his social status suffered for some days.

The war came closer on 29 November when all service personnel were ordered back to camp and on 1 December 1941 a state of emergency was declared throughout Malaya and Singapore. Mild panic set in as the squadron reflected on the limited training they had received since their arrival.

The following day the squadron was ordered to move all aircraft to the dispersal areas that had already been prepared around the perimeter of the airfield. These were

Aircrew on standby: Pilot Officers Butch Hesketh and Jack Godsiff with Sergeant Eddie Kuhn wait in the aircrew dispersal hut for the order to get airborne.

sandbagged, and blast wall protective areas built for each aircraft, spaced at roughly 200 m intervals. No further work was to be done in the hangars as these would be prime targets during a raid. There was a downside for the groundcrew as they would no longer have the weather cover afforded by the hangars and would need to work out in the open.

Pilot Officers GL 'Butch' Hesketh and Jack Oakden joined 488 Squadron in a posting from 243 Squadron. The aircrew spent the next three days practising dogfights and 'plane-on-plane' attacks. On 6 December a small 'war' erupted on Kallang when the airfield perimeter guards opened fire for no apparent reason. One of the army units protecting 488 Squadron's area fired a shot at Sergeant Dennis Pharazyn, fortunately missing, as he did his rounds as the night duty NCO. The tension was rising and reached fever pitch the next day when a first state of emergency was declared. All leave was cancelled.

The build-up of armaments and constant talk of war gave these young men plenty to speculate about and it was obvious something was brewing. Bert would never have

Pilot Officer Jack Oakden.
*Air Force Museum, Christchurch*

contemplated the coming storm that was about to descend. All the talk was centred around the threat of the Japanese and their quest for oil and rubber, both plentiful in South East Asia. The British High Command had a defence plan for Singapore and Malaya built on the expectation of a sea-based attack on the southern coasts and all their defences were established accordingly. Winston Churchill had decided that a strong navy presence in South East Asia would be a sufficient deterrent to any expansionist plans of Japan. Huge resources had been put into upgrading the naval dockyard at Sembawang on the north coast of the island and the British High Command considered this sufficient to defend the region. How wrong they were!

Mackenzie about to lead off A Flight.
*RNZAF Official*

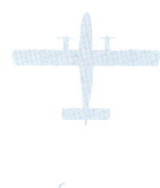

four

# The arrival of the storm

### THE JAPANESE INVASION

The signs had been obvious. Japan's intentions with respect to the Far East had been widely known for many years. Its expansion had started in 1931 with the invasion and seizure of Manchuria, followed by northern China. With a population explosion and insufficient raw materials to sustain its economy Japan had huge ambitions to expand. It relied heavily on the United States for up to 80 per cent of oil with another 20 per cent being sourced from the Dutch East Indies. The Vichy French Government ruled Indochina and acceded to Japan's demands to have a military presence there. The Japanese cunningly stirred up trouble and raised the nationalistic urge in the people to throw off the shackles of the French colonial power. They moved troops into the area and quietly and steadily built up ports and airfields as a part of what they called a 'policing' action in the region. This allowed them to have strike bases, both air and sea, within 1100 km of Singapore. When the Allied governments realised what was happening in the region they placed an embargo on trading assets in their respective countries and almost overnight Japan lost its entire supply of oil. From that time on, war was inevitable.

Japan at that stage had the world's third largest navy and they also had in Asia an estimated 200,000 well-trained troops waiting for the signal to move. Winston Churchill ordered a naval force to proceed to Singapore post haste and the stand-off began. A huge Japanese fleet was assembling in Japan's Inland Sea. The United States continued with talks trying to prise the Japanese out of Indochina. The talks broke down and the rest is history.

On 6 December 1941 the general alert had been given. An Australian Hudson bomber had reported a large convoy of Japanese ships in the South China Sea heading southwards towards the east coast of Malaya, which arrived just before midnight. On the morning of 7 December, US time, the Japanese attacked the American naval base at Pearl Harbor in Hawaii and destroyed the American Pacific Fleet.

Bert Clayton's war started at 2.30am Singapore time on 8 December 1941, with a crash that had him instantly standing beside his barracks bed at Kallang like a stunned mullet. Just a few kilometres away the Japanese were bombing the port of Singapore. What had woken Bert was the rattle of the anti-aircraft fire that had started as the bombers made their initial run over the city. When he realised what was happening he and the others vacated their billets and sprinted for the foxholes they had dug. This was to be the pattern for them for many more nights to come. Bert remembers squatting in the bottom of the trench listening to the explosions, the sound dying away, the noise of the aircraft departing and only then, as the silence returned, the air raid sirens in the city starting to wail their belated warning. The city was lit up like a Christmas tree, every neon light and streetlight burning brightly, showing up the city as the perfect target. Singapore was totally unprepared. Bert was now at war. 488 Squadron was still not fully operational.

John Hutcheson was the station duty officer that night. He was woken at 2am and informed that the Japanese had

Sergeant Jim MacIntosh.
*Air Force Museum, Christchurch*

attacked and were landing troops off the coast of Malaya. He probably reacted with some trepidation but with a tinge of excitement as he rushed around informing everyone of the situation. His colleague and fellow flight commander, John Mackenzie, on being woken by an excited Hutch, told him to shove off and went back to sleep. When the bombs started dropping over the city just a kilometre or two away he shed his dignity and joined the others in a nearby drain.

Jim MacIntosh was by this time in a high state of excitement. He followed Hutch around, chanting 'Come on Hutch, what are we waiting for? Let's go'. Around 5am they piled into Mac's old Austin and headed for the airfield. They were stopped by the local militia and ordered to put out their lights despite the city being fully

## ✈ Entering the war

*Unbeknown to Bert, some significant events had taken place which impacted on the Singapore saga and significantly contributed to the island's fall. One of the major reasons for the subsequent loss of Singapore happened much earlier than Japan's entry into the war. On 24 September 1940 the unarmed cargo ship SS* Automedon *sailed from the UK carrying a top-secret Chief of Staff's Report on the defence situation in the Far East. It was destined for the High Command in Malaya. In the mid Indian Ocean she was attacked by the German surface raider* Atlantis *and after a brief skirmish was boarded and the ship's papers uplifted. The report was subsequently forwarded to the Japanese Government. It basically said that the British Government could not rely on the support of the Dutch or the Americans in South East Asia. There were significant concerns that the newly built naval base on Singapore Island could not be stocked with sufficient vessels to offer support in the event of an attack by the Japanese. The Japanese were overjoyed by the report and consequently upgraded their invasion plans. Why this report was sent in an unarmed merchant ship has never been explained. Clearly the crew had no knowledge of the papers they were entrusted with or these would have been destroyed to prevent them from falling into enemy hands. The first salvo fired from the* Atlantis *wiped out the bridge and killed all the senior officers on board and that may explain why the papers were not destroyed.*

*The second major factor was the total collapse of the northern airfields in the first two days of the Japanese invasion. Malaya had a series of airfields strategically placed, but poorly defended, on the coast and in its northern regions close to its border with Siam (or Thailand as it was soon to be known). The Japanese bombers that were heading towards Singapore at this time had flown all the way from airfields 600 km north of Saigon. This was the limit of their range and the Japanese had set as a very high priority the acquisition of the airfields in the north of Malaya. They were well prepared to take these using troops rather than destroying them with bombing raids, but never could they have imagined how easy the securing of them would be. Not only was there no opposition but they found them abandoned, in some cases complete with munitions and fuel.*

illuminated; in fact, the road was so well lit that they had little need of lights anyway. The street lights, of course, had been blazing brightly throughout the bombing raid. By the time they reached their dispersal area at Kallang the groundcrew had all the aircraft, some with motors running, ready to go, but the Japanese by this time were long gone and no order was given to move. At daybreak the men were still waiting. The rest of the day was spent in total readiness with some patrols hitting the sky as aircraft were spotted, but these all proved to be 'friendlies'.

488 Squadron was eventually the first squadron to fly in the defence of Singapore Island. Most of the bomb damage in the early-morning raid was centred on Raffles Place in the city where many civilians were killed. Hutch wryly noted that he was sure the city would have lights off the next night. Other than that first bombing raid the Japanese were nowhere to be seen. At Kallang the aircrew were 'champing at the bit' and both Noel Sharp and Jim MacIntosh asked the question: 'When will the bastards come?'

Masanobu Tsuji, the Japanese colonel and chief of staff of operations, had planned the invasion carefully. He had flown over the northern airfields on 20 November 1941, three weeks before the planned landings, and realised the importance of securing these installations. In his now classic account of the invasion he recounted his excitement while overrunning these airfields with the attacking forces and finding huge stockpiles of arms and munitions laid out ready for the taking.[1] At Alor Star, he claims there were bubbling pots of hot food, giving some indication of the speed of the departing personnel. Heartened by the relative ease of these early victories the Japanese pushed on quickly, overrunning their key objectives in hours rather than days. The huge stock of munitions, fuel and food gave rise to

Pilot Officer Noel Sharp.
*Air Force Museum, Christchurch*

Opposite: Location of principal areas discussed in this narrative.

the expression 'Churchill Supplies'. The well-fed Japanese Army then used the munitions and fuel with devastating effect against the British forces in northern Malaya. In fact, the Japanese survived on these supplies all the way down the Malayan Peninsula until they replenished them from their own sources on reaching the final staging post at Johore, across the water from Singapore.

In the meantime the RAAF had Hudson bombers ready and waiting at Kota Bharu — and wait they did. By the time orders came through to attack, the first of the Japanese had landed on the coast. They were so close to the airfield that one member of the Aussie crew remembers lighting a cigarette as they took off and stubbing it out as they landed back to reload, after dropping a load of bombs on the Japanese transports just off the coast. Refuelling was not needed. The groundcrews worked like Formula One pit crews, rearming the bombers as they returned in an endless stream. The first day of the Japanese invasion clearly went to the defenders.

The following day things quickly changed. With their fighter aircraft now based on closer airfields in Thailand the Japanese slowly took control, causing considerable damage to the Allied aircraft defending the coast. Thus began the British collapse and by the evening of 9 December only 50 aircraft out of 110 were available throughout the whole of the Malayan Peninsula, including Singapore Island. Support from the Singapore aircraft may have changed the balance somewhat. A large number of the aircraft were destroyed on the ground and recent information suggests that the Japanese had advance knowledge of their whereabouts but, worse, that they were guided by fifth-columnists led by a British officer who was eventually captured and summarily executed.[2]

The surviving Kota Bharu aircraft of No. 1 Squadron RAAF were diverted by Air Operations to Kuantan.

The next day Kota Bharu became the first airfield to fall, literally given away not by the defending army but by the Australian groundcrews abandoning the airfield and fleeing south. When the army units realised what had happened they were left to destroy the fuel dumps before retreating.

The walkout of the groundcrews was said to have started among the fitters and riggers. While working on aircraft out in the open for the last two days, they were convinced they were being shot at by fifth-columnists. The men were jumpy and apprehension soon spread. The officer commanding the airfield left to confer with the local army commander. When he returned he was amazed to find the squadron operations room abandoned and that the groundcrew had set fire to the attap roofs of their buildings. In his absence someone had contacted air headquarters in Singapore, convinced them that they were being overrun, and had received permission to evacuate.

The local army commander arrived at the base to see the air force groundcrew clambering aboard trucks, shouting as they fled the scene that the Japanese were over on the eastern boundary of the airfield. The commander cautiously moved over there to find only Indian troops who said they had had no contact with the Japanese, and had been bemused and bewildered by the antics of the Aussie groundcrews. The Australian decision to evacuate was a pathetic ending to a day that had appeared so promising.

It got worse. The groundcrews were trucked south leaving behind two intact Hudson bombers, 60 aerial torpedoes, some bombs and a high-octane fuel dump. The Kota Bharu crews headed towards Kuantan to meet up with their aircraft but, some 30 km from Kuantan, met up with another convoy of trucks packed with the Kuantan groundcrews from No. 8 Squadron RAAF.

They informed the Kota Bharu crews that they had been bombed that morning, all their serviceable aircraft had flown to Singapore and they were on their way to join them. There was not a Japanese within 100 km of Kuantan at that time — in fact, Kuantan was not overrun by the Japanese until 3 January. It was the first reported case of desertion during the Malayan Campaign.[3] A number of the groundcrew had stolen some civilian transport as dawn broke, and by the time the first Japanese bombers arrived three hours later they were well on their way to Singapore. The rot continued as similar scenarios took place in other areas.

On the afternoon of 9 December, Sungai Patani was abandoned by No. 21 Squadron RAAF, and No. 27 Squadron RAF at Alor Star followed next morning, despite no Japanese being near. Later that afternoon Butterworth was abandoned. Air cover was desperately needed at this time and the loss of these airfields was to have a significant outcome on the future of Singapore. The abandonment of Kuantan, particularly, took away from the navy any hope of protection from events that were about to happen off the east coast of Malaya. Paddy Cromie, an RAF groundcrew member who was to later join 488 Squadron, recalls in his memoirs the movement south of the Australians. He was to join them on 10 December when his RAF squadron was officially disbanded.

When the news of the Japanese landing at Kota Bharu filtered through early on the morning of 8 December, a British naval force which had reached Singapore several days before left the naval base at Sembawang around 4pm and headed up the coast to intercept an expected seaborne attack on Singapore Island. The naval group known as Force Z, commanded by Admiral Sir Tom Phillips, consisted of the battle cruiser HMS *Repulse* and the battleship HMS *Prince of Wales* with four destroyers:

*Electra*, *Express*, *Vampire* and *Tenedos*.

Despite an offer by Wilf Clouston to provide air cover, Admiral Phillips took the ships out to sea. Clouston and his two flight commanders, Mackenzie and Hutcheson, had formulated a plan whereby 488 Squadron would provide air cover to the fleet. The operation, called 'Get Mobile', was to give air cover off the coast during daylight hours by leapfrogging flights up and down the east coast of Malaya using the many airfields available. When the fleet arrived in port, Clouston and his flight commanders attended a meeting at Air Operations and presented their proposal. The plan was rejected out of hand by the naval personnel.

The British fleet headed north up the coast. A Catalina aircraft flew low and signalled that the Japanese were landing at Singora, on the east coast of the Malayan Peninsula. Admiral Phillips decided that the weather conditions, low cloud and misty rain, would deter any attack by enemy aircraft so he continued on northwards to Singora. The ships in the fleet then began to report activity from Japanese aircraft overhead and these aircraft tracked their movements until nightfall. After nightfall, Phillips decided to call off the run towards Singora and turned southward. Around midnight he received a signal that the Japanese were landing at Kuantan, which was on the coast between the fleet and Singapore. Phillips sent a signal to Singapore that he would head there. One of the searching destroyers reported no such landing taking place and that the area was quiet. There were no further communications from the fleet.

Meanwhile, on Singapore at Kallang Air Base, aircraft were on standby to provide air cover for the fleet if needed. Soon after dawn on 10 December action stations were called to all the ships, due to a big increase in overhead aircraft activity by the Japanese. Still the

Singapore squadrons sat waiting for the call! In the air was a Japanese strike force of 34 high-level bombers and 51 torpedo bombers. They were looking for the fleet. The strike force travelled as far south as Singapore then headed back up the coast until they came across the fleet, totally unprotected from the air. The first wave of bombers made their run at 11am at around 10,000 feet, over the *Repulse* and then the *Prince of Wales*. Chaos reigned as groups of torpedo bombers came in low and fast. By 12.30pm the *Repulse* had been ripped apart and sunk by bombing and torpedo strikes. An hour later the *Prince of Wales* followed her to the bottom. Inexplicably, until an hour after the first attack no call went out for air assistance. Another half hour passed before word of the disaster reached the operations room at Air Headquarters in Singapore. In just a few hours Japan had destroyed the Allied naval strike force and now ruled the oceans in South East Asia.

At Kallang, the squadron had been ordered to stand by for a big assignment but no one knew what was in the wind. It was early afternoon when finally the call came, and after a long wait Flight Lieutenant John Mackenzie and Sergeant Jim MacIntosh took off and headed towards the last reported position of Force Z. They knew by the co-ordinates given that they would be heading out to sea and the first inkling of a disaster began to sink in. Until much later in the day they were not to know its extent. Of course, they were much too late. Four separate patrols of two aircraft went out during the day, but all they could do was provide air cover for the destroyers picking up survivors from the Japanese raid. The sea in the area was littered with debris and survivors waiting to be picked up by escorting destroyers. The disaster that had taken place was the forerunner of what was to come for the island of Singapore.

Meantime, for the groundcrew at Kallang work

continued. There was constant pressure to repair and generally make serviceable any aircraft available. It would have been difficult in peacetime conditions anywhere in the world, but working in the tropics brought its own problems. The heat was debilitating. Coupled with pilots arriving back with badly damaged aircraft and the threatening presence of Japanese bombers, life was a complete and utter misery for these men. As well as aircraft servicing, the groundcrew were kept busy responding to the earlier warning they had received from their commanding officer to dig foxholes. The high water table at Kallang created problems and to minimise flooding they would only partially dig the holes and layer sandbags and compacted earth to create room for at least two men per shelter. Max Boyd observed that the area looked like a rabbit warren. The men were getting more and more jittery, with the long hours and the constant tension. A typical day would start with wakeup at 4.15am. Breakfast was somewhat pathetic — half a slice of fried bread with a strip of fatty bacon and very little else, not

Pilot Officer Noel Sharp, one of the characters of 488 Squadron, shown with his aircraft, which was probably the best known of the Buffaloes, W8138 NF-O. Note the fashion statement with the infamous white overalls worn for a short time by all aircrews.
*Burton family/Paul Sortehaug*

a good start to the day. They would be transported or walk the 20 minutes across the airfield to the work areas, arriving just on daybreak.

The aircraft on call that day would be prepared, the engines started by the groundcrew prior to the pilots' arrival and then, after the flight was airborne, the wait began for the return, which may have been just minutes or several hours depending on what was found. When they returned, there was refuelling and rearming, and the various support services did their bit to ensure a quick turn-round so that the aircraft would be ready for the next callout. There was no way of planning ahead and this work continued until after dark almost every day. The men returned to the billets around 8.30 most nights and the cycle continued at 4.15 the next morning, only being broken with compulsory rostered guard duty for each man every fourth night.

The key to their day's work was to keep an eye on what became known as the 'recco' plane. This Japanese reconnaissance aircraft made its daily run over the island at a height of over 30,000 feet with impunity. None of the serviceable aircraft on Singapore could reach the height of this machine. Many times the Brewster Buffaloes of 488 went up early with the intention of knocking the plane out of the sky, but, fighting oil pressure problems and overheating motors, they only managed a height of 20,000 feet. The Japanese observers on board must have been laughing. It was no laughing matter on the ground, however, as a couple of hours later the bombs would start falling and it was time to make that great sprint to the foxholes and relative safety.

The stressful situation worsened when the Japanese started night bombing. Despite the immediate Kallang area being spared bombing at this time, the squadron were still forced to respond to all the alarms, or they lay there at night listening closely to the ominous drone that signalled aircraft overhead and hoping that the target for that night would be elsewhere. The observer system was very primitive and as the island was so small there was never going to be any guarantee of which area would be targeted. The closeness of targets all round them meant little sleep and certainly no relaxation.

Every day was a work day — not even Sundays were spared. In fact, Sunday, 14 December started for most at 4am and ended with them in total collapse that night around 8.30pm.

Flight Lieutenant Mackenzie was totally frustrated with the rate of climb of the Brewster Buffalo and he asked Bert and his crew to strip his aircraft of its armour plating and take out all armaments except one gun. Even the transmitters were removed. Much lighter and with fabric over the barrel of his single gun to counter moisture at altitude, he headed off, determined to bring down 'that damned recco plane'. He reached 27,000 feet, still 3000 feet below his antagonist, and returned even more frustrated and angry.

When the bombers inevitably arrived over Kallang the foxholes were okay for protection from shrapnel but provided no protection from a direct hit. There were some lighter moments, though. One of Bert's mates, Bert Dunn, was quick off the mark one morning and led the sprint to

Top: Flight Lieutenant John Mackenzie DFC, 488 Squadron's second Commanding Officer from 23 January 1942.
*RNZAF Official*

Above: A very bedraggled and wet Bert Dunn trying to dry off after his dive into a water-filled foxhole.

the foxholes. He arrived first and dived headlong into a pit full to the brim with water! The trick was to be second, to avoid a repetition of Bert Dunn's experience, but to ensure that — like musical chairs — you were never in a position of running from one full foxhole to another to find one with room for one more. Often they found themselves caught in the open and had to lie hard pressed to the ground against any shelter they could find.

In the days following the *Repulse* and *Prince of Wales* debacle, the squadron prepared for the coming onslaught. All were in readiness and patrols were carried out. The Japanese were very quiet with no contacts made, but there were several false alarms. On Saturday, 13 December there was great excitement and panic as a large number of unidentified aircraft were reported heading for Singapore. Every available machine from the squadrons at Kallang were scrambled, 30 aircraft in all. The resulting take-off was a shambles with aircraft milling around trying to get into flight formation. It turned out to be a false alarm as four unidentified aircraft were reported as 44. Squadron Leader Clouston was livid at the undisciplined way the squadron took off and more than reprimanded his flight commanders.

The quiet continued over the following four days but the peace was broken on 18 December, when the squadron had their first fatality. They lost Sergeant Alexander Craig during a formation landing at Kallang. Bert was particularly saddened by his death. Flight Lieutenant John Mackenzie had been training Sergeant Craig and one other pilot in formation landing. The groundcrew watched as they approached very low, just clearing the tops of a row of trees. As they were about to pass over a second row Craig's starboard wing struck a slightly higher tree, the nose pulled down, the aircraft hooked around to starboard and he crashed to the ground. (This was the official version of events but, as Bert Clayton recalls it, Craig's aircraft struck the roof of a house and ploughed through a brick wall before striking the ground. Photographs taken of Kallang prior to the incident tend to support his story. There were no trees on this section of the perimeter, which was very close to Bert's foxhole position.) The aircraft exploded into flames and, despite the efforts of the groundcrew, nothing could be done to save him. He was remembered as a big, jovial and kindly fellow. They were flying into the sun at the time and it was thought that Craig was blinded at a crucial moment while concentrating on maintaining his position in the formation.

The next two days were spent trying to set a trap for the recco plane. Sixteen aircraft were in the air on Friday, 19 December but the altitude and speed of this pest defeated them. Despite their efforts they never got close as he was just too high and too fast. The groundcrew could only watch with frustration, willing the Buffaloes on to close in on the clearly visible vapour trails. Apart from extremely wet weather on 21 December all was quiet up to Christmas Eve. There was some hilarity among the boys on 22 December as trucks arrived with dummy wooden anti-aircraft guns which were positioned around the airfield in an attempt to fool the Japanese. The 488 boys would have felt much more comfortable if they had been real ones. You have to wonder at the mentality of those decision makers who determined this action. It may have been a show of force but instead it would have encouraged the Japanese bombers to intensify bombing to destroy what must have looked like the real thing. There was a huge air raid on Singapore City on the night of 23 December but no bombs fell near Kallang.

Des Hargreaves, in his memoirs, mentioned spending Christmas Eve in an air raid shelter while a single Japanese aircraft bombed the island. Christmas Day started very quietly, fine and warm. A Japanese aircraft dropped leaflets over Kallang but no bombing disturbed the peace. As the day progressed, the parties started. Everybody was talking about what they did last Christmas, some a little homesick but most wanting to get started and have a crack at the Japanese. A big party was held in the Officers' Mess. The Kallang OC, Wing Commander Chignell, 488 Squadron OC Wilf Clouston and some Netherlands East Indies squadron officers enjoyed a repertoire of 'risqué songs' sung mostly by Hutch.

John Mackenzie, Butch Hesketh, Noel Sharp, Jack Meharry and Terry Honan went out on the town later that night in Mac's old Austin, 'Galloping Gertie'. They arrived at the Alhambra Movie Theatre and managed to 'souvenir' a large portrait of movie actress Kay Francis. This was smuggled down the stairs and placed in 'Gertie'. Next followed a bigger portrait of Paulette Goddard, which was concealed under Mackenzie's overcoat, through a crowd and down two flights of stairs. While they were scouting for more loot some spoilsport stole 'Gertie' and drove off into the night with Noel Sharp in hot pursuit on foot. The five weary warriors consoled themselves with a few more beers at the Adelphi Hotel before being driven back to base by a sympathetic Aussie. From all accounts the airmen on the base had a quiet night, although there are several comments on record of plenty of beer being drunk in the NAAFI. Gifts of cigarettes and butterscotch were distributed, having been sent from home by the New Zealand Patriotic Society. They were greatly appreciated.

Good news came the next morning when 'Galloping Gertie' was found complete with souvenired portraits. Christmas Day dinner was celebrated with a visit to a local hotel where, despite the war, there was a lot of hilarity. The evening 'smoke concert' in the Airmen's Mess hall at Katong degenerated into a 'de-bagging' session with the senior NCO, Flight Sergeant Eric Patterson being the first to lose his trousers, followed in quick succession by Andy Chandler, Noel Sharp, John Hutcheson and finally the CO, Wilf Clouston. It was recorded as being a very enjoyable evening and happily there were no bombing raids by the Japanese. The event was organised by Flying Officer Cecil Franks. The guests included two Netherlands East Indies (NEI) Air Force officers and 'Judge' Foreman, Kallang's engineering officer. Toasts were proposed by Cecil Franks, Bunt Pettit, and one of the NEI officers. Squadron Leader Clouston read a Christmas greeting from Air Chief Marshall Sir Cyril Newall, which everyone autographed, and it was subsequently mailed back to him in New Zealand. Wilf Clouston thanked the men for their tremendous effort in getting the squadron airworthy in such a short time. The concert then got off to a roaring start. The evening was a time of great jubilation but most of the younger men facing their first Christmas away would have been thinking of loved ones at home.

Unfortunately for the revellers, the war continued on Boxing Day. The recco plane was back on the normal run between 8 and 9am despite rumours that it had been shot down. It was painted silver and initially identified as a JU88, a German aircraft, stripped of all armaments and far quicker than anything available to the Allies. The craft was later revealed to be the Japanese army's new 'wonder plane', the Army Type 100 Command reconnaisance aircraft, known by its Allied name, 'Dinah'. The height that it operated at had them all beaten and any Allied aircraft could be outrun with ease. Anti-aircraft fire was ineffective and if any got close the pilot would frustrate the gunners completely by turning circles around the shell burst and making rings with his vapour trail. The next couple of days were very quiet, with just a few aircraft

## A ditty for Christmas Day

One of the features of the night was the rendition of a ditty put together by some of the squadron.[4] Despite the verse being a bit dodgy and the tune unreported, it is worth recording as it features some of the characters who served in the squadron.

**And Some Have Greatness Thrust Upon Them**
*488 we wish you all the best of cheer*
*For this funny Christmas and the coming year*
*So, our guests of honour, we're glad you're here tonight*
*And hope that you will get welly muchee tight.*

*Now we're going to give you some exclusive squadron gen*
*That has not been twisted by the censor's pen,*
*But remember, gentlemen, that even walls may hear*
*So don't retell these secrets, if a stranger should be near.*

*Our CO Squadron Leader is a very decent chap*
*He took a strong objection to a recent squadron phlap,*
*There were forty Buffs a-buzzing like a swarm of angry bees*
*Without regard for windsocks, blackballs or landing tees.*

*Then we have an Adjutant who likes to aggravate us*
*With King's Regulations and questions on our status,*
*He puffs and blows and blusters and strokes his ruddy chin*
*But if you want to knock him back just send Flight Chandler in.*

*Flight Lieut. 'Flash Mackenzie' has a DFC*
*A most amazing auto and a phlap propensity,*
*With his stock of doubtful stories and his wicked gambling way*
*His pilot's cash balances get smaller every day.*

*'Hutch' is quite a problem to tell you all about*
*Because he works so slyly he never gets found out,*

Dallies with the ladies at the swimming club
And … hmm … hmm … hmm … hmm.

Fly. Off. Franks, equipment, of his new braid so proud,
He would be the funny man in any sort of crowd,
He rides a snappy bicycle and scorches here and there
The only thing he doesn't do is find us any gear.

One day Eddie Kuhn was coming into land,
The joystick of his Buffalo grasped firmly in his hand,
And being in a playful mood he blipped the landing tee
But, he said, my eyes were dim I had no specs with me.

A tribute to our maintenance we feel that we must pay
For they work so very hard to help in every way,
They pull a kite to pieces and build it up again
But you should hear their language when they see the salvage crane.

One day upon the tarmac the armourers were bored
And they started making war on their own accord,
They lined up square a Buffalo and pressed the tit with glee
And bloody near exterminated good old 243.

Rugged front row forward Jack Rees is in 'A' Flight,
He is one big moan from morning until night,
Dug himself a funk hole nearly six feet deep
But now it's full of water and he can't get in to sleep.

Old Flight Sgt. Stevie is the daddy of the lot
With his scanty foliage and his little pot,
He potters here and there as busy as can be
And does precisely nothing as far as we can see.

And now we close this ditty with the heart felt prayer
That you may all have a prosperous New Year,
The ruddy little Japanese may make things mighty warm
But you just watch them scatter, when 488 strikes back.

| | |
|---|---|
| *Composer* | *Plt. Off. Cox* |
| *Asst. Composer* | *Plt. Off. Pettit* |
| *Director* | *Fly. Off. Franks* |
| *Music by* | *Anonymous* |

A footnote attached reads: 'This colossal production was presented by the composers on the occasion, on the momentous occasion of the squadron's 1941 Christmas Smoke Concert. The writers deny the rumour that they have been offered Hollywood contracts.'

New Zealand Fighter Squadron.

SMOKE CONCERT.
KALLANG,
SINGAPORE, MALAYA.

CHRISTMAS NIGHT,
DECEMBER 25,

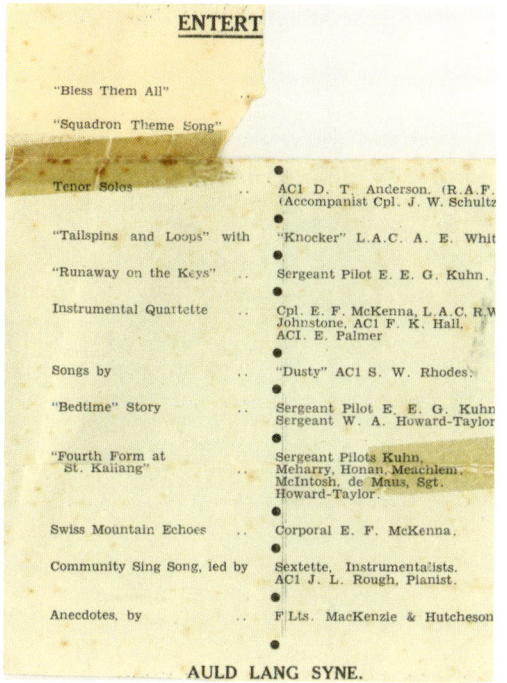 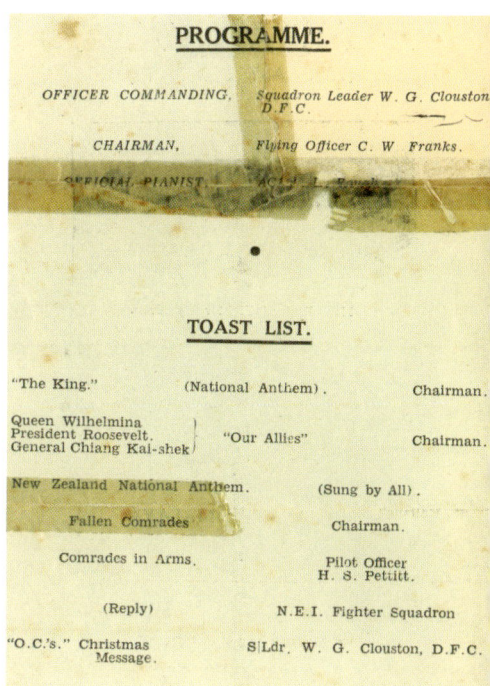

Opposite and above: One of the original Smoke Concert programmes. *Collection of Jim Cromie*

making practice runs and flight tests. The general feeling among 488 Squadron was boredom with being constantly on readiness, but the squadron diarist reminded everyone that their turn would soon come and 'we will all have as much combat as we desire'.

The squadron had a visit from MGM and CINESOUND News cameramen on 28 December and were filmed co-operating with the Netherlands East Indies pilots, all this with a war raging to the north of them. The day dawned hot and fine but by early afternoon there was a cloudburst and the airfield was completely flooded. There was some comfort for them as the weather conditions meant they would be spared an attack from the air.

Sergeant WR 'Bunny' de Maus had a lucky escape on Monday, 29 December. He collided with a Gipsy Moth of the Malay Volunteer Air Force over the city. He managed to return to Kallang with only minor damage but the Gipsy Moth had a wing torn off and crashed onto Lavender Street in the city, killing its pilot and pupil. The pilot was a New Zealander serving with the Malay Volunteers, Pilot Officer WWG Felton. His pupil was a naval officer who had survived the sinking of HMS *Repulse*, Petty Officer W Smith.

The city was later heavily bombed and big fires were seen from Kallang. The air raid warning was as usual too late and the bombing aircraft too high for the defending Buffaloes to get there. Later that night a Blenheim twin-engined bomber overshot the runway making a night landing and finished up in the boundary drain after destroying one of the Dutch Buffaloes. The Dutch were not amused.

On Tuesday, 30 December both A Flight and B Flight flew offensive operations over Kluang without contacting the enemy. Most of the Dutch squadron left to return to Java to reinforce defences against threatened

Sergeant 'Bunny' de Maus.
*Air Force Museum, Christchurch*

Japanese attacks. They would have been missed by the New Zealanders as a good rapport had been established between the squadrons.

New Year was observed by most of the aircrew, who celebrated the occasion at the Cathay Restaurant, but for the groundcrew it was work as usual. The pilfering continued as some of the pilots again visited the Alhambra Cinema and lifted another two portraits of female movie stars. Those left at the Cathay managed to retrieve most of the Christmas/New Year decorations, which later adorned the roof of the 488 dispersal hut at Kallang.

New Year's Day continued as normal in the city and many of the squadron went to the movies. In the early morning a Japanese dive bomber had come in low over the airfield at high speed, his bombs missing the hangars but hitting one of the many petrol dumps. Max Boyd reported with some mischievous pleasure that one of the bombs damaged the Happy World, a house of ill repute on the outskirts of Kallang. Martial law was declared in Singapore and the curfew at night was rigidly enforced. Clem Randall recalls on New Year's Eve sharing a bottle of cherry brandy with one of the sergeant armourers who had received word that his wife had given birth to a baby girl. He remembers there being a full moon and the sky being clear — a perfect night for bombers, but fortunately none arrived to spoil the occasion.

The calm around Kallang continued, except that on Friday, 2 January the airfield's anti-aircraft gunners opened up on two of 488 Squadron's planes returning to base. Their accuracy was such that they missed by a wide mark but definitely did not endear themselves to those in the aircraft. The squadron diary noted that the 488 dispersal hut had the appearance of an art gallery with all the portraits of movie stars still hanging from the walls.

The weather closed in on Saturday, 3 January but the

squadron flew five patrols during the daylight hours, providing cover for a convoy bringing reinforcements into Singapore. The poor visibility meant flying below 1000 feet, but the bad weather did offer some protection from Japanese bombers looking for targets. The squadron flew patrols as far south as the Banka Straits and took turns to escort the convoy right through until it reached the Straits of Johore. Hutch commented that the men felt the strain of the long-range patrol work as they had to fly over unfamiliar territory, mostly out of sight of land, using Dutch maps and having no radio contact with base or each other.

Pilot Officer Jack Godsiff unintentionally provided considerable excitement on Sunday, 4 January when, during his landing approach, he suffered engine failure and crashed into a house on the perimeter of the airfield. Some of his fellow officers including his CO were playing cards in the aircrew dispersal hut when they saw Godsiff heading directly towards them, at very low altitude and with a very sick motor. There was a scramble for the door, which Wilf Clouston reached first. Godsiff, fighting for altitude, just cleared the hut and some trees behind, but collected the roof of an adjacent house. They rushed over and dragged him out. He was very lucky to have sustained only a broken nose and a slight fracture of the forehead, so received very little sympathy. The group playing cards likened the sound of Godsiff's arrival to that of a horse and cart going through a glasshouse. Bert remembers one of the fitters cutting a wire in the engine bay and having to step back very quickly when the engine crashed to the ground. Needless to say, the aircraft was a complete write-off.

The mishaps continued. Bert remembers vividly that the following day, 5 January, he and some of his mates were walking back to the barracks and had to walk around

Final resting place of W8223 after Jack Godsiff's little 'whoops'.

Groundcrew salvaging the best bits and trying to put Jack Godsiff's aircraft together again.

behind a 243 Squadron Buffalo waiting to take off. They noticed a second aircraft coming in to land but instead of turning off the runway it continued to taxi down towards the waiting aircraft. Suddenly the latter plane gunned its motor and headed off down the runway. Less than 100 m from where Bert and his mates stood watching in horror, the two planes met with a tremendous explosion. An oxygen bottle shot like a rocket into the sky and fell back into the inferno below. The two pilots, who were from

*Pilot Officer Len Farr supervises the ground handling of his aircraft.*
*RNZAF Official*

243 Squadron, both New Zealanders from Wellington, died instantly. Sergeant Paul Lester 'Shorty' Elliot had only just turned 19; his mate, Pilot Officer Ronald Spencer Shield, was older at 23. Elliot had earlier taken off with others to intercept an incoming raid but had broken formation to return to Kallang. There was smoke over the airfield and this was thought to have been a significant factor. Bert, however, was convinced that poor forward visibility due to the Buffalo's extra-large motor contributed to the disaster. Both Elliot and Shield had just had birthdays and died too young. The shock of

Mackenzie about to lead off A Flight. *RNZAF Official*

that incident was just the precursor of similar tragedies.

On 6 January, Mackenzie and Butch Hesketh, while on convoy patrol, were ordered to have a close look at a vessel with strange markings, which proved to be Dutch. The aircrew were issued with white overalls this day, giving the impression of a squad of paperhangers. The white suits were intended to save the pilots from flash burns should fire break out in their aircraft. The following days, 7 and 8 January, were very quiet, the calm before the storm as it eventuated. The groundcrew spent most of both days sleeping under the wings of their respective aircraft; they were on call but their services were not needed. It was a welcome break. Around them the clouds of war were gathering.

Aircrew sheltering from the rain under a Buffalo wing (from left): Grahame White, Jack Godsiff, Bunt Pettit, Jack Burton, Perce Killick, Eddie Kuhn, Wally Greenhalgh, Tony Cox, Frank Johnstone, Bruce Herbert (groundcrew), Len Farr and Jim Macintosh (squatting).

## five

# The beginning of the end

### A DEFENSIVE COLLAPSE — TOO LITTLE, TOO LATE

Seletar, on Singapore's northeast coast had its first major raid on 9 January 1942. The squadron headquarters, equipment store, oil and ammunition store were hit and destroyed. As much gear as possible was salvaged from the damaged buildings and stored in nearby houses, which had been evacuated the day before this attack. It was a pattern of recovery and survival that those at Kallang would soon face. The casualties among the civilians employed on the base were high. They seemed to think that if they hid themselves in the long grass and bushes they would be safe. Patrols from Kallang continued over the next two days but 488 Squadron reported no contact with the Japanese. The only excitement was caused by faulty interrupter gear on Pete Gifford's Buffalo putting a bullet through the propeller. Hutch commented that the plane must have got sick of waiting for some action and decided to take matters into its own hands.

The first time a Kallang flight had contact with enemy aircraft was on 12 January. Led by A Flight commander Flight Lieutenant John Mackenzie, it left Kallang with eight Buffaloes and climbed to the northwest to intercept a raid of 27 bombers heading towards Singapore. This contact would be the first of many. Almost always the formations targeting Singapore were of 27 planes — three flights of nine each. Mackenzie and his flight reached

Scramble of flight at Kallang.

Pilot Officer Harry 'Bunt' Pettit.
*Collection of Bunt Pettit*

12,000 feet but the Japanese were still 3000 feet above them. The Buffaloes were totally outnumbered and could only disperse as the fighters protecting the bombers dived down onto them en masse. The superior speed and turn of the Japanese Zero fighters meant that, despite taking evasive action, the Buffalo pilots could only try to outrun them, look for safety in clouds or head into the sun. Sergeants Terry Honan and Rod MacMillan were shot down immediately, both managing to bale out and land safely about 20 km from Johore on the Malayan mainland. Bunt Pettit was hit, suffering a bullet hole in his arm. He reported his injury, but feeling okay despite losing a lot of blood, carried on patrolling close to Kallang. When he eventually landed he was unable to climb out and several of the groundcrew were reported to have been close to passing out when they saw the amount of blood in the cockpit.

Pilot Officer Jack McAneny took a bullet through his fuel tank, fortunately without catching fire, and force-landed on Sembawang airfield. Pilot Officer Grahame White was shot through the prop and fuselage and Sergeant Jim MacIntosh found himself in a head-on position with three Japanese bombers but frustratingly his guns failed to fire at the crucial moment and he was forced to pull away.

Five other Buffaloes were damaged, two of the pilots being wounded. Mackenzie and Sergeant Perce Killick turned on their attackers but were so heavily outnumbered they had to break off and head for home. Lots of lessons were learnt this day and the tactics quickly changed from bravado to survival. The feeling was that there would be trying times ahead.

Led by Flight Lieutenant John Hutcheson, a second formation of six aircraft took off a half hour after Mackenzie but only the leader Hutcheson made contact

Sergeant Terry Honan.
*Air Force Museum, Christchurch*

with the enemy. After being outmanoeuvred by a Zero, Hutch broke off the engagement and also headed back. In the meantime Singapore City was taking a pasting. On the same day, two later interception flights took to the air but were unable to reach sufficient height to make contact. One aircraft was lost, crashing into a swamp after engine failure but the pilot, Sergeant Vern Meaclem, escaped unhurt.

This day was not a very good start to combat operations by 488 Squadron; unfortunately, it set the scene for the rest of their campaign in Singapore. The Brewster Buffalo was hopelessly outclassed as a fighter aircraft. It could not sustain maximum power while climbing at full throttle without suffering from overheating and a drop in oil pressure, which caused the propeller oil seals to give way and blow oil all over the aircraft. The Buffalo could not operate above 25,000 feet but, worse than that, had to be nursed up to that height, a process that took 35 minutes. The Japanese aircraft were faster and more manoeuvrable; our pilots were disadvantaged from the very first day.

The groundcrew played a big part in the lives of the aircrew. These pilots were often younger than the groundcrew that strapped them in. The process was a ritual, four straps in all, one over each shoulder and one

Sergeant Perce Killick.
*Air Force Museum, Christchurch*

around each leg. The straps were fastened to a central pin and Max Boyd remembers a young pilot's hands shaking so much that he had to fit the straps over the pin himself. One of Bert's fellow groundcrew commented that the last contact each pilot had was with his flight rigger and flight mechanic. Pilots often left their wallets and personal possessions with their groundcrew, with instructions on what to do if they did not return. The trust was implicit and the non-return of a pilot was keenly felt by those awaiting his safe reappearance.

A second large sea convoy arrived in Singapore Harbour on 13 January bringing further troop reinforcements, 20 more pilots and 51 new Hurricane fighters packed in cases. RAF Squadron No. 232 was to bring some relief to the Singapore squadrons. By this time the Japanese Army was in the upper reaches of Johore, less than 100 km from Singapore, and the supplies brought much-needed relief and hope to the beleaguered city. The work out of Kallang went on as normal. The day started early with Pilot Officer Butch Hesketh leading four aircraft of A Flight out at 6.30am, but no contact was made with any enemy aircraft. They had to be airborne early, particularly with the convoys arriving with further supplies. Eddie Kuhn did not return by air from this flight. His engine seized during the early-morning climb and caught fire, causing him to bale out into the sea. He was rescued by some Chinese fishermen in a sampan and returned to shore.

John Mackenzie took a flight of eight aircraft up on patrol at 10am but had no contact with enemy aircraft.

At 11am John Hutcheson took off with a third flight of another eight aircraft, including some from a Dutch squadron recently arrived at Kallang. They made contact with a flight of Japanese bombers but the tail-gun defence proved too damaging for the attacking flight. Gradually, they dropped off and, despite being only marginally faster than the bomber formation, Hutch persisted and kept on. Such was the mettle of this man he continued alone trying desperately to bring down at least one of them. In the end he was forced to break off the action and managed to crash-land his badly shot up aircraft on Kallang airfield. Pilot Officer Jack Oakden was shot down into the sea and eventually rescued by sampan. Sergeant Don Clow was also shot down and had to swim to an island, being returned to Kallang two days later. Two of this flight reported gun failures. Five aircraft were written off, so it was another bad day for 488 Squadron.

Because the Buffaloes' top speed was only marginally superior to that of the bombers they were chasing, when they were overtaken it was almost impossible for the New Zealanders to get into an attacking position, and thus there was little they could do to defend themselves against the bombers' superior tail-gun defence. As a result, in the first two days of active service seven aircraft were lost from the original 21.

However, despite being seriously disadvantaged in every respect, the squadron doggedly continued to defend Singapore to the best of its ability. Between raids from above, the groundcrew worked constantly, repairing and

Sergeant Don Clow.
*Air Force Museum, Christchurch*

patching the aircraft ready for the next scramble.

After being shot up and unable to land at Kallang, due to damage to the airfield, Flight Lieutenant Hutcheson got into trouble again, being forced to make an emergency landing at Tengah air base. When he and two of his fellow pilots landed the airfield was deserted because of an air raid warning. He and his two mates made their way to the empty Officers' Mess and helped themselves to a very welcome drink. After some time, the all clear sounded and slowly, from the surrounding trees and shelters, the station personnel came out of hiding. Hutch was confronted by an apoplectic station commander, Group Captain Watts, who shouted at him and demanded he move his aircraft immediately because his aircraft parked there 'would encourage the Japanese bombers to return'. It was recorded that Hutch was not amused.

It was this day's entry in the squadron diary that first commented on the shortcomings of the Brewster Buffalo as a fighting machine. Imagine the feelings of the pilots knowing that they would forever be outclassed during any contact with the enemy. The groundcrew would also have been very much aware of the situation. I wonder how many of them would have had second thoughts about getting an aircraft back to airworthiness knowing that they would be sending the pilots back into the air with such a dangerous and life-threatening disadvantage. For the pilots it could only be hit-and-run tactics to gain surprise by ambush from cloud cover, striking quickly and again using the cloud as a means of escape to outrun their faster and more manoeuvrable opponents. Consequently, the New Zealanders developed a unique survival manoeuvre. When attacked from behind they immediately threw the Buffalo into a full-power vertical dive. The Japanese pilots were reluctant to follow on account of their dive-speed limitations. There was a downside, however, as Pilot Officer Peter Gifford discovered when he returned from a sortie with a twisted aircraft and bent wings after a pullout from a high-speed dive.

January 14 was notable for the huge python caught by the boys at the back of their billets — not a very welcome break but it did provide some distraction. The photo shows it looking alive and lethal but Bert assures me that it was in fact very dead and was posed for the picture. It was at least 3 m long. Des Hargreaves commented in his diary notes that, thankfully, the weather was particularly bad with heavy rain squalls throughout the day and into the evening, which kept the Japanese quiet.

488 Squadron had its first combat loss on the morning of 15 January. Pilot Officer Butch Hesketh led a flight to intercept a bombing raid and his flight was attacked by a swarm of Japanese fighters. Those who survived returned with badly damaged aircraft. According to the diary of Des Hargreaves, Butch Hesketh was shot at least nine times and died in his cockpit after crash-landing. His aircraft was seen flying low out of control over the city and eventually

George Clancy and a python caught behind the barracks.

Sergeant Eddie Kuhn.
*Air Force Museum, Christchurch*

crash-landed on a narrow strip of land alongside some oil tanks not far from Alexandra Hospital.

Sergeant Eddie Kuhn recorded 488 Squadron's first kill on the same day, sending a Japanese Type 97 fighter crashing to the ground. Bert saw the battle from Kallang and he remembers watching from a distance three aircraft in succession diving steeply towards the ground. Two crashed but the third pulled out of the dive at the last minute and returned to the fray. Bert later learnt that the first two were Japanese fighters, the third being Geoff Fisken, a New Zealander with 243 Squadron who followed his victims all the way down to make sure of the kill. Another interested observer was a young Eurasian lad, Romanus Miles, who watched from his home close to Kallang. He saw several Brewster Buffaloes shot down by the Japanese Zeros, the Buffaloes making a distinct whistling noise as they turned tightly trying to get into an attacking position against the Zeros. Unfortunately, the sheer weight of numbers meant that they had no chance.

Singapore City was saturation-bombed from high altitude on 16 January. The city defences were pitiful, with the First World War-vintage anti-aircraft guns unable to reach anywhere near the height of the aggressors. 488

The aircrew dispersal hut at Kallang.
*Art Donahue*

Squadron, with just six serviceable aircraft on this day, took off with three of the remaining Dutch aircraft, initially for patrol and escort duties for shipping, but they were diverted to intercept some approaching aircraft. However, air operations knew that due to their heavy fuel loads they would have no chance if they chose to engage the Japanese bombers and ordered them to head out to sea. The Dutch pilots, however, left the formation and headed back to Kallang with disastrous results. Two were shot down in flames and the third barely made it back to base. A raid at 3am ruined a night's sleep for everyone and this was followed by a large concentration of bombs which landed on the end of the airfield around 9.45 later that morning.

Pilot Officer Frank Johnstone ran into some bother during take-off from Kallang on 17 January. After putting his Buffalo into a steep climb his engine failed and he was forced to bale out. Fortunately, he was high enough and landed by parachute, shaken but unhurt, in the sea just off the coast close to a Chinese junk. He tried to attract the attention of the crew by firing shots from his revolver but after the third shot his revolver jammed. When he was returned to Kallang he handed in his revolver for cleaning. None of the shots he had fired had left the barrel and he was lucky it did not explode in his hands. Later in the day the Japanese made a huge bombing raid on the island. Kallang was spared the worst of it but Sembawang and Seletar were plastered. The aircraft losses on those bases were considerable.

The only day that the 488 Buffaloes managed to get above the Japanese aircraft was 18 January, and was therefore the most successful in terms of the number of enemy aircraft shot down. Pilot Officer Noel Sharp, however, was an early casualty, managing to shepherd his riddled aircraft back to Kallang with most of its rudder shot away. As related earlier, Pilot Officer Pete Gifford tried the classic vertical dive during this engagement to avoid a Zero hot on his tail. Unfortunately, in the excitement of the moment he forgot his machine was still trimmed for climbing. The force on his control stick became too much for him to cope with and the stick was snatched from his hand. The aircraft automatically corrected instantaneously, did a snap pullout and headed back up in the direction from where he had just come. His attacker must have got one hell of a fright. Hutch commented that the pullout from the dive must have been very sudden as when Gifford returned to base the groundcrew found his whole machine was twisted. Gifford suffered a stiff neck as a result. In the squadron records, listing damage to various aircraft, a single entry of 'W8173 Plt. Off. Gifford — Warped' appears. (Stu Smart recalls that Peter Gifford blacked out with the suddenness of the dive and a fellow pilot also in a dive recalls Gifford diving past his aircraft at

Pilot Officer Pete Gifford.
*Collection of Bunt Pettit*

such a speed that he felt that he was standing still. It was Stu Smart that noticed the dihedral effect of the wings on Gifford's aircraft while it was parked waiting for propeller repairs later that day. Stu had stopped for a smoke while sitting on the blast bank in front of the aircraft and what he observed caused him to investigate further.)

The damage to Gifford's aircraft gave some idea of the sturdiness of the Buffalo design, one of its few redeeming characteristics. Very early in the piece, the pilots of each Buffalo in the squadron used this tactic to avoid confrontation with the Japanese Navy Zero fighter as they knew that they would not be followed down due to the lighter built Zero having a propensity for wing collapse in high-speed dives. There were many instances recorded of the Japanese aircraft wings folding against the body of the aircraft while diving, with disastrous results for both aircraft and pilot.

Late in the morning Hutcheson led a flight to meet an incoming raid but fell foul of two Zeros who latched onto him. One was still firing at him as he crash-landed among trees on the shore of a small island about 15 km south of Kallang. He was hospitably received by the resident Dutch official on the island, fed and tidied up, and subsequently picked up by an air-sea rescue launch and returned to Kallang in a borrowed suit of fine white material, looking every inch the pukka sahib.

Another casualty was Pilot Officer Tony Cox, aged just 22, whose plane was last seen diving into cloud. He was posted missing at the time but his body was never found. The whole of the engagement had taken place over Kallang, which was badly hit by bombing later around 1pm. Squadron Leader Clouston left the RAF operations room where he had been working and waited on the airfield for the return of the surviving combatants. Japanese bombing of the naval base oil tanks resulted in huge fires which covered the island in thick smoke — a foretaste of the disaster which eventually overcame Singapore. The newly arrived 232 Squadron tried out their new Hurricanes this day and Hutch drily commented that it was a pity they were not operational enough to help out in the air.

On 19 January the squadron lost Pilot Officer Jack McAneny and Sergeant Deryck Charters. McAneny was shot down and killed just out of Muar township on the west coast of Malaya. He was 19 years of age. Charters survived after parachuting from his stricken aircraft and was taken prisoner by the Japanese. He was originally listed as missing believed killed, but the International Red Cross later informed his family that he was in a POW camp in Thailand where he died of dysentery on Christmas Day, 1943.

Bert recalls sitting quietly with the maintenance crew on the aircraft wheel chocks feeling sick with apprehension waiting for the aircraft to return, a feeling that would be experienced many times over the coming weeks. The groundcrew all knew the flying time available on a tank of fuel and dreaded the deadline, returning quietly to their work if it had passed, hoping the pilot had baled out safely. Many did not make it but others were returned to the squadron days later to the relief of their comrades. There was immense camaraderie among the

Top: Pilot Officer Jack McAneny.
*Air Force Museum, Christchurch*

Above: Sergeant Deryck Charters.
*Air Force Museum, Christchurch*

groundcrew and the pilots, who had great trust in their 'fixit' men to provide a safe aircraft.

The loss of McAneny and Charters was a sad one as they were not seen going down and made no RT call to indicate they were in trouble. Most of the aircrew were keen to return to search for them but there were no aircraft available. Later in the day Mac Mackenzie (just released from hospital) and Jack Meharry did head north on a reconnaissance trip to Kuala Lumpur. On the ground at one airfield they sighted more enemy aircraft than the entire remaining Allied aircraft in Singapore. They saw no sign of their comrades.

The Dutch fighter squadron that had been at Kallang for just over a month returned to Palembang in southern Sumatra. This left just 243 Squadron RAF and 488 (NZ) Squadron at Kallang and on them fell the whole responsibility for the defence of Singapore. There were two RAAF squadrons, 21 and 453, at Sembawang but they were used mostly by the army and for escorting the few Hudson bombers still in service.

On 20 January, more Hurricanes arrived at Kallang but three were wiped out by bombing during the day, leaving only eight. There were three raids in waves of 27 followed by great excitement at Kallang when one of the Japanese bombers was shot down by anti-aircraft fire. Singapore City took the brunt of the attacks with the Orchard Road area being plastered. Patrols were sent north to Muar and, with several machines from 243 Squadron, managed to head off a bombing raid by six Type 97 bombers, forcing them to jettison their loads over the jungle. They kept a close eye out for any sign of McAneny and Charters but none was found.

Bombing continued on Wednesday, 21 January, mainly on the city, although Hutch was sure that the attack was intended to hit Kallang but the bombers appeared to be deterred by the anti-aircraft fire. The first formations arrived over the city at around 10.30am. Max Boyd remembers the bomb doors all opening simultaneously and even at that great height you could see the flash of the sun reflecting off them. The bombing covered a large area, stretching for 100 m from the Kallang airfield perimeter all the way into the city centre. Some big 500-pound bombs were dropped. People on the receiving end found it difficult to cope when a string of bombs commenced exploding several kilometres away and came rattling towards them in a direct line.

Paddy Cromie went into town at midday and saw first hand the bombing damage on civilian targets. He recalls the seafront stretching back along to Kallang being hit during the raids. North Bridge Road leading to the ANZAC Club was singled out, with many bodies lying on the road. He lunched at the ANZAC Club with 'Red' Maloney, having to hitch a ride back to Katong as all the taxis in the town had disappeared. He later went back to the movies with 'Squib' Newcombe. Life in the city continued as usual, which must have seemed quite unreal at the time. Kallang lost another two Hurricanes this day but one of the attacking Japanese bombers exploded in midair.

The new foxholes, only partially completed, were just 18 inches deep due to the water table. The extra sandbags were not yet in place to build up the sides and the guys felt very vulnerable lying in them, listening to the bombs whistling down. Hutch was highly amused when a visit by the Church of England padre coincided with a bombing raid. The padre learnt a lot about the ancestry of the Japanese people from the cursing bodies darting in all directions seeking a safe place to shelter.

Max Boyd used the expression 'Hell on Earth' to describe this day. The squadron had its biggest attack from the air on Thursday, 22 January (Jack 'Hopper' Mant's birthday). The day dawned fine and clear with clumps of cloud scattered over the sky. Around 10.30am, at what was becoming the regular arrival time, Bert counted over a hundred aircraft approaching in a tight formation. The early-warning radar system had long broken down and the first indication of trouble was a pulsating drone coming louder and louder from the northeast. It meant only one thing, and the men dropped everything for the quick sprint to cover. Mac Mackenzie and three of his flight, Eddie Kuhn, Don Clow and Len Farr, were waiting with motors running when the first stick of bombs hit. Today all these bombers were targeting Kallang. Usually, Seletar airfield or the naval base on the other side of the island were hit first and this gave those at Kallang some warning. Not this time.

Mackenzie quickly waved the chocks away and his groundcrew raced for the foxholes. Mackenzie and two of his flight managed to open throttles and take off through a shower of bombs but Len Farr and two of Eddie Kuhn's groundcrew left it too late and were swallowed up in the conflagration. Len Farr desperately tried to get airborne, but while under full power his aircraft was first blown into one of the houses on the end of the strip and then onto a petrol storage dump on the other side of the Geylang River, landing on top of hundreds of drums of high-octane fuel. Miraculously, there was no fire but Len was hit by shrapnel, one piece lodging in his back against his spine. He survived the crash but died of his injuries three days later. One of the groundcrew killed was aircraftman Andy Anderson, just 21 years old, from Dannevirke; the other was an RAF groundcrew member with 488 Squadron, Archie Service. Both were buried in a common grave at a burial ground off the Bukit Timah Road.

The death of Archie Service was keenly felt by his

mates from 488 Squadron. Clem Randall was particularly saddened by his death. Archie, who was from Renfrewshire in Scotland, was engaged to a lass back home and that compounded the loss for Clem. He had promised to show Archie the Southern Cross constellation, which could be seen on the horizon to the south at dawn. Archie, of course, had never seen the Southern Cross as it is unique to the southern hemisphere. It was not to be and Archie never got to see it. Archie had posted a letter to Clem's parents that very morning, but Clem had to write to them later that day to pass on the sad news.

The two squadrons, 243 and 488, worked side by side. Most of the aircrew from 243 were Kiwis. Harry O'May and Paddy Cromie packed up all Archie's belongings. About 30 of Archie's mates left Katong at 3pm for the funeral of the two who died. Harry O'May, Jim Delap, Hugh Stewart, George Pritchard, Frank Howell and Paddy Cromie were pallbearers for Archie.

For the men on the ground the first ear-splitting crash became a familiar pattern usually followed by a series of terrific detonations that sounded as if the whole of Singapore was being levelled. The ground trembled as though hit by a gigantic hammer and the air filled with dust. Explosions grew progressively louder until they felt their eardrums could withstand no more. At the height of the loudest explosions, bomb fragments or shrapnel could clearly be heard pinging off concrete and surrounding hard surfaces. Their fists would be clenched tightly as every man tried to push his body into the ground.

Sandy St George had a narrow escape when a 250-pound bomb landed a couple of metres from his foxhole. The blast blew the top off his shelter and sucked him bodily out. He suffered permanent damage to his wrists with shrapnel lacerations and was fortunate to survive. Paddy Cromie was sheltering in a foxhole just 20 m from

## ✈ *A fortunate return*

*Clem Randall and Stan Guiniven saved some of their fellow squadron members this day. The squadron had a deliberate policy of allowing on the airfield only those personnel immediately required to service the aircraft on call that day. Once the planes were airborne, if an air raid alert sounded anyone not essential to operations was taken as far away from the airfield as possible in an old Dodge bus and several trucks, which the squadron had lately acquired. If Kallang was the target of the approaching bombers it was somewhat of a rush, but if not there was sometimes more time to disperse.*

*Those people not immediately required were taken to a bomb shelter a short distance away known as 'Gammons Shelter', built by a local engineering firm. Clem and Stan had already dropped off a load at the shelter, and, with no bombers in sight, decided to make one more trip back to the airfield to pick up anyone left after getting the last of the squadron's aircraft away. There was a substantial shelter built close to the flight dispersal area but this was only used in an emergency as it was close to obvious target areas on the airfield. By this time, it had to be said, some complacency had set in and many of the groundcrew stayed close or in this shelter rather than have the continuous disruption of fleeing after the constant air raid alarms, many of which were false. Clem and Stan took a terrible risk by travelling back across the airstrip, but Clem stayed on the open back of the truck watching the sky, knowing that if bombers appeared he and Stan would have to take their chances by diving into any drain or ground opening for protection. They reached the dispersal area unharmed but at that very moment a large formation of Japanese bombers arrived. They had to use some choice language to get the six or seven men sheltering there to come out in the open and onto the back of the truck. They tore back across the airfield arriving at Gammons Shelter just as the first of the bombs landed.*

*After that raid was over they went back to the dispersal area to find that the shelter recently vacated had taken a direct hit and was completely destroyed. Clem Randall felt good about that decision and I guess there were six or seven of his fellow groundcrew feeling even better. Clem remembered a very shaken Sandy St George emerging from the destruction. They had missed Sandy on their final pickup but later realised he would probably have been already in his foxhole with fingers in his ears. He would consequently have missed the calls from Clem and Stan as they picked up the others.*

Bert's toolbox is under the burning aircraft with the stranded fire truck to the right.

Taking a break after taking a plastering.
*Collection of Jim Cromie*

Clouston's car showing the effects of one bombing raid.

the nearest bomb and commented that it was as close as he ever wanted to be.

At the time of the bombing attack Bert had been working on an aircraft. As the first wave of bombs hit he headed for an empty foxhole and curled up in a ball with his fingers in his ears. The noise and the concussion were incredible. The ground rolled and heaved with the explosions. He lost consciousness and when he came to he was upside down in the hole, badly shaken but amazingly unhurt. He called out to the two Hall brothers in the foxhole next to him to see if they were okay. The aircraft he had been working on was no more. It had taken an almost direct hit and was burning furiously. Bert was angry as his toolkit, which had been left under the aircraft, was destroyed. He had built it up from nothing in the preceding weeks. Parked beside his aircraft was one of the squadron's fire trucks. Most of its crew were wounded and one was blown to pieces. The truck was peppered with bomb fragments and unable to be used.

Bert saw many unexploded bombs after the attack still smoking. They left distinctive neat holes in the ground even though the surrounding surface was intact. John Mackenzie remembered the bombs landing all around him as he made his take-off down the runway that day, 'hundreds of little anti-personnel ones which seemed to race us across the airfield'.

Sergeants Yanovich and Payne, Leading Aircraftman Duffin and three other of the groundcrew bravely attacked a fire that had broken out in the armament filling room and managed to contain it despite exploding ammunition. The aircrew boys sheltering in their foxholes were amazed and full of praise for the groundcrew, who were working out in the open, despite bombs falling all around them, to ensure the safety and protection of their aircraft.

Stu Smart recalled that he had been carrying out repairs

to one of the aircraft and climbed into the cockpit to run the motor following routine maintenance. As he did so the NAAFI wagon pulled up. He tossed up as to whether he should continue with the 'run up' or stop for morning tea. Morning tea won so he shut down the engine, climbed out of the cockpit and went over towards the NAAFI truck. As he walked around the rear of the aircraft he looked over towards the Happy World establishment and saw to his horror a flight of Japanese bombers coming in low and fast. He ran for the nearest shelter and curled up through the maelstrom that followed. After the bombers had left he tentatively climbed out to find the aircraft he had been working on had completely disappeared. It must have taken a direct hit as all that was left was the alloy oil tank sitting on the tarmac, still half full with clean oil. As with Bert, all his tools and gear that had been around the aircraft had disappeared. Clem Randall later returned his four-inch crescent spanner that he found over 800 m away. He considers himself very lucky as had he stayed in the cockpit of that aircraft with the engine running he would not have had a chance.

This day's intensive bombing finished off any buildings that had remained standing after previous raids. The groundcrew barracks were totally destroyed and every window in the old airport building was blown out. Even worse, the airfield was too badly damaged to allow any aircraft to take off or land. The three remaining fighters were still aloft somewhere waiting to return. The normal civilian repair crew had long since disappeared, so the groundcrew with as much salvaged equipment as they could find, filled in the craters for the returning aircraft. They managed to find one bulldozer, undamaged and in working condition, and spent the next couple of hours doing the necessary repairs.

In his diary, Max Boyd commented on the appalling

state of affairs that day, particularly the lack of warning given to those on Kallang. The deaths of those caught on the ground caused a lot of bitterness among the 488 boys. The RAF Operations staff responsible for the warnings admitted afterwards they had made a terrible blunder, but it was too late for any kind of remorse. Geylang, the civilian area close to Kallang and the city, also took a hammering for which the Japanese supposedly apologised later. Many of the bombs hit without exploding and it took considerable skill to avoid these areas. Some members of 243 Squadron game enough to poke their heads up were sufficiently frustrated to fire revolver shots at the passing aircraft. The 488 boys soon put a stop to that as many of the bullets were landing in the 488 area. Max Boyd reported that Happy World had again 'copped a beauty' and now ceased to exist.

There were many stories among the groundcrew of near misses, and the soft boggy ground saved many. A considerable number of the bombs had penetrated deeply but failed to explode. The Japanese had decided to limit damage to the infrastructure of the airfields by cunningly using incendiary, delayed action and shrapnel bombs rather than high-explosive types. Although the shrapnel bombs were devastating above ground, one was generally safe in a shelter below ground level.

Top: Telok Kurau School in Katong: Bert's first night and on guard duty.

Above: Telok Kurau School the scene of a dreadful massacre just days after Bert left.

The recreational area set up near the Kallang billets, pictured before being destroyed by bombing.

Bert and his groundcrew mates returned exhausted to the sad sight of their destroyed barracks and mess hall. They collected up what was left of their belongings and were trucked away after dark to the Telok Kurau English School at nearby Katong. The men crowded into the tiny classrooms, thankful at least to be away from the targeted area at Kallang. The school accommodation was basic, although the bath and toilet facilities were inadequate. Several of the squadron reminisced about the showers or lack of them. They rigged up a temporary shower where there was a garden tap outside, enclosing the area with fronds and branches. Unfortunately, after a couple of days the once-green vegetation wilted and died and the local population on the other side of a wire mesh fence found out what Kiwis really looked like!

Ted West and two of his mates missed the trucks taking them back to Telok Kurau that night and while waiting on the side of the road spotted an ambulance approaching. They hailed it and the driver offered to take them into Katong. Ted commented it was then they realised that they were not the only passengers, as the driver asked them to help with the wounded. In the back were women and children who had been caught in the bombing. It was the first time that Ted had seen the effects of bomb damage on innocent civilians and it is something that still distresses him after all these years.

The following day they travelled back to Kallang to view the damage. As the airfield was still considered operational a big clean-up was started.

Squadron Leader Wilf Clouston was officially posted to Headquarters Operations Room on Friday, 23 January and the command of 488 Squadron passed to the newly promoted Squadron Leader, Mac Mackenzie. By this time the squadron was almost destroyed, having, on any one day, only up to four very patched and reworked aircraft available. They joined forces with the other Kallang-based squadron, No. 243, which was only marginally better off. Later in the day they were visited by two very low flying aircraft which they all thought were returning Hurricanes of 243 Squadron. They came in low over the airfield boundary and turned out to be Japanese. By the time the anti-aircraft gunners spotted them they were well away.

Life continued on for those at Kallang. The day's routine was interrupted in a big way with the arrival of the Japanese bombers, but any activities were run around these events where possible. Propaganda leaflets were dropped by the Japanese telling 488 Squadron that they would be bombed and shelled on 25 January. They were able to do this with impunity as the island's defences were just about non-existent.

On Saturday, 24 January, 488 Squadron was re-equipped with nine Hurricane fighters from one of the convoys for which they had flown air cover. Their arrival was timely as they were down to the last three Buffaloes, which were handed over to 243 Squadron. The Hurricane was a vastly

Pilot Officer Len Farr.
*Air Force Museum, Christchurch*

superior fighter aircraft to the old Buffalo and both ground- and aircrews got stuck into bringing these nine aircraft on line. Hurricanes were being assembled in scattered dispersal areas all over the island. The learning curve for the squadron started all over again with the arrival of the new aircraft. Having just got familiar with the idiosyncrasies of the Buffalo these young men now had to face a new challenge and learn to fly a new aircraft with simply no time to practise other than flying operationally. All made solos the following day.

Sadly, news was received on Sunday, 25 January that Len Farr had passed away at midday from his injuries received earlier on 22 January. 488 were now in the thick of it. The day started with a tropical downpour. The rainstorm was centred over Kallang and Flight Lieutenant Hutcheson was in the middle of the morning briefing when, without warning, bombs started crashing down around them. Most stayed for a short while but eventually the room cleared and everyone headed for the foxholes. The bombs seemingly came about quite by accident. Unbeknown to them, No. 232 Squadron based at Seletar had managed to get airborne and intercepted the Japanese squadron. In their haste to get away the Japanese carried out their normal tactic and jettisoned their bomb loads — right over Kallang. It could be said that Kallang had advance warning from the leaflets that had been dropped earlier. Paddy Cromie remembers a stick of bombs crashing into the sea just off the airfield perimeter and him unashamedly sprinting like a madman towards the nearest shelter. Further interception patrols were carried out later in the day and many Japanese bombers were cut off before they reached Singapore and forced to jettison their loads before turning back and fleeing for their lives. The squadron later carried out ground attacks against Japanese troop transports on the road north of Batu Pahat.

Max Boyd remembered the bombs that day coming out of nowhere, but felt it was no accident and that fifth-columnists were at work. It seemed to him to be too much of a coincidence that the day after the new Hurricanes arrived they were targeted in conditions that normally would have meant no bombing due to the lack of visibility. He also reported the increasing nervousness among the groundcrew, particularly those on first flight section that were working out in the open and needed an extra few minutes' warning to get to safety. He commented on one man in his flight who even showered in his steel helmet and one other that always put his steel helmet over his backside while cowering on the ground as he felt that this was the highest part of his anatomy and as such the most vulnerable!

Len Farr was buried on 26 January 1942. Len was just 24 years of age and was buried at 8am on a hilltop overlooking the straits of Johore. His funeral was attended by members of his squadron and the service was led by Squadron Leader Hardy of the RAF. There was a sad postscript to Len Farr's story. After the war attempts were made to locate his grave, without success. He is commemorated on the Singapore Memorial at Kranji.

A farewell party was held in the Airport Hotel that night for Wilf Clouston. It was a time of mixed emotions

The first of the much-needed Hurricane fighters.

for the squadron, but the festivities were a welcome break from the sadness of the last few days. There was much alcohol drunk, with the champagne being donated by the hotel manager, who had taken an interest in the squadron, in fact putting up free bottles of the stuff for any pilot that downed a Japanese aircraft. There was a heavy raid that night and the bombs fell close to the new billets at Telok Kurau School.

The groundcrew worked impossible hours readying the Hurricanes under the most trying of conditions. When the aircraft were rolled out on the morning of 27 January for refuelling there was an unmitigated disaster. Out of the clouds came a formation of 27 Japanese bombers, dropping their entire load on Kallang. Two of the new planes were destroyed outright and the remaining seven

Not too many salvageable parts left following another bombing raid.

badly damaged. Eight of the pilots waiting during the refuelling in a sandbagged gun emplacement were buried when a bomb burst close by, but they were hauled out relatively unharmed, although most suffered from ear damage. Flight Lieutenant Mackenzie seemed to have suffered the most. The concussion had made him stone deaf and when he recovered a fortnight later he had difficulty even hearing his engine when he resumed flying. He suffered with his hearing for the rest of his life. No. 243 Squadron also took a plastering, losing what was left of its Buffaloes. The bombs set fire to grass in the dispersal areas and considerable effort was needed to

Looking across Kallang airfield to the north just after bombing.
*Art Donahue*

control the flames, which were putting their remaining machines at risk.

Just 40 minutes later a second wave of bombers came over from the opposite direction and completely obliterated the aerodrome runway, destroying most of the aircraft on the ground, three petrol tankers laden with fuel, and most of the motor transport still left. One tanker was parked close to the dispersal hut and had a jet of flame shooting about 12 m in the air out of its centre section. Some pilots watched in amazement as a large group of groundcrew pushed the burning tanker about 200 m away where it eventually exploded and burnt out completely. One of the tankers had been riddled with shrapnel and fuel was streaming out of it like little fountains. Clem Randall remembers how funny it looked at the time, but a frantic effort ensued to plug the holes with bits of wood, handkerchiefs, rag or anything that would stem the flow. Over a 10-day period the airfield lost 10 tankers to the bombing. Paddy Cromie reports several near misses following the three raids over Kallang. Anti-personnel bombs straddled the shelters, missing by only several metres. Phosphorus bombs set a pile of matting alight in the hangar and it was all hands on deck to get it extinguished.

It was a miracle no one was killed. Aircrew members Eddie Kuhn, Don Clow, John Hutcheson and Harry Petitt helped the groundcrew relocate the ammunition threatened by the flames after Flight Sergeant Guiniven had the good idea of shifting the ammo rather than trying to control the fire. Max Boyd and two of his mates had squeezed into a foxhole dug for two only. Fortunately for them, because of the high water table on the reclaimed ground of Kallang, the foxhole had been built quite shallow but built up with sandbags and earth. One of the blazing petrol tankers was only a short distance away,

## ✈ Daisy Cutter bombs

*The Japanese by this time were using 'Daisy Cutter' bombs and bombing from a height of 20,000 feet, well above anti-aircraft defences on the island. These were long, narrow bombs with a protruding spike which detonated when it touched, usually a couple of feet above the ground, and spread shrapnel over a wide area. Mackenzie remembers the after-effects of one of these bombs landing close to a truckload of women heading off to factory work down the airfield road. Several were cut to pieces by the blast.*

*The Daisy Cutters figured a few days later when an Indian works company was employed filling in the bomb craters on the main runway. They generally worked during the night but had decided to work during the day between raids. The English officer in charge was warned that there was a very small margin of time between the air raid alarm warning and the actual arrival of the bombs — sometimes only minutes. He sneered that running for the shelters would be unnecessary as they would simply lie down flat on the concrete and accept the possibility that a couple of them would be injured. When the next raid came the whole works company lay down on the ground as instructed and were wiped out almost to the man. The fate of the officer was unknown but in a way it reflected the colonial madness of the time, which had entrenched the notion that men were expendable.*

*Clem Randall in relaxed mood on one of the few serviceable Hurricanes.*
Collection of Stu Smart

and the burning fuel came right up to the built-up ground. Had it been a fully excavated hole they undoubtedly would have perished. Hutch remembered one of the station civilian fire crew turning up long after the bombers had left and starting to throw his weight around. He was soon given short shrift and left very quickly. Hutch reckoned rather laconically that the 'heat was too much for him'.

The third and final raid of the day destroyed most of the remaining aircraft. Max Boyd was even more convinced they were being targeted through the efforts of someone on the ground, as only the aircraft that had been left intact and largely hidden from the air were systematically destroyed or very badly damaged. The despondency in his diary notes comes through at this time and he commented that he was resigned to being overrun by the Japanese Army in a very short while.

A large number of civilian Chinese workers were killed while sheltering under the concrete flying boat slipway when a bomb blasted through the concrete. Many more were killed trying to hide in the long grass out in the open. The remaining groundcrew barracks were destroyed along with the recreation hall and NAAFI canteen. Des Hargreaves, Jack Mant, Harry O'May and 'Smiler' Patterson all took advantage of the demise of the NAAFI. Beer was collected in empty petrol cans, and it was a long and boisterous night for those men. Jack Mant also managed to score a couple of cartons of smokes.

Shortly after the last raid of the day, a Blenheim aircraft of 27 Squadron, flown by a New Zealander, tried to land at Kallang with no brakes. The only clear and undamaged ground was around where three surviving Hurricanes were parked. As he desperately tried to avoid the parked aircraft it was reported later by one of the bystanders that Wilf Clouston shouted out, 'Here comes a bloody idiot,' drew out his revolver and said he would 'shoot the bastard if he as much as touched one of the parked aircraft'. Fortunately, the Blenheim missed all three by the closest of margins and the pilot taxied his aircraft away, blissfully unaware of what his fate could have been. The same Blenheim pilot later commented that all the trees on the perimeter road of the airfield had been cut down so that the road could be used as a runway.

By Wednesday, 28 January, the pilots, attended by their groundcrew, would sit waiting in the cockpits for the orders to take off rather than stand by in the dispersal hut. They needed that extra time to get airborne rather than face the delay of reaching the aircraft and run the risk of being caught on the ground or in the process of taking off. The Japanese had developed a regular pattern with the bombing and the same scene was repeated day after day. The recco plane was spotted always between 9 and 9.30am. This was followed around 10.30am by the first of the bombing waves so it was not too difficult to anticipate the next flight of bombers. There was little systematic bombing carried out in the afternoons at this time, although as the days progressed the intensity lifted and one raid seemed to follow another. The Japanese clearly saw Kallang as a threat to their advance and dealt with the airfield appropriately. Kallang at this stage was out of shelling range unlike Seletar, Sembawang and Tengah, so

## ✈ Keeping planes flying

*Most of the aircraft still flying were hybrids put together from parts taken from different aircraft. Wings were joined to fuselages and motors from different sources, mostly from damaged or written-off aircraft. When a badly damaged plane reached Kallang and crash-landed it was immediately descended upon by maintenance groundcrew who, within hours, dismantled and removed all its still usable parts. As the days went by and this source of parts dried up, they went further afield around the island looting parts off known crash sites. Bert referred to many of these wrecks as 'Christmas Trees' in his memoirs. Equipment was even removed from Japanese wrecks and reused where it was either compatible or could be modified to fit. There was nothing to touch the ingenuity of the 488 Squadron groundcrew. Bernard Grindrod recalls commandeering a Chinese truck to go to the city for food and tools. Later in the day they scrounged some rum from the stores at the devastated naval base and were arrested on their return for stealing the truck. Hutch told the provosts who had made the arrests to get lost and they did!*

it attracted continuing bombing attacks to try to nullify any resistance.

The individual aircraft were dispersed all over the airfield to minimise the damage from bombing. This had the effect of spreading the support for each aircraft, and the pilot and his immediate groundcrew assigned to that particular aircraft became very close units. Ironically, it was safer for the aircrew to be in the air and away from the bombing than it was for the groundcrew left defenceless on the ground to face being caught in the firestorm that arrived from the air. It was hell for the maintenance guys led by Andy Chandler.

Although there were three air raid alerts this day, no bombs reached Kallang. Seletar and Katong instead took a plastering. The groundcrews took advantage of the break from getting aircraft airborne. Totally without the help of the long-departed civilian labour, they worked like madmen to fill in the bomb craters and repair any aircraft considered salvageable. When the air raid alarms sounded, the squadron personnel, where possible, were evacuated away from the airfield, generally towards Katong where they waited out the raids and returned when the all clear sounded. This time, though, the first load of bombs was dropped on Katong village just a short distance away. Harry O'May was caught in Katong and spent an uncomfortable 15 minutes cowering in a stormwater drain. He survived without injury, despite having part of a building come down over him. Clem Randall remembers the incident at Kallang with Harry O'May with some humour, although he was sure that Harry

Salvaging parts off the destroyed Hurricane of Squadron Leader Llewellyn, who was killed while taking off from Kallang. He struck the mast of a junk in the adjacent canal and buried his aircraft into a boatshed on the seaward side of Kallang.

The beginning of the end 137

*Waiting in a rubber plantation near Katong for a bombing raid on Kallang to pass over.*
Collection of Stu Smart

was caught out in the open. The Japanese were dropping a lot of incendiary bombs at that time. These were full of a mixture of phosphorus and rubber that emitted huge clouds of a thick yellow-green smoke which stuck to everything. Although Harry was not injured he emerged from the devastation looking like something out of a pantomime, covered in a sticky yellow-green residue.

Paddy Cromie commented on Thursday, 29 January that initially a lot of the groundcrew were clearing out on the trucks back to Katong well before the raids came over. As time passed on, however, more and more got very blasé about the possible outcome and stayed at Kallang and rode out the storm. The Japanese were by this time also targeting Katong and nearby Geylang village with increasing frequency, so it was becoming very debatable where the safest place was. The day was spent repairing the remaining aircraft in what dispersal bays were still undamaged, and the rest of the aircraft were distributed away from the airfield, under trees and in back yards of surrounding properties. Not one of the aircraft was flyable. The bombing increased in frequency over Katong. Paddy Cromie and some of his mates had to take cover in a shallow trench near the canal. They felt very unsafe there and decided in the end to make a break for the trenches nearer their camp.

Kallang was completely unusable after the three latest raids but the groundcrews worked tirelessly filling in the bomb craters and clearing the shrapnel off the runway areas. Flight Lieutenant Hutcheson noted in his diary that all the civilian labour had cleared out, so both the aircrew and groundcrew were forced to carry out repairs to the runways and buildings as well as repair damage to, and service, the remaining aircraft. He commented also that the only ones other than the air force personnel that stood their ground were the Malay Police and the Indian troops who were guarding the airfield.

By Friday, 30 January they managed to get three Hurricanes in the air again, but bomb damage to Kallang meant the three could only land at Tengah airfield. Bert left with the inimitable Flight Sergeant Andy Chandler and a couple of other groundcrew looking for spares for their Buffaloes. They travelled out to some RAF stores close to the causeway. It was a desperate measure, given that the roads were being constantly shelled and bombed. The stores were situated right under the nose of the watching Japanese. The madness of the situation was compounded by the person in charge of the RAF stores insisting on procedural matters being carried out, saying that it would take two days to arrange delivery to Kallang. Not to be outdone, and in the true Kiwi manner, Andy Chandler distracted the stores officer and Bert and his mates effectively stole a Buffalo propeller and spares, and loaded them onto the back of their truck. As they sped away back to Kallang, bombs started falling and the area they were just leaving was blown apart, including a small hospital they had just passed. What spares that were still left in the stores were to fall into Japanese hands a couple of days later when they gained a foothold on the island.

Pilot Officer Peter Gifford.
*Air Force Museum, Christchurch*

Back at Kallang an increased frequency of bombing was alternated with leaflets being dropped, calling on the British to surrender. The three serviceable Hurricanes flown by Hutch, Jim MacIntosh and Jack Meharry took off on interception but were too late to prevent Kallang being plastered again. They were ordered to fly to Tengah as there was no way they could land back at Kallang because of the damage. Jack Meharry crashed his aircraft while on final approach to land at Tengah. The two surviving aircraft of Hutch and Jim MacIntosh flew patrol work with some of 232 Squadron from Tengah.

No one seemed to be in charge of the groundcrew

One of the early Hurricanes.
*Collection of Jim Cromie*

at this stage with most orders and instructions coming from the flight sergeants. Nearly all the groundcrew were wandering the airfield repairing bomb damage. Most of the foxholes were beyond repair so a truck was sent out to slowly circulate the airfield. When a 'bombers approaching' warning sounded it moved among the personnel out in the open picking up everybody without transport and taking them into the nearby rubber plantations until the all clear was sounded.

The naval base oil installation at Sembawang burning day after day.

## six

# The end draws near

### OBLITERATION OF THE AIRFIELDS AND AIRCRAFT, EVACUATING TO SUMATRA

The situation was getting desperate on Singapore, with constant shelling and bombing. The Japanese were now consolidating in Johore just a few kilometres from the island. On Saturday, 31 January, the last of the retreating British troops crossed the causeway onto Singapore Island and army sappers blew a breach in the causeway to slow the Japanese advance. John Hutcheson was at Tengah Air Base at the time and when the explosives detonated he thought he had been shot. He commented that he thought his nerves were by that time well and truly damaged.

The other airfields on the island, Seletar and Sembawang, were being obliterated, as the Japanese artillery was now just 2.5 km from them. It was decided that any remaining serviceable aircraft from those airfields were to be flown back to Kallang. Of the 51 Hurricane fighters that had arrived in the middle of January only 20 were still in action, the rest having been damaged or destroyed. Only six of the original Buffaloes were still airworthy. The bombing patterns were changing by now and instead of the regular daytime and after-nightfall formations, the Japanese were sending small flights or just single aircraft during the night-time hours. In the definitive work by Masanobu Tsuji, who wrote the Japanese version of events leading to the fall of Singapore, he tells of Staff Officer Kawashima, who carried out bombing attacks in a single-seater fighter aircraft over Singapore. He went out alone at night with the intention of causing psychological damage to the Allies at a time when the onset of darkness was supposed to bring relief from attack from the air. It was a cunning ploy and one that worked very well. One man was therefore capable of disturbing the peace of countless thousands on the ground, waiting and listening for the sound of falling bombs. The night was lit like daylight with the many burning fires and the glow from the wreck of the still-burning *Empress of Asia* just off the coast. It was, as many of the men commented, possible to read at night from the glow.

All around the island explosions could be heard, particularly from Johore and the naval base at Sembawang, and it was obvious now to all those at Kallang that a 'scorched earth' policy was being adopted and units everywhere were firing their fuel and explosive dumps.

Japanese tail fin from one that didn't get away. Clem Randall on the left and Robbie Nixon behind the tailplane.
*Collection of Stu Smart*

The end of Singapore as a British outpost was obviously very near.

At 9pm on Saturday, 31 January, Squadron Leader Mackenzie was told that 488 Squadron was to pack up and be ready to move immediately. All the Hurricane spares were packed into cases and all the tools and personal gear were loaded onto the backs of trucks ready for the move and hidden away in the rubber plantations around the airfield. This work was stopped many times during the night due to the continuous bombing. When dawn arrived the next day the weary men were told that they were not leaving after all and that the 488 groundcrew were to remain to service what aircraft were left of No. 232 RAF Squadron. Most of the groundcrew personnel from 232 Squadron had already left for Palembang in Sumatra on the coaster *Perak*. Decisions had been made by Air Operations to rationalise the situation on Singapore by leaving just a core group to fight on while as many men, aircraft and resources as possible were to be sent away to establish a new line of defence in Sumatra. The groundcrew of 488 Squadron were now to be the only air force maintenance personnel left on the island; they had to face the near certainty they would be left to be prisoners of the Japanese or worse.

This incident still upsets members of 488 Squadron I interviewed, as they found out later that ranking British officers had given 232 RAF Squadron groundcrew precedence over the New Zealanders and sent their own RAF personnel to safety. This galled, particularly as the British groundcrews would be servicing 488 pilots and planes in their fallback position in Sumatra. Unhappily, though, for the 232 Squadron groundcrew this arrangement proved disastrous. The ship that they, rather than the 488 boys, were on, the *Perak*, was caught by the Japanese and sunk, and most of the 232 Squadron groundcrew members that survived the sinking were imprisoned for the duration of the war. Many of them in fact did not see their homes or loved ones again, dying in the death camps set up by the Japanese throughout Java and Sumatra.

As it turned out, the British High Command did the New Zealanders a favour, and this incident was the first of many fortuitous events that favoured Bert and his mates. They at least were still together though still in mortal danger. They held on desperately to the hope that they would eventually be repatriated to catch up again with their departed aircrews and reform as a fighting unit. There was still considerable coming and going of aircraft with flights of two or three aircraft returning from Sumatra for a couple of days before setting off back to the relative safety of the two airfields set up at Palembang.

The intensity of the bombing raids increased on Sunday, 1 February, with the Japanese being almost totally unopposed. The few British aircraft that were still flying took to the air in a futile but brave attempt to defend the island against overwhelming odds. Bert, still today, becomes quite emotional when he recounts seeing those young men taking off, sometimes a lone aircraft to attack what seemed at the time to be a sky full of Japanese bombers and fighters. Most of these aircraft literally limped into the air looking like patchwork quilts, outnumbered and outgunned. Each of those young fighter pilots would have known that their days were numbered but still took to the skies night and day and often without being ordered to. The Hurricane aircraft they were now flying were completely new to them and they did not have the benefit of any conversion training. It was simply a case of climbing aboard and trusting that they could build up some training hours in the air before striking combat conditions. Their problems were further

Reg Hall and Jim Boddy standing in the crater of a 'big one' that landed beside the foxhole of Stu Smart, Errol Law and Johnny Helmore. The cover in the foreground is over the timber roof of their shelter at ground level. Miraculously all escaped without injury.

compounded by the horror of having to land their aircraft on an airfield that was looking no better than a turnip field from the saturation bombing they had endured over the past weeks.

Many of the groundcrew boys by this time were not coping too well with the situation. They were spending more time away from the immediate area of the airfield to keep clear of the bombing. Once their aircraft had left on a flight, they headed back to shelter among the rubber trees away from the airfield, leaving only a skeleton crew behind. When their aircraft returned they moved back to Kallang. Tempers were fraying badly at this time due to the stress of the situation, the constant bombing, the now increased shelling, the heat and the exhaustion. None of those factors was lessening with the onset of darkness. There was simply no way of getting away from the feeling of hopelessness and coping with the uncertainty of their situation. Food, or the lack of it, was by now becoming a major problem. Max Boyd remembers that most of the guys went out at night to the local village shops from their billets at Telok Kurau School hunting for food to supplement the meagre supplies given to them during the day. They felt they had been literally abandoned.

The naval base was under constant bombardment at this

A direct hit on the Kallang Airport building. The tents shown were used by the Indian Army airfield guards as temporary shelters.
*Collection of Stu Smart*

time and the pall of dense black smoke from the burning oil storage tanks was to be an ongoing feature over the following days. It was, in fact, a scene that later was to constantly reappear in countless books and publications describing the last days of Singapore. The volume of smoke took on the appearance of a volcanic eruption. The Allied aircrews, even when desperately trying to use cloud cover to avoid being seen by the enemy, would not fly through it. The intensity and heat was so great that they claimed that solid burning oil was being carried thousands of metres in the air and to fly through it risked disaster.

Rebuilding the airfield was now a constant daily task. The groundcrews worked in unbelievable conditions to keep the aircraft flying. The 488 boys managed to get another four Hurricanes patched up on Monday, 2 February and they were flown out to Palembang in Sumatra by Noel Sharp, Grahame White, Wally Greenhalgh and Eddie Kuhn.

In the following days as an aircraft became serviceable it

## ✈ The big guns

A lot of talk at the time, and for many years since, has been about the big naval defence guns pointing out to sea and this being the reason the Japanese managed to take Singapore with relative ease. While the siting of the guns contributed to the loss of Singapore, it was more the Japanese planning circumventing their effectiveness by not attacking from the sea that made the invasion so successful. Churchill had effectively put all his eggs in one basket by declaring that the naval task force combined with coastal defences was all that would be required to protect the area.

British arrogance in assuming the Japanese had no experience of jungle fighting and that they could not use tanks or armoured vehicles in such conditions was a big factor. The Japanese achieved both, and the early loss of the Repulse and the Prince of Wales ended any British capacity to defend Malaya and Singapore successfully. The big coastal guns were used in defence of the island, as they had a 360-degree traverse, but were in effect shooting blind. A further factor was a total loss of effectiveness as they were only set up with armour-piercing shells and these simply buried themselves into soft jungle ground. Those at Kallang worked under the trajectory of these shells, which had a massive muzzle explosion, followed by the whine of the shell passing over. As Bert said it was just more interruption to what little sleep they were getting at night.

Top: Sergeant Wally Greenhalgh.
*Air Force Museum, Christchurch*

Above: Trying to clear the mess after one of the raids.
*Collection of Jim Cromie*

was flown out. Not that there was any great number — in fact, only some Hurricanes and just the two Buffaloes. These were flown by Pete Gifford and 'Bunny' de Maus over to Seletar. Nerves were on edge now and many of the groundcrew took to sleeping in the foxholes. The Japanese by this time seemed to be concentrating on shelling and bombing the dock areas and the city, just a few kilometres away, was under constant attack.

Squadron Leader Clouston returned to Kallang on a visit on Tuesday, 3 February and gave a talk to all the 488 personnel. He told them that they were to stay at their posts as a maintenance unit, as he was sure that the island could be defended and that they would be required to service aircraft returning from Sumatra. Most listening thought at the time that there was now no chance and it was hard to imagine that Clouston really believed what he was saying at the time.

Most of the daylight hours were spent salvaging parts off destroyed Buffaloes mainly to give the men something to do. There were simply no serviceable aircraft left at Kallang. Most realised by now the futility of the work but it took one's mind off the approaching storm. Some took the opportunity to catch up on what little sleep they had had in the past week. Hutch found the waiting totally demoralising and found it easier to just potter around doing anything to keep the mind occupied and keep morale up. They were receiving no instructions at all by this stage. Notes made at that time by Bernard Grindrod told of him going into the city with two mates, Leading Aircraftman Herb Ashley-Jones and Aircraftman Vern Oakey, during a bombing raid, looking for a drink and finding the Raffles Hotel deserted except for one barman. Servicemen except for officers were normally banned from the hotel but they defied standing orders and ordered the famous 'Singapore Sling' at the Long Bar before the barman finally scampered away to the nearest bomb shelter. Bombs were still falling on the streets outside when they left to return to Kallang — without paying, I might add.

On Wednesday, 4 February, Pilot Officer Peter Gifford and Flight Sergeant John Rees took Andy Chandler, Bert and a party of men across to Sembawang to patch up any aircraft they could find, left from the recently departed 232 Squadron. As they arrived, the Japanese must have spotted them and started shelling from across the straits. They were effectively in no-man's-land as any personnel on the base had long since gone. They worked on when they were able during the night, and early next morning attempted to fly what aircraft they could back to Kallang. Bert remembers no feeling of being scared as they had endured many days of continuous bombing at Kallang, although being shelled by artillery was a new experience. The aircraft had been hidden in temporary dispersal areas and when next morning, at first light, they were wheeled out into the open, the Japanese shelling intensified.

The aircraft took off in a hail of shells. One plane was hit while taxiing and the pilot, Pilot Officer Frank Johnstone, leapt out and grabbed another undamaged one and managed to take off. The groundcrew all left in a great hurry when the aircraft were airborne and managed to leave behind one of their number, Aircraftman Fitzgerald.

He turned up a day later at Kallang not a very happy chappie. He had found a rifle during his travels and had spent most of the night dodging Japanese shells landing in among the rubber trees where he was trying to shelter. Later that day the same group crossed the island to Tengah and flew out all serviceable aircraft there at great risk to their lives. At the very least they had stopped the aircraft falling into the hands of the Japanese when they finally arrived a couple of days later.

Thursday, 5 February was a busy day with aircraft flown by the aircrew survivors of 243 and 232 squadrons arriving and taking off all day. The weather had packed up completely with torrential rainstorms throughout the day, making landing and taking off more hazardous and just adding to the problems caused by bombing damage to the surface of the airfield. One of the arriving Buffaloes landed downwind at high speed and turned a complete somersault. Twelve new Hurricanes arrived in the morning with another 18 aircraft in the afternoon. Hutch was sent at dawn over to Seletar to try to recover some Hurricanes that had been hidden away in the rubber trees. Again their arrival sent the Japanese artillery into a frenzy of shelling, categorised by Hutch as 'very uncomfortable'. They were forced to wait for a lull in the shelling before moving the aircraft out into the open and trying for a very hurried departure back to Kallang. All the hidden aircraft were shifted without incident. The only injury during the day was a lump of earth falling on Sergeant Claude Halkett's helmet and giving him a mighty headache. Hutch had earlier driven over to Sembawang to check on Peter Gifford and John Rees and their party carrying out the same sort of recovery under very heavy shellfire. Shelling during the day caused problems, with many personnel travelling to Tengah to escape the worst of it. Clem Randall went across to Tengah with others

# Reflex action

*The 488 boys had been warned to watch out for low-flying Japanese fighters sneaking in over the treetops at high speed and strafing the boundaries. Clem tells the following story:*

*At this stage of our activities, for our own protection we knew exactly where the nearest slit trench, underground shelter, bomb crater or effective shelter against blast and shrapnel was, in relation to our position. Just on dusk I was buttoning down a Hurricane for the night and to lock the controls you had to reach down into the floor of the cockpit, centralise the control column and the pedals, then unlatch the locking bar, swing it up and over 180 degrees and engage the pedals and column in the appropriate slots. I was head down bum up and concentrating on getting everything into place when there was a rumble of aircraft engines. I looked up and sure enough there they were, a light bomber flanked by four fighters just coming over the brow of a low hill and swinging down onto the boundary. In a flash I was down off that Hurricane and headed flat out for my friendly bomb crater. Heading for the crater I was surprised that there wasn't a hail of bullets and cannon shells going past me. I looked around again and saw that the planes were ours, in fact a Hudson flanked by four Hurricanes and not a Japanese plane in sight.*

*Clem did think it was curtains for him but remembers no feeling of terror at the time; he described his feelings as just doing automatically what he had been conditioned to do by circumstances. No fear, just an automatic reflex response.*

# A 'heartbreaking' mess

Arthur Gerald Donahue, an American pilot with 232 Squadron, had arrived following the closure of Seletar, Tengah and Sembawang. The remnants of his squadron's aircraft had arrived ahead of him as he had chosen to drive across to Kallang. He described driving in through the gates of what had been Singapore's only civilian airport. He was appalled at the devastation. The airfield appeared to be in no better condition than the devastated one he had just left.

*The vast concrete aprons between and in front of the hangars were torn and pitted with bomb craters, as was the entire field. The saddest sight of all was the remains of several Hurricanes and Buffaloes, as well as three or four trucks and tank wagons, around the outside of the field — sorry-looking, smashed and twisted wreckages, mostly burnt out, the victims of bombing and machine-gun attacks. It was heartbreaking.*

When he reached the ruins of the Officers' Mess he found several squadron members still raking around in the smouldering ruins recovering bottles of beer and liquor from the damaged but intact refrigerators. By this time, a new mess had been set up at the 'Seaview Hotel' some kilometres away on the coast road closer to the city.

(Donahue, a native of Minnesota, had travelled to the UK at the outbreak of the war with Germany and joined the RAF as a fighter pilot. He was shot *down and wounded both during the Battle of Britain and later in Sumatra. After his escape from Sumatra back to the UK he was finally lost tragically when his Spitfire crashed into the English Channel on 11 September 1942.)*

to help service some aircraft sent there due to Kallang being in such a mess. The Japanese had an observation balloon overlooking Tengah so they knew every move being made by those on the ground.

Hutch returned later that day from Tengah to Kallang in time to see the result of the Officers' Mess having been destroyed, by a single bomb that had hit dead centre. The rest of the bombs had landed in a line from the end of the runway extension all the way up to the mess building. Hutch had left the mess in a hurry to take cover earlier that day and tried later on his return to recover something from the building, but the burning ruin put a stop to

Pilot Officer Frank Johnstone.
*Air Force Museum, Chrstchurch*

The board that says it all, just the 488 Squadron groundcrew and no aircraft are left to defend the island of Singapore. George Clancy, Ray Stephenson and Pat Chadwick looking more cheerful than they must have felt at the time! Note the two naughty words altered on this photograph but not on the original sighted by the author.

that. He recalled with some humour two of his fellow officers climbing out of the sewer after the bombers had left. Later in the day Hutch returned to Sembawang with Jack Oakden to see if they could find some runway marker boards to use back at Kallang. Sembawang by this time was almost deserted. He met up with Frank Johnstone, who was sitting in a car on the perimeter track watching a Japanese dive bomber making repeated bombing and strafing runs at Sembawang station's mess buildings.

No. 232 Squadron aircraft were now in place at Kallang and the remainder of their aircraft were being serviced by 488 groundcrew. All 488 pilots were heading south to Sumatra with any flyable aircraft supposedly to be serviced by 232 groundcrews who had left for Palembang — but, of course, they were never to reach their destination.

There was a lot of dissent among 488 groundcrew at the time due to the changeover as they had hoped to stay together and reform as a complete unit with their own aircrew. The powers that be had ordained otherwise. The Commanding Officer of RAF Station Tengah, Group Captain FG Watts, shot himself at Tengah air base so it wasn't only the groundcrews that were under stress. Watts had been station commander at Tengah for two years and had suffered the stress of seeing his squadrons being decimated and his airfield destroyed. His groundcrew wandered around aimlessly and the considerable Chinese labour force he had built up would only work at gunpoint; in fact, several had been shot to prevent the rest from fleeing. His behaviour had become increasingly bizarre. During the many Japanese high-level bombing attacks while everyone else was taking shelter, he could be seen walking about the airfield out in the open. It was said that following a 'Please explain' from headquarters that related to the failure by his squadron to get sufficient aircraft in the air, he had a quiet drink with some of his aircrew, finished his drink, quietly excused himself and went to his room and shot himself.

Back at Kallang a pattern of survival had been established by the groundcrew. Once the alarm for enemy aircraft sounded, all the serviceable aircraft were sent off and the groundcrew cleared out. They used any means of transport available, some simply travelling by truck down the coast road while others fled for the rubber plantations — anywhere to get away from the target area of the bombing.

On the evening of Friday, 6 February, all the remaining 488 Squadron pilots, except Jack Oakden and John Hutcheson and four others, left on the cruiser HMS *Danae* for Batavia where they were hoping to be re-equipped with new aircraft and set up a new defensive line. Both New Zealand and Australia were in the path of the Japanese advance and these men would have been very much aware of this fact. Hutcheson and Oakden, together with Squadron Leader Brooker, spent the day searching the dispersal areas at Tengah, Sembawang and Seletar again for any serviceable aircraft still left but were unsuccessful. All three bases were being shelled out of existence. They left later that day themselves on the SS *City of Canterbury*, sailing for Batavia at eleven o'clock that night. Bunt Pettit said that there was considerable anger among them that their groundcrew were going to be left behind.¹ Hutch and his small group had some difficulty as they were initially not allowed to embark and had to drive back to Kallang and get Group Captain Rice to issue orders by telephone to the Embarkation Officer on the wharfside. Returning to Kallang was somewhat difficult as the airfield was taking a real pasting with six bombing raids in the three hours before midnight.

Four of the remaining Kallang Hurricanes had earlier been written off, all within sight of the base, mostly returning from action elsewhere. The new commanding officer of 232 Squadron, Squadron Leader Llewellyn, was killed taking off from Kallang after he hit the mast of a junk that was passing up the main canal at the side of the airfield. The aircraft somersaulted into the ground and Llewellyn was killed instantly. One other aircraft sustained a bullet through its engine and crash-landed without power, one crash-landed on the beach and the fourth landed but tipped up on its nose. Not a productive day.

Art Donahue and three of his 232 Squadron members had earlier asked for some time off to get things sorted and their new CO, Squadron Leader Llewellyn, had told them to take the rest of the day off. They had left by car to travel into the city. After some touring around and looking at the sights they had ended up at the Alhambra Movie Theatre where they watched the movie, staying there even through a bombing raid. By the time they returned to Kallang just a few hours later, they found to their horror that Llewellyn was dead.

Art Donahue was an old friend of John Mackenzie from their early days with the RAF in England. He was shocked by the appearance of Mackenzie, finding he was 'so worn and haggard and had lost so much weight I hardly recognised him'. Mackenzie at the time was still recovering from the near-miss bombing and burial that across the island. The Japanese artillery, after a quiet day beforehand, certainly made up for it this day. Not the quiet Sunday that many would have liked. The last of the 232 Squadron aircraft, patched and broken, were flown off to Sumatra with the aircrews intending to return with new aircraft. Flight Sergeant Andy Chandler had a crew working to get one more serviceable Hurricane ready for Squadron Leader Clouston to fly to escape from Singapore if the surrender to the Japanese became inevitable. For the next couple of days the 488 groundcrew took shelter from the intensity of the attacks and listened to the awful sounds of the war getting closer to them. They were constantly on their guard as advance parties of Japanese troops had been seen close by. They waited in vain for the return of the aircraft from Batavia to pick them up but it was not to be. They were effectively trapped. Nerves and tempers were frayed, although morale was high among the men, considering the circumstances. Even the dropping of a tin helmet caused panic. Two or three of the groundcrew had not been near the airfield for at least two weeks and had taken to sleeping up on a hillside nearby.

There was heavy fighting close to Kallang. There was also general disbelief among the men that the British had not arranged bomber coverage, particularly at the time the Japanese had massed for their final push with huge concentrations of troops and equipment around the Johore area. What a target that would have made. There were clearly no civilians in the area as the leaflets dropped over it made that quite plain, so there would be no risk of 'collateral damage'.

Max Boyd wrote that each day that the Kallang aircraft were in the air the groundcrew were leaving the airfield and taking shelter in the rubber trees. He worried about the time needed to hand-wind the starters on their Hurricane aircraft, particularly when speed was needed to

## ✈ Last visit from Allied Commander

Bert probably had his best chance to offer his opinion directly to the British High Command on Monday, 9 February. The Allied Commander, General Wavell, landed on his last visit to the beleaguered island from his headquarters in Dutch Sumatra. Ironically, he arrived at Kallang at about the same time that his Japanese counterpart, General Yamashita, waded ashore on the northern beaches of the island. Wavell's Catalina flying boat landed between raids at the old Imperial Airways slipway just off the main runway at Kallang. He noted the destruction at Kallang and would have seen the last of the serviceable aircraft taking off from the mostly destroyed runway to head for safer pastures in Sumatra. Work on these aircraft had been almost impossible over the preceding days of bombing raids. Fifth-columnists were also causing problems on the ground with reported cases of sabotage. Latex rubber was found in more than one fuel tank.

Wavell waited and wandered around at Kallang for some time before he and his staff hitched a ride to the Allied Headquarters at Sime Road close to the Bukit Timah Golf Course. They drove through lines of Australian troops, mostly unarmed and covered in oil and soot, heading away from the front lines and *into Singapore City. He stayed only long enough to establish that the end was near and later that day flew back to Sumatra. His leaving was not without incident. As he got out of his staff car on the ramp where his aircraft waited, he fell backwards off the ramp, a 2-m fall, landing on barbed wire and broken concrete. Among other injuries he broke two bones in his back and had to be carried onto the waiting Catalina. It appeared to sum up the situation at the time.*

get the planes in the air after the warning had been given that enemy aircraft were approaching. He commented that very little of the original runway was now left and even filling holes was no answer as by the next morning the filled holes in the sodden ground had settled, leaving further depressions. Much damage resulted to landing gear and propellers. Trees had been cleared from Grove Road which ran close to the airfield perimeter with the idea that this could be used as an alternative runway. With the Japanese now so close there was next to no warning of approaching bombers and the situation was almost impossible. However, the aircraft still left Kallang continuously in twos and threes in a vain attempt to stall the Japanese advance. The main target was the massed formations of bombers, but all too often the fighter escorts prevented them getting

### DECREE.

1. It is strictly requested that any civilian, who is living within the area extending from Pontian Kechil - Kulai - Kota Tinggi - Tengarline to the Strait of Johore, should evacuate from the above-specified zone on or before 1st February, 1942.
2. Any one who is against the above order is to be considered as a combatant and shall be bonbed or shot.

*January, 2602.*
*The Commander of the Nippon Army.*

佈告

大日本軍司令官

（一）邦影，古來，古打鼎而，丁瓦等，以南至柔佛水喉之間一概居住的非戰鬥員者限到二月一日准要退去

（二）如不從命令者看做戰鬥員必須爆並炸銃殺勿悞

皇紀二千六百二年

### MEMBERI TAHU.

1. Di nyatakan dengan keras, bahwa masing² penduduk yang tinggil di antara Pontian - Kechil, Kulai, Kota - Tinggi, Tengar dan Selat Johore harus mengundurkan diri, selambat² nja sampai pada hari 1 February 1942.
2. Pada siapa yang melanggar kenyataan ini hendak di pandang sebagai musuh dan hendak di bom atawa di tenbak.

*Tahun Nippon 2602,*
*Tuan Penglima Tentera Dai Nippon.*

Japanese Army pamphlet dropped over Johore in Malaya, ahead of the Japanese advance.

anywhere close. The odds of survival by these pilots were practically nil and Air Vice Marshal Maltby ordered a halt to all aircraft defensive actions and insisted on all aircraft and pilots leaving for Palembang at once.

By mid-morning on Tuesday, 10 February 1942, the Japanese Army was stalled just 10 km from Raffles Place in central Singapore. They had been badly held up by the surviving Argyll and Sutherland Highland troops and this had caused some frustration for the Supreme Japanese Commander, General Yamashita. It was his declared aim to have taken Singapore on the day of Kigensetsu ('Empire Day'), the anniversary of the founding of the Japanese Empire 2602 years before. Bert and his fellow 488 Squadron groundcrew were still at Kallang listening to the battle raging literally just down the road. The Allied army by this time was in a complete rout, and surviving members of assorted battalions were pouring down the Bukit Timah Road, the main road into the city. The remaining eight Hurricanes had departed for Palembang in Java at dawn after the groundcrews had worked through the night to get them ready. Kallang was visited by the Air Officer Commanding, RAF Far East Air Vice Marshal CWH Pulford. He was loud in his praise of them, but given that the Japanese were sending up to 250 aircraft daily over to Singapore, those eight remaining Allied aircraft had no show and he had been forced to order them off to Palembang.

The new leader of 232 Squadron, Flight Lieutenant Julian, was loud in his praise of the 488 groundcrew. Such was the discipline of the 488 men that they had rallied around to get the planes in an airworthy condition, despite knowing that there was never going to be a chance for them to escape with the last of the aircraft.

Notwithstanding the shambles all around them the New Zealand groundcrew still had problems with RAF

Unloading cans of aviation fuel by hand from the squadron's fuel dumps: Geoff Hocken, Ray Stephenson and Bill Howard-Taylor.

Headquarters staff officers trying to throw their weight around. Max Boyd remembers Flight Sergeant Stan Guiniven refuelling a Hurricane by standing on a wing and pouring fuel from a can. A passing staff officer told him he was risking the aircraft; Stan told him to 'bugger off' as the plane was needed in a hurry and he was holding him up. Just then the daily recco plane passed over, followed by the anti-aircraft guns opening up and the staff officer quickly disappeared from sight. Through all the commotion Stan just kept pouring the fuel.

The squadron's fuel supply at the flying boat base had now run out and cans of fuel had to be unloaded from the supply dumps located around the airfield and poured by hand into the surviving tankers for transferring to the aircraft. It was long, hard and dangerous work, which exposed the groundcrews while working out in the open. They worked on into the night and when they finally got back to the billets at the school, Max Boyd and Leading Aircraftman Wally Murray, rather than take the risk of sleeping during the daylight hours in the school buildings, decided to find a safer place among the rubber trees and scrub where they knew a trench had been dug. They were woken a short while later by the sound of gunfire. They had a look around and came across three Australian Army troops who said they were the sole survivors of their company that had just been attacked by the Japanese. Max and Wally hurried back to their billets to tell the others.

The groundcrew were issued with ancient American five-shot rifles and bayonets. There were not enough to go round so they drew lots. Wally Murray missed out so Max Boyd gave him his bayonet to make him feel better! They were divided up into sections under an NCO and deployed to meet the Japanese Army, who were now on the other side of a canal in an adjacent rubber plantation. Max remembers being separated from Wally. His NCO was Sergeant Yanovich and he remembers Aircraftman Stan 'Dusty' Rhodes being alongside him as they took positions opposite where they thought the Japanese were. He recalled later the despondency he felt at the time, being totally unprepared for this action and cursing the British High Command that had got them into this mess. The men were totally untrained for this fighting; some had never used a firearm. Another small group consisting of Des Hargreaves, Smiler Patterson, Jack Mant and Harry O'May settled down nervously to wait, sharing rifles but having a good supply of ammunition. 488 Squadron were effectively caught in no-man's-land, with the British front line now behind them and the Japanese in front and on either side.

The day of Kigensetsu had dawned on Wednesday, 11 February. All around Kallang was desolation. The air was black with smoke from burning dumps, a heady mixture of burning oil and rubber, and the dawn brought a renewed intensity of bombing and shelling. Bert must have thought it was the end of the world and have wondered if he would ever see his beloved Phyl or his family again. Three more Hurricanes had been patched

One of the Kallang Mk 2 Hurricanes that just made it back to base. The aircraft is believed to be that flown by Squadron Leader Richard 'Boy' Brooker (seen standing alongside) due to its coding visible in the photograph. This aircraft, BE208, was later recovered by the Japanese, repaired, flown and evaluated for use by the Japanese air force. *Art Donahue*

up overnight and made ready for flying out. Two of them were at Seletar. The groundcrews had been all over the island searching for aircraft that could be made flyable. A general instruction had been issued for any pilots left to fly all available aircraft away to Palembang. Two 232 Squadron pilots travelled from Kallang to Seletar before dawn and brought the two Hurricanes back to Kallang. They described the situation at Seletar as 'creepy', as the airfield had been captured earlier by the Japanese but had been retaken by the British Army some time later. After they left, the army was preparing to destroy everything as they realised the inevitability of the base being lost again. Back at Kallang, the only aircraft in the air were by now Japanese. The squadron had an early-morning visit from a very low flying aircraft that came in off the coast at rooftop level, scaring the life out of everyone, but dropping only leaflets.

Art Donahue was ordered by Squadron Leader Clouston at Air Operations to select two other pilots and take the three remaining Hurricanes and fly them off the island to Palembang. By the time they had reached the airfield from the operations room, which was by this time in the front room of one of the local houses, pandemonium reigned. They were met by the duty officer at Kallang, who was in a panic as the Japanese were very close. As the

## ✈ The indomitable 488 groundcrew

*Art Donahue praised the 488 groundcrew:*

The aircraft had been patched by the New Zealand groundcrews who had got them serviceable and had done all they could for them. Whatever we accomplished in those last few days of operating at Kallang, we owed largely to these groundcrews — who worked night and day and through bombing and machine-gun attacks, never losing spirit and always keeping our machines in shape if it was humanly possible. The groundcrews at Kallang Airdrome were a real fighting bunch.[2]

*Praise also came from another of the 232 Squadron pilots, Sergeant Terence Kelly:*

Meanwhile, the squadron at Kallang continued to operate and not at all unsuccessfully and curiously, as distinct from elsewhere, the ground staff was by all accounts pugnacious. With the Japanese already on the island and with all the other airfields occupied by the Japanese or under attack, they found a sense of purpose which allowed flying to continue until February 10th 1942.[3]

This from a man who, with a fellow pilot, had earlier in the week drawn his pistol and threatened to shoot RAAF groundcrew who were walking away from servicing his aircraft at Tengah Air Base. The recco plane had appeared overhead and they downed tools and were about to clear out and leave the aircraft stranded despite knowing that they would not be under

> *attack for at least a couple of hours. (Kelly was later captured by the Japanese in Java and transported to Japan with Eddie Kuhn.)*

three Hurricanes taxied to take off they were joined by a very battered Buffalo that one of the remaining pilots had found.

The Japanese by this time had set up artillery in a small grove of trees just to the northeast of the airfield and started shelling Kallang with shrapnel shells set to explode above the centre of the field. Donahue, who while frantically loading his aircraft, remembers the crack of rifle fire and thought the rifles were being fired from only about a half kilometre away. He recalls bullets passing close by overhead, but the Japanese were hidden by the shrubbery around the airfield perimeter. It was a bizarre experience for him as two Japanese reconnaissance planes were flying very low over the city, slowly, purposefully and unhindered. A little biplane with British markings came cruising over at about 1500 feet and he recognised it as a training aircraft from Tengah Air Base, probably being flown by a Japanese pilot. The gun in the grove turned its attention onto the biplane so for the moment the heat was off Donahue and his mates. 488 Squadron member Red Nelson recalled the biplane and was sure it was a Tiger Moth. (Stu Smart confirms that the aircraft was a Tiger Moth painted yellow, and it did drop at least one hand grenade over what was left of the aircraft dispersal area at Kallang.) At the time he spotted it, on the same day as Donahue, the aircraft was flying overhead in the port area and was being watched very carefully by those on the ground as it was reported that hand grenades or

*What is reputed to be the last Allied photograph taken from the air over Singapore before the surrender to the Japanese forces.*
*Art Donahue*

small anti-personnel bombs were being dropped from the vintage machine.

The sole Buffalo by this time had fired up and was trundling down the runway. Donahue was helped by two of the groundcrew who he knew would be left to face the Japanese. As Donahue and his small flight took off they were very conscious of the closeness of the Japanese around the perimeter of the airfield and as they circled around they were fired at by Japanese anti-aircraft guns on the northern perimeter of Kallang. He remarked somewhat drily that it was rather traumatic 'being shot at from his own airfield'. As the four aircraft gained altitude they looked back at the island. Donahue took a couple of photographs as he left, knowing full well the significance of the moment. His final memory of Singapore was:

*Looking back for one last time, my memory is of a bright*

Sergeant Bill Howard-Taylor in the foreground, with Kallang airport building and bomb damage behind.
*Collection of Bob Wright.*

*green little country, resting on the edge of the bluest sea I'd ever seen, lovely in the morning sunlight except where the dark tragic mantle of smoke ran across its middle and beyond, covering and darkening the city on the seashore. The city itself, with huge leaping red fires in its north and south parts, appeared to rest on the floor of a vast cavern formed by the sinister curtains of black smoke which rose from beyond and towered over it, prophetically, like a great overhanging cloak of doom.*

As Art Donahue flew away, below him the groundcrew of 488 Squadron were left to face whatever was to come their way. They had no chance with the Japanese within sight of them, and they must have felt the end for them was near.

The MV *Empire Star* in better days.

seven

# Flight from the storm

### AN IGNOMINIOUS DEPARTURE, EVACUATION ON THE *EMPIRE STAR* AND ESCAPE FROM THE JAPANESE

Captain Selwyn N Capon OBE had brought the Blue Star Line MV *Empire Star* alongside the wharf at Tanjong Pagar Docks in Keppel Harbour. That is, what was left of the docks. The *Empire Star* had arrived early in the morning of 29 January 1942 with guns, trucks, tanks and 200 tons of munitions for the British Army. They arrived in convoy BM11 from Bombay in India following a route that took them in a long loop to the south before heading back up to Singapore. Japanese warships, submarines and bombers ruled the waves right down the east coast of Indochina, the Malayan Peninsula and the Gulf of Siam.

The *Empire Star* had been requisitioned by the British Government. It was a refrigerated vessel of 12,656 tons and had normally plied its trade on a regular run from London to Lyttelton in New Zealand and back since its launching in 1935.

It was obvious to all those on board the *Empire Star* that they were much too late in arriving. The wharf sheds were reduced to rubble and the wharf labourers had long since disappeared. The entire dock area seemed to be on fire, the glow being seen from far out to sea as they approached as part of a large convoy. The *Empire Star* spent the early part of her stay anchored in

Keppel Harbour's Dangerous Goods area. The crew had a grandstand view of the desolation in the city and around the dock area. She was purposely moored away from the docks as just one hit from a Japanese bomber would have caused massive destruction. It was thought at the time that the Japanese had advance knowledge of her cargo as no attacks were made on her, not even a near miss, although many of ships anchored around them were targeted. The Japanese would have been very keen to get hold of her cargo rather than have it destroyed as their munitions supplies were badly depleted. The other scenario was they may well have wanted the ship alongside the wharf in order to optimise the damage to their targeted areas with the ship and its cargo of munitions being capable of taking out half the wharf area if it was struck.

The *Empire Star* moved under cover of darkness on the night of 6 February into a berth in the wharf area. The ship's crew began to unload and they had barely started when the bombers returned, which looked suspiciously like a planned move on the part of the Japanese. It was panic stations with ropes being cast off and the ship moved rapidly back to its earlier anchorage. When some normalcy returned they moved back to the wharf area and worked all the next day and well into the night unloading the dangerous cargo. The crew had no choice, since the wharf labourers and stevedores had vanished. The British Army reserves of munitions were being overrun by the Japanese so the *Empire Star*'s cargo became more important with each passing hour. A member of the crew remembers unloading the munitions while bombs fell and shells whistled all around them. All the surrounding wharf sheds were burning and he recalls the surreal scene at the time. It was, he noted, the fastest cargo unload that they had ever been part of. To a man, the crew had very mixed feelings about unloading as all felt at the time that they were simply gifting the munitions to the Japanese.

Captain Capon had ordered the unloading for a very good reason. He had come to the conclusion that his ship would be required to take on board a new cargo, a cargo of a human kind. Even at that time there were milling mobs of people waiting to climb on board to escape the madness around them. Feeding what he knew would be a large group of people was going to be a problem. The ship had intended to reprovision on its arrival in Singapore but that was never going to happen. The captain sent foraging parties out through the ransacked warehouses looking for supplies and managed to source some food and provisions.

Singapore was in its last throes. The wharf area was decimated, with teeming mobs of people desperately trying to get aboard any ship that could take them away from the Japanese who were now advancing steadily across the island from the Malayan mainland. Abandoned vehicles littered the wharf area, including luxury cars left by their civilian owners. Large areas of the godowns were on fire. A huge pall of smoke hung over the naval base at Sembawang: the navy had finally fired their oil supplies to make sure the Japanese did not get their hands on them. There were huge supplies of rubber stored in the wharf area awaiting export and these were ordered to be fired. The resulting smoke

Captain Selwyn N Capon OBE, later CBE, master of the MV *Empire Star*.

and fumes almost closed off the sun from over the city.

By now the British had withdrawn to a semicircle of a defence line following roughly the outskirts of the city perimeter. The city was close to capitulation.

Back at Kallang, Bert and those that were left of his fellow groundcrew travelled from their billets in Telak Kurau School to the aerodrome in the hope that the spare aircraft had flown in from Sumatra to evacuate them. This was not to be and after waiting around for some time they headed back to the school. They were the last air force personnel left on the island and simply had no aircraft left. Any of those that had been flyable had already been flown off to air bases in Batavia. The saying doing the rounds at that time was: 'You will never get off the island, mate!' Proof of that was shown when some very wet and bedraggled troops had staggered through the jungle area at Kallang from the direction of the coast. They told Bert they were the survivors of one of the larger ships, the *Empress of Asia*, sunk about a kilometre offshore by Japanese bombers as it arrived with reinforcements for the defence of Singapore.

There was much confusion at this time. Bert remembers an officer of the Argyll and Sutherland Highlanders arriving out of the rubber plantation asking them where their rifles were and ordering them into sections to dig trenches to help ward off the Japanese advance. He then promptly disappeared. Bert thinks to this day that the officer was a deserter but the Argyll and Sutherland Highland Regiment had taken a fearful battering in the defence of Malaya. They had been ordered by the British High Command to fight a rearguard action when it was obvious that the Japanese advance was too powerful and could not be contained.

The delaying tactics of the Argylls and their sheer bravery gave many, including Bert, the chance to escape

## The Argylls' rearguard action

The Argylls were the last to cross the causeway before it was blown. They bravely fought a very disciplined retreat, taking fearful casualties and forcing the Japanese to fight for every inch of the way into Singapore City itself. The Argylls caused huge casualties among the Japanese military, to the point that any Argyll captured by the Japanese hid his regimental identification for fear of reprisal.

Their headquarters in Britain were based at Stirling Castle and they drew most of their recruits from the working-class areas of Glasgow and Edinburgh. In the final days the regiment almost ceased to exist, despite their numbers being boosted by the Royal Marines who survived the sinking of the Repulse and the Prince of Wales. Towards the end of their campaign the regiment was named the Plymouth Argylls to acknowledge the Marine content of their fighting force. Continuing their rearguard action across Singapore, eventually they dug in around the perimeter of their old barracks at Tyersall on Bukit Timah Road, where they fought almost to the last man. From here, small groups of Argylls were sent into the dock area to help police the evacuation, and it was one of these groups led by Captain Eric Moss that later cleared, at gunpoint, Australian Army personnel thought to be deserters, off the Empire Star.

and survive to fight another day. As Bert was to find out later, the Japanese were at that time all around them and even between them and the port, which was their only avenue of escape.

The Japanese by now controlled the centre ground of the island and were sending troops ahead on the coastal flanks to form a pincer movement. They had stated loudly and clearly that they would never let the British have another Dunkirk. They had total command of the air and total control of the sea around the southern approaches to Singapore. Escape, even at this stage, was almost an impossibility.

All of 488 Squadron aircrew had flown out in what aircraft were still serviceable, heading for Batavia or had gone ahead to get on to whatever shipping was still leaving port. Bert and his fellow groundcrew were left to become prisoners of the Japanese, and when they were figuring ways to prevent this happening a strange event took place. They were approached by their earlier commanding officer, Squadron Leader Wilf Clouston, who just a few weeks before had been posted to the Air Operations Headquarters. He wanted to make a deal. The deal was that if they could get a plane serviceable for him to fly off he would get them a passage off the island. This incident has surfaced several times in diary notes and in discussions with ex-488 Squadron members and added to the intrigue of the situation on Singapore at that time. Passages on evacuation ships were rigidly controlled due to limited berths being available and the only way through the wharf gates was with official passes. Clouston, in the end, did not fly out as arranged, although an aircraft was available for him, but instead he attempted to escape with fellow Air Operations staff officers on board a ship that was subsequently sunk. He ended up captured by the Japanese and was returned to Singapore as a prisoner of

Photo taken just seconds before Bert was fired upon.

war. It is only speculation at this stage but his part of the bargain was later honoured. Word came through that the groundcrew who remained on Kallang were to organise transport to get them all down to the wharf area as soon as possible.

It was late in the afternoon of 11 February and Bert was working on the last aircraft left at Kallang. He was sure that this was the aircraft they had prepared for Clouston. The aircraft had bullet damage to its fuel tank and he had just the one last patch to fit to make it airworthy. He still remembers the feeling of being very vulnerable and alone. He kept moving out into the open and checking the sky for aircraft and scanning the airfield perimeter for any sign of Japanese troops moving in. He had good reason to be concerned. Some days before, he had been working on an aircraft and had walked a short distance away. While doing this he heard a shot and the bullet whistled past between him and the aircraft. He yelled at his mates working on the plane to take cover and dived behind the nose cowl. As he dived to the ground, three or four more shots were fired. They had no arms between them but someone in the control tower saw what was happening and made contact with a machine-gun crew to the left of the aircraft and they opened up on a group of houses behind them. Such was the situation at that time that no further investigation was made and Bert never found out who had fired at them.

Bert was resigned to the dreadful reality that in a very short space of time he would be a prisoner of war. The sound of an approaching truck travelling at speed brought him out into the open again. As the truck approached, Bert was relieved to see that it was the squadron munitions truck being driven by Andy Chandler. He shouted at Bert to get on board. They drove back to the billets at Telok Kurau School and picked up one other person. Bert was sure it was Clem Randall but his memory is hazy due to the stress of the moment. Bert only had time to grab his best drill uniform, some toilet gear, a towel and some photographs and camera and throw them together into a kitbag before they left. He was not to know it then but Kallang was overrun by the Japanese Army the very next morning. Even today, Bert speaks with gratitude of the fact that Andy Chandler returned for him. Chandler could have left with the others when they got the call to leave for the port. He knew Bert was working alone and drove at great risk back from Katong to Kallang to pick him up. The Japanese had already crossed the canal behind the school and were heading towards the city centre.

Ted West was detailed with several others to go down to Kallang and carry out any demolition of aircraft that could be repaired. They were only given 15 minutes to do this. Because of the proximity of the aircraft hidden in dispersal areas to some local housing, they were told to not burn the aircraft but smash them up with hammers. While this was happening, like Bert, Ted clearly remembers worrying about not being picked up and missing out on getting away to the docks with the rest of his squadron.

Bert found himself scrambling on board the squadron munitions truck with his meagre possessions. The truck still had a load of ammunition on board so they joined

## Massacre of the Chinese

*The Telok Kurau English School at Katong took on a new and macabre life just a few days after Bert and his fellow squadron members left. In the early days of the Japanese occupation of Singapore the Japanese military were keen to press on to Sumatra and gain control of the Indonesian oil fields. They had huge concerns about the Chinese in Singapore. The Chinese had defended the island tenaciously, being profoundly anti-Japanese, and the Japanese military had planned to leave Singapore under the control of a token force with the minimum number of troops needed to ensure stability on the island. There were some concerns that Chinese resistance would prove difficult to control, so all Chinese citizens were ordered to report to various centres around the island at noon on 21 February 1942. Telok Kurau English School was one of these centres. This clean-up operation was known as Sook-Ching and was designed to root out all the anti-Japanese elements among the Chinese population.*

*A most brutal massacre took place. Truckloads of Chinese males were taken from these centres to various points around the island and machine-gunned or bayoneted to death. There is great confusion even today about how many died but the estimates range from the War Crimes Tribunal figures of 5000 to 10 times that number, as claimed by the Chinese community.*

*The Japanese intention was clear: to kill off all adult males between the ages of 16 and 50 to prevent any resistance to their occupation so they could free up more troops for active service duty. All other centres were reported to be selective of their victims, choosing tattooed men, members of gangster gangs, or anyone having membership of any Chinese organisation. Not so for the Japanese Kempeitai (Secret Police) Officer in charge of Telok Kurau. During the day, he ordered all the males segregated into groups on the sports field by a 'hands up' method: teachers in one group, doctors in another, government servants and so on. No personal interviews for him. At the end of the day the selected groups were herded into the classrooms recently vacated by 488 Squadron and during the night trucked away in their groups to the 12-km marker on the Siglap Road and massacred. They were machine-gunned to death and those wounded but still alive were bayoneted as they lay on the ground. I shudder to think what Bert and his mates might have faced had they not moved on when they did.*

the end of a convoy heading for the port. As they left, the Fighter Operations room at Kallang was also being abandoned and the senior radio officer, Flight Lieutenant Carter, was destroying all the radar documentation and codes to stop them falling into Japanese hands. Bert sat in the front of the munitions truck taking some comfort from the fact that they had plenty of ammunition if they needed it. They carried rifles with them but probably understood the futility of even using them under these circumstances. The munitions, though, proved a problem as the heavily loaded truck was soon left far behind in the traffic and bedlam of people on the congested roads. They came to a crossroads at one stage and waited while a party of Japanese soldiers carrying rifles crossed in front of them. The soldiers appeared not to notice them so they turned the truck and headed off in a different direction. Further up the road they spotted more groups of Japanese all heading in the same direction. They could only keep going and in the confusion they were not challenged.

The port area was a shambles. Singapore resembled something out of Dante's 'Inferno'. Most of the city seemed to be afire, the flames reaching skyward; fire-fighting services or intact water mains were simply non-existent. Great clouds of black smoke covered the sky, and out of that sky continually came Japanese dive bombers, completely unopposed, bombing and machine-gunning the crowded streets. Stanley Falk, in his book *Seventy Days to Singapore* described it as:

> *Streets blocked by craters, fallen telegraph poles, wrecked and burning vehicles, and by long lines of slowly moving military convoys. The streets were littered with rubbish and unburied bodies, and covered with great piles of electric cables and telegraph and telephone lines. Demolitions under way in factories and other installations added to the flames, noise and smoke. Singapore had ceased to function.*

Bert and his mates had to jettison the munitions truck as Japanese dive bombers struck just as they reached the port. In the scramble to get clear of the vehicles, Wally Murray was seen to remove a manhole cover from the middle of the road, climb down into the hole and pull the cover back over him. Bert and his mates dived into the nearest ditch, and when the aircraft had departed set off on foot looking for the number seven godown and the berth of the MV *Empire Star*. It wasn't too hard to find as it was the last of the bigger ships still left in port. They reached the vessel just on dusk and somehow, probably due to the influence of their late CO, the now departed Wilf Clouston, were allowed to board the already overloaded ship. Their rifles were taken off them at the gangway by the Military Police, which Bert thought was a bit odd. They were later returned to them. He would have been one of the last of his squadron to get on board. Bert and his mate Pat Chadwick noticed a guy struggling to get up the gangway with a large load of belongings. They went back down to help and this guy pulled out a revolver and threatened to shoot them if they touched one of the bags. They back-pedalled up the gangway and let him carry his own kitbag. As he neared the top he threw the kitbag in the water and the Military Police took his revolver. Bert

Godowns in Keppel Harbour burning following a bombing raid.

never found out what was in the bag. Loot of some kind was the guess.

Singapore at this time appeared to be in its death throes. Compacted in this small port area were masses of civilians trying to flee the Japanese advance. Within a 3 km zone from the city centre it was estimated that a million people were crowded, trying to stay away from the conflagration that was squeezing in by the hour. Up to 2000 people a day were dying in the bombing raids and the bodies were so numerous in the streets that they were left where they fell. More sinisterly, there were considerable numbers of army personnel who would normally have been expected to be defending the island from the Japanese invaders seeking shelter in the alleys and basements. The call had already been made for all military personnel to report to the area of the Botanical Gardens to form a last line of defence. Military Police were rounding up stragglers and directing them to that meeting point. Winston Churchill had already ordered the British High Command to fight to the last man 'for the honour and glory of the British Empire'. These were the prevailing orders but thousands of British and Australian troops had taken matters into their own hands and had retreated from the advancing Japanese Army. They were, in effect, deserters. They had left behind their weapons and stripped off their uniforms; they were also seen looting shops and houses as they headed down to the wharf area intent on leaving the island by boat.

Today, each country still blames the other for what was one of the greatest losses ever for the Allies in the Second World War. Many senior-ranking officers in the Far East Allied armies accused Australian soldiers of mass desertion, wholesale looting, rape and cold-blooded murder. It was reported that at least 200 Australian deserters forced their way on to the *Empire Star* just before it left the docks. Bert recalls a large party of Australian soldiers being on board but he is sure that most disembarked and left before the ship sailed.

The *Empire Star* was the last of the so-called big ships left in port on 11 February 1942. Singapore was just four days away from total capitulation. The Allied High Command was still holding on to the hope that they could defend even the port area and the inner city until reinforcements could be brought in from outside. It was revealed much later that the Japanese forces were comprehensively outnumbered and very short of ammunition and essential supplies. History has shown that the collapse of the Australian defences on the northwestern side of the island was a major reason for the fall of Singapore. The Australian troops seemed to be out of control in the city and large groups of these deserters roamed the streets looting and pillaging. They were in many cases armed and very drunk.

Dockside, among the chaos of the civilians trying to escape the island, large bands of the Australians were attempting to commandeer any vessels that could take them away. Embarkation onto the *Empire Star* had continued throughout the day and well into the night, illuminated by the burning wharf buildings and accompanied by the

Groups of nurses from Alexandra Hospital joined other evacuees on board the *Empire Star*.

shells passing overhead. Some were fired by the Japanese, but most were from the British naval guns on Blakang Mati Island (now known as Sentosa). From noon, groups of women and children had been boarding, leaving behind their menfolk. It was a sad and emotional scene as families were separated.

At this point Captain Capon ordered the crew to find whatever food they could get their hands on in the destroyed wharf buildings. A steward on the *Empire Star*, Eddie Green, noted that one of the larger groups to board were 60 Australian nurses from Alexandra Military Hospital who had been ordered to leave for fear that they may become victims of atrocities similar to those committed by Japanese troops earlier in the war. Those fears were well founded as those nurses left behind to stay with their patients were cruelly massacred by the Japanese just two days later.

Eddie Green recalls another group of 20 to 25 New Zealand air force pilots and a large group of 'non-officer air force technicians'. This would have been Bert's group, although Bert and his mate had arrived a long time after the main group. Green also remembers a party of armed Argyll and Sutherland Highlanders coming on board earlier in the afternoon. Among these soldiers was Captain Eric Moss, who had been ordered down to the wharf area to clear off the Australian troops who had forced their way on board. He moved around the ship rounding up these deserters. According to Captain Moss large numbers of Australians were sent packing at gunpoint. He waited on board until the gangway was about to be lifted to be sure that none found their way back on again and at the last minute jumped off the crowded ship onto the wharf. The ropes had been slipped but one remained attached. Climbing up it monkey-like was an Australian infantry sergeant. Moss called on him to return and, when he refused, Moss pulled out his revolver and fired at him. He was not certain if he hit him or not but the sergeant fell into the water.

In the rush to get away, the mooring ropes were let go before the *Empire Star* had a chance to come up to speed and Captain Capon had a few anxious moments before he got control of the ship. As the ship left the wharf those on board must have been thankful that they were not to

## The 'drunken' Aussies

*One of the RAF technicians recalled that when his group arrived to board the* Empire Star, *they encountered British Army armed guards all over the wharf area, trying desperately to maintain some order. Drunken Australians were swarming up the mooring ropes trying to get on board. They had been looting the dockland warehouses and were determined to get away come hell or high water.*

*Much has been made of the so-called drunken Aussie deserters during this period and claims and counter-claims have flown back and forth over the years. It was a chaotic situation and people could hardly be blamed for wanting to escape the impending storm. History has shown the treatment the Japanese forces handed out to their prisoners, and earlier significant events in China and the British colony of Hong Kong would have been known to all those potentially trapped on the island. It is clear, however, that a group of Australians, armed and drunk, did force their way on board but* the numbers from all accounts were not significant. There were 125 Australian Imperial Force personnel from the Australian Army Service Corps (AASC), most of whom had marched up the gangplank under the command of a Captain Wooldridge. Wooldridge, rightly or wrongly, had ordered the embarkation on board, but this appeared to be much earlier in the day. It was reported that they had actually left the ship with crew members to forage for food and provisions in the bombed-out godowns alongside the docks. There appeared to be no move by Captain Capon or his crew to stop them from boarding initially or later when they returned from the food-foraging expeditions. They were subsequently, at the captain's request, asked to drain fuel from tankers and vehicles still on board and as such could not in any way be branded as uncooperative deserters.

One of the last to leave Seletar airfield, Sergeant Eric Bott of the RAF travelled to the dock area to also find the chaos that others experienced. He described it as the most 'God-awful' mêlée of people that you could ever imagine. People of all nationalities were trying to board the Empire Star; abandoned cars were everywhere. Troops were trying to clear the congested wharf area by tipping the vehicles over into the sea. British Military Police were guarding the gangway, but Bott claims he watched as a large group of Australian soldiers literally clubbed their way on board using rifle butts. *(This scene has been described in many written accounts of the last hour before the departure of the Empire Star.)* The Military Police fought back but were badly outnumbered. Any attempt to rush the ship would have resulted in bloodshed in view of the mood that this group of Australians was in.

One of the airmen on board, John Dodd, was on the ship early but because of the sheer numbers boarding found himself forced against the rail overlooking the wharf below, which was packed with a surging mass of people. He watched as a young European woman with a small child and two suitcases was arguing with officials at the bottom of the gangplank. They wanted her to leave behind the suitcases but she refused. While this was going on he recalled a group of about 20 armed Australian soldiers pushing past the woman and also clubbing their way past the officials, up the gangplank and on to the ship. All this anecdotal evidence supports the view that a core group of Australians forced their way on board.

A stand-off was inevitable and it was reported that, fearing bloodshed, Captain Capon allowed them to stay. According to the ship's log, he signalled Captain Cazalet on the cruiser escort HMS Durban that he had unwelcome visitors on board. Arrangements were made for the ship to be met at Batavia by the military. John Dodd recalls the ship sailing away and seeing the distraught woman and child still waiting on the wharf.

share the fate of those left behind, but they still faced the uncertainty of whether they would reach their destination in safety.

The *Empire Star* pulled away from the wharf and what was left of No. 7 Godown as darkness fell. The darkness was not too much protection for the ship as the fires from the burning wharf area lit up the night sky like daylight. When they were about 400 m from the wharf there were two long bursts from a machine-gun. At the time it was thought to be either someone disgruntled at being left behind or a Japanese patrol. One of the New Zealand groundcrew from another squadron also reported the machine-gunning of the ship as it departed, which confirms Bert's memory of events. A further confirmation comes from one of Wooldridge's Australian Army Service Corps men, Archie Mitchell. He and 14 others from his unit had got separated from the original group earlier in the day. They arrived on the dock just in time to see the *Empire Star* pulling away. They hopped into a small boat, paddled out to the ship and scrambled up a boarding net onto the deck. As they were doing this a volley of machine-gun fire passed close by overhead. Rumours at the time, and since, allege it was the work of disgruntled Aussies left behind on the docks. It seems, though, that the culprits were recognised by their kilts as Argyll and Sutherland Highlanders who had been instructed to guard the docks and the ship embarkations and were in fact just doing that by trying to discourage those already on the water from attempting to board the few boats left. Max Boyd, in his diary, reports a different version: one of the Australian troops that was forced to leave the *Empire Star* shouted at the New Zealanders to throw down one of the Tommy guns on board as he needed a firearm if he had to stay. When this was done he fired a burst at the side of the ship to vent his frustration and anger. Red Nelson remembers also that the culprit was an Australian Army soldier.

The heavy artillery guns on the outlying islands of the harbour suddenly stopped firing. A brief period of quiet was welcomed by those who had put up with the incessant racket for days. The silence, unfortunately, was short-lived as the relative peace was shattered by a massive explosion as the army destroyed their guns. A little later there were further massive explosions from Pulau Bukum and Sabarok islands as the Royal Navy and staff of the Asiatic Petroleum Company fired the oil tanks to prevent them from falling into Japanese hands. Although they were over a kilometre away, Bert still remembers the force of the explosion. A thick oily blast of smoke and heat swept over the waiting flotilla followed by a huge conflagration that sent flames roaring hundreds of metres into the air.

Captain Capon was keen for his ship to continue on out of the harbour that night but was forced to anchor in the stream due to the fact that the light buoy, known as the Raffles light, which guided ships through the minefield, had disappeared and he was loath to take the risk in the darkness with his fully laden ship. He officially had 2161 people on board, on a ship that had accommodation for only 23 passengers. This was later disputed by many of those on board as attempted head counts during the voyage reached at least 3500. Captain Capon in his official report acknowledged that his count may have been low, but his list included 1573 air force, army and navy personnel, 139 Australian infantry (the Wooldridge AASC group?), 133 nursing sisters and signals personnel, 199 civilian evacuees (128 women, 35 children, 36 men), 29 civilian passengers (mostly women authorised to travel as passengers) and 88 crew members including 4 surviving seamen from the bombed and sunk *Empress of Asia*. The Australian nurses were from the 10th and 13th Australian General Hospitals based at Alexandra, now overrun by the Japanese. It would appear from Capon's list that the only unauthorised passengers would have been the Australian infantry group. The other scenario is that he only included authorised passengers in his list and the unauthorised passengers were those that clearly gave the impression to many of those on board that the ship numbers were well in excess of the official count.

The passengers would have spent an anxious, uncomfortable night trying to sleep but not being able to take their eyes from the burning city of Singapore.

The ship, although from the merchant navy, was armed with a six-inch long-range surface gun, one three-inch high-angle anti-aircraft gun, four twin Lewis machine-guns plus a Hotchkiss and several Lewis machine-guns brought on board by air force personnel. Most of the 488 boys, being the last group on board, slept on deck that night and were thankful that they were not squashed in among the hundreds crammed into the holds.

The *Empire Star* left at first light on the morning of Thursday, 12 February 1942 and Captain Capon headed on a southerly course to try to put as much distance as possible between the Japanese bombers and his ship. The Japanese Army by this stage was just a kilometre from the city centre, temporarily held up by fierce fighting on the part of the 44th Indian Brigade and the 1st Malayan Brigade. His course took him towards and into the Durian Straits. They were accompanied by two escort ships, HMS *Durban* and HMS *Kedah*, and a flotilla of smaller vessels.

*Kedah* led the small convoy out of the harbour with *Durban* bringing up the rear to give fire cover if the convoy was attacked. Later in the day *Durban* left with the larger, faster vessels, including the *Empire Star*, and set off at high speed down the coast of Sumatra heading towards Java. The slower vessels, which numbered 12, made their own way independently, heading towards the

Banka Straits after the convoy was split up. One of the passengers on HMS *Kedah* remembered:

> *leaving with the convoy just after dawn and passing between two huge pillars of fire, to the starboard were the burning oil tanks on Pulau Bukum while to the port there was a mass of flames and smoke from Pulau Sambu. Looking back, away to the north were the blazing tanks of the now abandoned naval base and other burning tanks near the causeway provided an impressive back-cloth to the hundreds of other fires burning along the waterfront.*

The flotilla was guided out of the channel by the escorting destroyers heading south towards the Durian Straits. The trip down through the straits was uneventful but as they reached the southern exit things started to happen.

Bert remembers being startled by a very low flying aircraft that swooped over the *Empire Star*. Most on board thought it was one of the British Sumatra-based Hudson bombers but Bert knew in his heart that it was a Japanese reconnaissance plane, probably a Kawasaki Ki-54 which looked very similar to a Hudson, and that they were about to get it. All his fears came to fruition when, at 9.10am, six dive bombers came hurtling down out of the sky from dead ahead. Most of their bombs straddled the small convoy but were close enough to rupture the eardrums of one of the nurses packed into the hold. Three, however, were direct hits. The first hit the after end of No. 5 hatch on the starboard side, the second punched through the poop deck abreast of No. 6 hatch and exploded in the poop space blasting off beams and wooden hatch covers. The third destroyed the Engineer Officers accommodation and seriously damaged No. 4 lifeboat. All areas caught fire but were quickly extinguished due to great work by the crew. The fire-fighting effort was hampered by the crowded conditions on the ship. While the Australian nurses attended to the wounded, the fire parties under the control of the Chief Officer, Mr Joseph Lindon Dawson, did a marvellous job under dangerous and difficult conditions. Captain Capon had very limited options during this first attack as he was in a relatively narrow channel and manoeuvring to avoid the attacks was difficult.

In this first attack by the dive bombers, according to Captain Capon's official report, 12 military personnel were killed and a further 17 military and ship's personnel were severely injured. Two of these badly injured military personnel subsequently died. All were buried at sea. Jim Cromie helped gather up at least six of the bodies in blankets. The ship's defences put up a terrific fight, bringing down one of the attackers and causing a second bomber to pull away, trailing smoke. The Australian nurses reported treating up to 35 badly injured people in their immediate area, so there must have been many more casualties spread around the ship.

The 488 personnel took cover where they could, some climbing down into the already packed holds. There were no foxholes to climb into now. Those with rifles stayed in the well deck area and were organised to fire in concentrated volleys. Those without rifles sat in the alleys leading to the forecastle and loaded magazines for the passed-back rifles. Stu Smart remembers the force of the bomb blasts, which lifted the rear of the ship so that the screw was clear of the water, causing it to rev up. Many of the hull plates were damaged with the strain and with the concussion from the near misses.

The bombing runs continued until late in the afternoon as successive waves of bombers of up to 57 aircraft tried to sink the ships. Each able-bodied man on the crowded decks fired into any of the low-flying aircraft, with the civilians and nurses down below also taking the empty rifles, reloading them and passing them back up. The Lewis machine-guns were tied to the ship's rail with rope to provide steadier support. After the initial bombing runs the Japanese planes tried low-level machine-gunning across the decks but the firepower from the *Empire Star* and the accompanying destroyers must have been effective as later bombers reverted to bombing runs from high altitude. This gave Captain Capon manoeuvring time to avoid the clusters that fell on either side of the ship. The *Empire Star* was one of only two vessels that were not sunk that day out of 16 ships that had left the port with them.

When the bombing and strafing started everyone had headed for shelter in the holds and anywhere there was cover. Inexplicably, there were still vehicles left on board taking up valuable space, with fuel still in their tanks but, worse than that, one fully laden petrol tanker. During breaks in the bombing some Australian troops were designated to drain the tanks and unload the tanker of fuel.

The ship had some Bofors guns and twin machine-guns for protection and these were manned and used until the barrels glowed red hot. It was, according to Captain Capon in his official report, a Hotchkiss anti-aircraft gun, mounted on the starboard wing of the navigating bridge and manned by RAF personnel, that accounted for the bomber shot down into the sea. One of those gunners was Aircraftman George Cottrill, a RAF groundcrew member attached to 488 Squadron. He was subsequently awarded the Military Medal. As many rifles as could be found were put into action and Bert found himself with many others desperately trying to put up sufficient firepower to bring down their attackers.

Captain Capon played a big part in their survival by

throwing the ship into evasive turns to avoid bomb strikes. Bernard Grindrod remembered the captain putting the ship into full reverse as the bombs left the bomb bays. The strain on the ship, its engines and the passengers must have been enormous but the sudden slowing of the vessel was enough to have the bomb aimers in the aircraft miss their target time and again. Captain Capon stood on the open bridge, exposed to his attackers. He had a crew member, Third Officer James Peter Smith, and Captain George Wright of the Singapore Pilot Service, who remained on the ship after clearing the harbour, lying on their backs with binoculars watching for the falling bombs leaving the aircraft. They were able to give him just enough warning to heel the ship away and avoid contact. This man saved many lives with his seamanship and it was such a tragedy when he went missing at sea just weeks later.

The high-level bombing runs were carried out by twin-engined heavy bombers with nearly 60 being counted on one run. A large number of bombs were dropped but fortunately were wide of the mark. With one such attack Bert thought the end had come. A stick of bombs straddled the ship, three each side, and with the explosions and violent twisting manoeuvres carried out by the captain, Bert thought the ship would overturn. The attacks lessened as they travelled out of the range of the bombers and everyone gradually relaxed. In this quiet time the dead were slipped overboard to the emotional strains of that old hymn 'Abide with Me'.

One of the wounded from Alexandra Hospital in Singapore was Second Lieutenant Stewart, a South African with No. 232 Squadron. He was taken with four others by a doctor and placed on board the *Empire Star*, in the Fourth Assistant Engineer's cabin with other wounded. One of the bombs from the first low-level attack came through the roof of the adjacent cabin just 10 m from

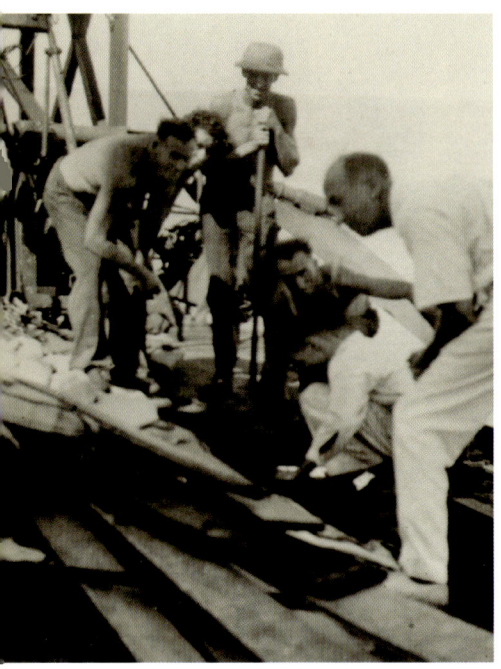

Bomb damage to the poop deck on the *Empire Star*.

him and killed the six occupants outright. Two of the badly wounded from a gun post that was hit were brought into their cabin for shelter wrapped in blankets. The blood was running through the blankets all over the floor of the cabin. The nurses brought in morphine to help ease them before they died. Each of the bombers made strafing runs, machine-gunning the decks with low-level attacks but without causing too many casualties. When the high-level attacks started Stewart was moved with the other wounded into a hold where all he could do was listen to the explosions coming nearer. The concussion of the closer ones was felt down in the holds. Everyone was singing at the tops of their voices trying to block out the dreadful noise, knowing full well that they were unable to do anything to help their situation.

Most on board, particularly out on the open decks, felt vulnerable and exposed and spent the time they were under attack cowering against any shelter they could find. Many prayers were said in the four-hour period of the attacks.

There were numerous instances of bravery during this time, none more so than among the Australian nurses on board. Two of their number were awarded gallantry medals for their work on this day. Sister Margaret Anderson was awarded the George Cross and Sister Veronica Torney the MBE. During the strafing attacks both nurses lay across wounded men they were attending on deck at the time to save them from further injury. One of the other nurses on board, Margaret Hamilton, helped the rest of the nurses in one of the holds to set up a makeshift hospital for the wounded. They had no equipment but helped make the injured as comfortable as possible. She remembers that they had very little food on board but recalls drinking tea out of a cigarette tin. She also remembers one of the air force personnel on board passing around a bottle of whisky.

The ship's crew toiled long and hard throughout the voyage, in particular putting a stop to the many fires that had broken out. There was no panic, just recognition that they had escaped a fate worse than death and that anything that happened from now on would be a bonus. Margaret remembers the singing on board, mostly hymns but many renditions of 'Waltzing Matilda'. She also remembers talking to Captain Capon on their eventual arrival in Australia:

> *We said goodbye to Captain Capon and thanked him. He told us that the ship had been in the evacuation of Greece and Crete, but he maintained it had never been in such a tight spot as it was coming out of Singapore. We knew that it was only by the mercy of God and the seamanship of the ship's master that we managed to get home safe and sound. As we said goodbye to Captain Capon he asked us to do two things every day of our lives: we were to thank God we were alive, and to never forget the Merchant Navy.*

The nurses from the 10th and 13th General Hospitals had been evacuated in three groups. One of the other groups, the last to leave, left on the SS *Vyner Brooke* the day after the *Empire Star*. They were sunk in the Banka Straits by the Japanese and the survivors were made to walk down the beach into the water and were machine-gunned to death. Only one survived. Unbelievably, there was much bitterness in Australia when the *Empire Star* nurses made it home and many were badly treated in their home towns, being accused of cowardice for having escaped and come back alive.

A good watch was carried out for submarines or surface raiders when the bombing attacks stopped but none was sighted. The Japanese blockade of the Banka Straits had been put in place just before the *Empire Star* passed through. Admiral Ozawa's fleet completely sealed the straits and very few ships that followed made it to safety. The size of the *Empire Star* would have made it a very good target. The Japanese would have been very much aware of the position of the ship but somehow did not get the blockade into position in time. It may have been due to the fact that the ship had been on fire following the earlier bombing attacks and the Japanese had thought that the ship had sunk during the night and so lessened their surveillance.

Something strange did happen, however. On the morning of 13 February a large convoy of approximately 11 ships appeared on their port side crossing over the front of them until disappearing over the horizon. The

488 Squadron's position in front of the bridge on the *Empire Star*.

'Roo' Robins, Ian Montgomerie, unknown, Stan Guiniven and Ernie De Suza.

convoy carried no flags or markings of any kind. Captain Capon edged the *Empire Star* over to the left, slipping away from the direction the convoy was taking. They found out later that the convoy was in fact Japanese and it was the invasion force heading towards Palembang in Sumatra. The fact that they were left alone was strange and many reasons were advanced. The consensus was that the Japanese thought they were one of them as Admiral Ozawa had sealed off all the escape routes from Singapore. Another possibility was that they did not see the *Empire Star* as a threat and had not wanted the planned invasion to be compromised. Either way, it was one of the quirks of fate that once again helped the men of 488 Squadron to survive.

Food was scarce on board. When the food call did come during the day 488 Squadron were not called. When they approached the crew for food they were told in no uncertain terms by a crew member that they should have stayed on Singapore. Bert still wonders how Wilf Clouston was able to pull strings that allowed them to escape with their lives. They did get a little food, a spoonful of stew and a piece of bread, which other than water was all they had for the three days it took them to reach Batavia.

The crowded port side foredeck of the *Empire Star*.

The *Empire Star* finally arrived in Tanjong Priok, Batavia, the port of what is now Jakarta City, around 6.15 on the evening of 13 February 1942. They had started out in a convoy of ships but one by one these vessels had been sunk, run aground, intercepted by the Japanese or simply disappeared without trace. It has been estimated that over 70 vessels carrying up to 5000 people that left Singapore did not make it to safety. The official casualty count on the *Empire Star* was 14 killed and 17 severely wounded, but many of the survivors claim many more were killed.

The Japanese had repeatedly said that they would use any means necessary to prevent the evacuation of Singapore, and they were very effective at that. Submarines, destroyers and gunboats prowled the straits and inlets and the many bays around the myriad of islands to the south of Singapore. The Japanese would have been enraged that the *Empire Star* had escaped as it was the largest ship in the area and the biggest to escape Singapore. Most of the smaller shipping travelled only by night and tried desperately to hide against the coast to prevent detection during the daylight hours. Many of those that survived the bombings and sinkings were picked up by the Japanese as they advanced southwards and died in captivity in the

Bert Clayton coming up for air from hold (at rear left), Ernie De Suza holding can with chap on his left moving in for some scraps of food.

prison camps. Many hundreds were simply butchered where they were captured.

Other than two destroyers and a parked Catalina flying boat the port of Tanjong Priok was empty. There would have been a feeling of inevitability among those on board that they were still in the eye of the storm. The Japanese were not that far away. Given the speed with which they had traversed the Malayan Peninsula, the islands of Sumatra and Java in the Dutch East Indies were just a quick hop away. Unbeknown to them the advance guard of the Japanese military were already on Java and preparing for their next move. The Japanese had total control of the air and almost complete control of the seaways so there was little cause for optimism among the personnel of 488 Squadron that they would be operational again. The ship anchored in the harbour overnight. The crew worked all night with pumps running due to damage to the hull plates.

When the ship eventually tied up alongside the wharf, an armed party numbering 200 men, British military and naval marines, met them at Tanjong Priok wharf. The officer commanding the detachment came on board with a large group of soldiers dressed in a ragtag collection of

On the wharf at Tanjong Priok, the port of Batavia, following the arrival of the *Empire Star*.

uniforms to confront the leaders of the deserting group. He reasoned that any collective show of force at that time may have led to bloodshed on the packed ship. His ruse worked as the surprised deserters were disarmed and marched off the ship to the armed marines waiting on the wharf. They were bussed away before any disembarkation took place. They thought they were being taken to an army camp but were more than a little surprised to find themselves escorted to a civilian prison. They were placed under the control of Brigadier CEM Lloyd of the Australian Army who had been ordered by Malaya Command to arrest and court-martial them. Without explanation, about six days later they were released. Still to this day there has been no official word as to what happened to these men. Reports persisted for many years that some or all were shot but no hard evidence has surfaced as yet to confirm or refute this. It is only the recent release of embargoed Australian Government documents that has confirmed that some deserters were apprehended but few other details are available.

All the other passengers then left the ship and were trucked away. The RAF personnel were ordered to disembark and were trucked off to help defend Java. Very few of this group survived; they died not from the Japanese attacks but from the desperate conditions in the prisoner of war camps that were set up around the island when they were eventually captured by the Japanese.

The 488 Squadron boys watched and waited for orders long after the last passenger had departed. It was clear that they had not been catered for so they remained on board. After everyone had left, Bert wandered around the ship. It was quite badly damaged in places and was in an unbelievable mess — like something left behind by a football crowd after a game. The flotsam and rubbish left behind by many hundreds of people was cleared up by squadron members. Red Nelson remembers vast quantities of used clothing and rubbish being emptied over the side. All the now departed RAF squadron's gear was also dumped into the harbour. He also remembered a case of booze being found but — tongue in cheek — could not recall where that ended up!

There had been many children among the evacuees on board the ship. Among the cargo carried on the original voyage into Singapore were boxes of Christmas presents. The captain had ordered them left on board and these were distributed among the children during the traumatic run to Java. This was typical of the man. Just five weeks before the loss of Captain Capon and the *Empire Star*, the captain and his crew were awarded a number of gallantry awards for their brave efforts on that final run out of Singapore (see Chapter 12). Captain Capon was also gifted a monetary award of £100 by his employer, the Blue Star Line.

The *Empire Star* stayed in Tanjong Priok for two days while emergency repairs were made. The ship eventually set sail for Fremantle, Western Australia, arriving there without further incident.

Open air dispersal at Tjililitan.
*Art Donahue*

eight

# In the eye of the storm

### ARRIVAL IN BATAVIA AND SETTING UP FOR A SECOND LINE OF DEFENCE

Among the rubbish left behind on the *Empire Star* were weapons and ammunition which were gathered up by the squadron, as there was still great uncertainty about their situation. They were, after all, born scavengers, given the last few months spent looking for componentry and equipment to ensure their survival in Singapore. Bert found himself with a brand-new .303 rifle and a Thompson sub-machine-gun while most of the others equipped themselves with similar weapons.

Later in the day a ranking British officer boarded the ship and demanded to know 'who these men are'. When told they were 488 Squadron from Kallang in Singapore he said in a very nasty manner that they had no right to be there and should have remained at their posts in Singapore to be prisoners of the Japanese. This statement by the officer just summed up the attitude of the hierarchy towards the 'colonials' that had existed in the services since the First World War. When challenged, he overlooked the fact that rather than be sacrificed, as he wanted, they were now here to get the chance to fight again.

Eventually, some accommodation was found. They were trucked away to a school which was already inhabited by members of an RAF squadron so it turned out to be very overcrowded. Later that evening, their commanding officer, Squadron Leader John Mackenzie, visited and welcomed them to Batavia. It was the first contact for some time with any of their aircrew. Bert was never sure whether it was getting good food for the first time in many days or drinking the local water but a mini epidemic of dysentery went through the ranks like wildfire.

The first night at the school at Carpentier Oleting was spent sleeping outside on the hard concrete verandas with just a blanket each for cover. It was a long and miserable night for most. They were still thankful to be safe on dry land but very uncertain as to how close the invading Japanese were. The next day the Dutch authorities organised workmen to make up two-tiered bamboo bunks, which were very well made but very hard to sleep on. These, coupled with the small, hot, unventilated classrooms, meant that most ended up sleeping back on the concrete verandas the next night.

They eventually had about four days at the school before being sent out to Tjililitan airfield in shifts to link up again with the rest of the 488 pilots who had left Singapore ahead of them and had been in a rest camp at Buitenzorg, about 50 km from Batavia. There they learnt that Singapore had fallen and now there was very deep concern among them that the storm was about to descend on Batavia and they would end up being trapped on an island again. The British High Command was endeavouring to set up a second line of defence. 488 Squadron was in effect still on active service and the plan was for a regrouping to use what aircraft, equipment and facilities were available. As it turned out, the short answer was there was none. They had no aircraft but again, being on the scrounge, found almost a full squadron of Hurricanes, damaged but parked up ready to be worked on. Spares and crated aircraft were found by hunting through the docks and warehouses in the port at Batavia so the hard work started all over again. They again faced the problem of no tools or gear but begged, borrowed and stole to such effect that in a very short time they had aircraft ready for flying.

Tjililitan airfield was about 15 km from the port of Tanjong Priok. It was a grassed strip with no actual runway. The pilots were not that thrilled as the strip was in one direction only with no cross runway for wind changes, and was raised up above the existing ground level in the centre, falling away at each end. Bunt Pettit described it as being formed by a small hill being flattened out and the fill simply bulldozed out towards each end. It was difficult to read when landing. The crew facilities were little better, being nothing more than attap huts sitting out in the open providing little shelter from the elements let alone protection from Japanese attack.

There was a huge effort put in by RAF commanders to reorganise the defences of Batavia in order to avoid a repeat of the debacle in Singapore. The lack of serviceable aircraft, of course, was the problem and the aircrew from the three surviving squadrons from Singapore, 232, 258 and 488, were non-operational and two new squadrons, 242 and 605, were formed. The overriding instruction was for the Japanese to occupy every individual island in order to slow up their advance, to give the Australian government time to organise defences on their northern shores. The New Zealand government also held grave concerns because of its lack of preparedness and the number of its military personnel serving overseas. The government was putting pressure on the British High Command to release units so that they could return to defend New Zealand.

There was some posting of the aircrews at this time as pilots outnumbered aircraft, and ballots were held to see who would stay and fight and who would be sent further south to reform when more aircraft became available. There were at that time many hundreds of servicemen in and around Batavia.

Six of the former 488 pilots were posted to 605 Squadron, with the squadron being divided into two flights. The limited number of aircraft meant that when one flight returned the second flight personnel took over the same aircraft. This put a huge strain on the servicing by groundcrew and the loss or the grounding of an aircraft for any reason meant two pilots being out of action.

When Hutch and his flight arrived earlier at Tanjong Priok they had been transported up to Buitenzorg. They had enjoyed the stay in what was a recreational area and he personally was accommodated in a luxurious lodge belonging to a Dutch planter family. He was able to meet with members of the East Indies air force crews that he had served alongside at Kallang. He and his fellow pilots were very well treated, but that situation was soon to change. Unfortunately, too soon for them, they were instructed to proceed back to Batavia where they met up with John Mackenzie and the rest of the pilots. Hutch and the surplus 488 pilots were sent to Kemajoran, where new Hurricanes were being assembled and test flown, and these were flown back to Tjililitan for use by the squadron.

John Hutcheson, Noel Sharp, Jack Meharry and six pilots from 232 Squadron left, heading north from Tjililitan airfield at first light on 14 February to run a delivery flight of Hurricanes to one of the two airfields at Palembang. Known at the time as P1 and P2, these were very basic strips set up by the RAF to provide air bases for what was to be the line of defence for Sumatra. Hutch mentioned his misgivings in his diary about the flight as maps were almost non-existent and he was relying on just a pencil tracing he had made of one of the few maps in the squadron's possession at the time. The flight was going to be further complicated by the fact that they had no radios fitted to their machines. The distance was right on the safe limit for fuel and after being in the air for over two hours there was a lot of consternation among his fellow pilots. He remembers them flying up alongside him every few minutes and signalling frantically with their hands that they were low on fuel. He frankly admits he was lost and had no idea where they were at the time.

He was considerably relieved when he sighted the Palembang River, the township and then the P1 airfield. When they finally reached the strip and were on final approach for landing, they found to their horror that the airfield was under attack by huge numbers of Japanese bombers accompanied by aircraft dropping troops by parachute. Japanese Zeros accompanying the bombers dived at them out of the clouds and they had no option but to defend themselves with what ammunition they had on board and face crash-landing once the fuel had expired. Hutch, by now in shock, was in his own words, 'finished'. In desperation he barged in among the troop carriers, firing at everything he came across until his ammunition ran out. He admitted later there was nothing 'good or calculated' about his attack. He said he felt like a cornered rat and acted accordingly.

When his guns stopped firing, he dived and headed south and, with the river behind him, his fuel-starved engine coughed and died, leaving him desperately looking for somewhere to bring his aircraft down. Hutch aimed for the only open ground, which looked very swampy. He locked open his canopy, tightened his straps and hit the water with a mighty jolt. To his surprise a wall of water surged into the cockpit and he had to quickly climb out and cling to the tailplane, which was the only part of the

## Escape from Sumatra

*Having landed in the water, John Hutcheson's biggest concern was crocodiles. He shouted out in the direction of some native huts and the occupants came out, took one look and ran off in the other direction. Hutch was forced to swim to shore. Some Sumatran natives reappeared and after many minutes of trying to understand one another confirmed that he was indeed 'British' and on their side. They took him back to a small stream and put him aboard a canoe. Hutch panicked as he realised they were taking him downriver towards Palembang where the noise of the battle was plainly evident, but they stopped after a while at a small village. A young Chinese chap appeared who spoke perfect English and asked Hutch what he wanted. Being as thirsty as hell he asked for a drink and they eventually brought him a bottle of beer. He made off through the jungle southwards on his own. After some days' travel across country in very trying jungle conditions, Hutch eventually found his way to the south coast of Sumatra. He linked up with Noel Sharp and they caught a ride across the straits to Batavia and the relative safety of their squadron. All Hutch arrived back with was his service revolver and logbook, both recovered from his ditched aircraft. (Very little information survives about the trek to the south coast. The journey of over 160 km would have*

> been a story of its own.) Hutch unfortunately caught malaria while in the mosquito-infested jungle during his escape, something that eventually stopped him from operational flying some years later. He ended up in hospital in Perth when the squadron eventually disembarked on their travels back to New Zealand.

aircraft above water by this time. Four of the nine aircraft that travelled to Palembang that day, having scattered rather than take on the Japanese aircraft, found their way back to Palembang and landed safely amid the chaos. One was thought to be that of Jack Meharry, the third New Zealander. The airfield was still under attack at that time and, although the bombers had gone, there were Japanese paratroops still hiding in the plantations surrounding the strip. It took some time for the servicing groundcrew to come out of hiding to refuel the aircraft. After refuelling the four took off again and were escorted to the second airfield at Palembang, known as P2. A further two were lost on landing there, one hooking its wing into the ground and the other being stood on its nose. It was not a very productive day.

Meanwhile, back at the groundcrew billets there was a parade held on the morning of 15 February to sort the squadron groundcrew into different groups. The squadron maintenance was split into two sections. The following morning everyone was ordered to report to the railway station with all their kit at 11.30am. They were all on the train when they were ordered off and sent back to their billets. There was some conjecture as to why this had happened, with one story being that they were to have been sent to Buitenzorg for rest and recreation but this was cancelled at the last moment due to serious incursions by the Japanese Army into the region, or that they were being sent to the front line to bolster the defences. The cynics in the group favoured the latter theory. Later in the afternoon all the fitters, riggers and armourers were ordered to parade as they were told they were being sent to an airfield. They waited around for about 15 minutes, no one turned up, and as Des Hargreaves succinctly put it, they gave up and 'buggered off'. Such was the shambles of the times.

Max Boyd met up at that time with some of the survivors of the groundcrew of 232 Squadron, who were favoured over the 488 men and evacuated from Singapore in the ship that 488 Squadron were originally supposed to have left in. They were the survivors from a Japanese attack that sunk the vessel. They were badly shocked, blistered, sunburnt and generally not in good shape. Many of their group had been killed in the attack, with the bulk being captured by the Japanese. Max was greatly relieved that they had not in the end been evacuated at that time, but this meeting must have increased his apprehension at the possible outcome for his own squadron.

A parade was ordered for Tuesday morning, 17 February, but such was the cynicism of the groundcrew that most did not bother turning up. Des Hargreaves reports that the men were totally demoralised by now, there was little food to be had and the sanitation was dreadful. There were three or four lavatories for between three and four thousand men. The British High Command refused 488 Squadron's request to organise their own cooking and sleeping facilities.

The first group of groundcrew, known as A Flight, eventually left for work at Tjililitan on the morning of 18 February. Squadron Leader Mackenzie and most of his A Flight aircrew had been based at Tjililitan since 9

February, while the second group led by Flight Lieutenant Hutcheson had been sent at that time on standby to the Buitenzorg rest camp. The remaining unallocated groundcrew filled in the day the best way they could. Most slept during the day and went into town at night.

Max Boyd recalls problems at that time having to queue for food. The bitterness comes out clearly in his diary notes, where, weary after the bad treatment by the authorities in Singapore, Max found the situation the same in Batavia, with the British RAF officers looking out for number one and the rest having to fend for themselves. The New Zealanders were forced to go into Tanjong Priok to get whatever food they could lay their hands on while the British officers were living in hotel accommodation in the town with as much food as they needed.

The groundcrew servicing B Flight aircraft were taken out to the airfield the next day at 6.30am, having breakfast on their arrival. The day was quiet with no alerts and time was filled in doing some maintenance work and digging foxholes alongside the aircraft they were working on. The meals at Tjililitan supplied by the Dutch authorities were a vast improvement from those supplied back at Carpentier Oleting School.

Flying Officer De Suza told the men that he would have some good news for the squadron in a day or two, and all thoughts again turned to home. The following two days were non-events with no action recorded, but late in the evening of 21 February they were told once more to be ready to leave at an hour's notice. There was some surprise among the men as, even with all the uncertainty of their situation, they thought they would have a longer stay in Batavia, but that was not to be. On Sunday, 22 February, late at night they were told that they would be leaving the next morning for Australia. Bert was never that sure at the time that this meant going home but he

Open-air dispersal situation at Tjililitan, showing the total lack of cover or protection for the parked aircraft.
*Art Donahue*

felt at least they were heading in the right direction.

The weather had really closed in the next morning as they were trucked away from the school down to the docks. Most got soaked to the skin but there were no complaints as they knew the weather would keep the Japanese bombers away and make their departure a bit easier and certainly safer. They were stood to on the docks until midday before being allowed to board. It was clear now that the whole of the Dutch East Indies was about to be overrun by the Japanese. Reason finally prevailed when the futility of the situation in Java was realised and the powers that be made the decision to withdraw totally and get the surviving men back to New Zealand. Anyone could have seen that Australia and New Zealand were clearly in the path of the invaders and these men would be more use back home regrouping, re-equipping and preparing to defend their homeland.

Aircraftman F Hall (left) and Leading Aircraftman Jim Boddy with their Buffalo at Kallang.

In the eye of the storm 217

Top left: Pilot Officer Jack Oakden; top right: Pilot Officer Noel Sharp DFC; centre left: Jim MacIntosh, *From Jim MacIntosh, The War Diary of a POW*; centre right: Sergeant Eddie Kuhn; above left: Pilot Officer Harry 'Bunt' Pettit, *collection of Bunt Pettit*; above right: Flight Lieutenant Grahame White, *collection of Bunt Pettit*.

nine

# Of those that were left behind

### THE FINAL STAND — SIX BRAVE MEN POWS IN JAVA

On the eve of 488 Squadron's evacuation from Batavia on 23 February 1942, six members of the aircrew were ordered to stay behind and carry on a rearguard action attached to No. 605 Squadron. They had been seconded to this squadron on 18 February 1942, a week after the aircrew's arrival from Singapore on 12 February. This reorganised squadron comprised two flights, of which A Flight were the ex-488 boys. The flight commander was Flying Officer Jack Oakden, with Pilot Officers Noel Sharp, Bunt Pettit, Grahame White and Sergeants Eddie Kuhn and Jim MacIntosh. A second squadron, No. 242, was reconstituted at the same time and both squadrons used the remaining aircraft and pilots of 232, 258 and 488 squadrons. Aircraft were not plentiful — 242 Squadron had 12 serviceable aircraft and 605 Squadron just the six.

There were thought to be two further 'stay behinds', both ex-RAF groundcrew members, who had joined 488 Squadron after being cleaned out by Japanese bombing in northern Malaya in early December 1941. Jim Cromie remembers them volunteering as drivers after an army officer had boarded the train, taking the squadron to the wharves on 23 January, requesting assistance. Both survived the death camps. One was Aircraftman Douglas Denham and the other was thought to be Aircraftman Jimmy

Delap. Jim Cromie did catch up with Douglas Denham in England after the war but lost track of him in later years.

Not much is known or recorded about this part in 488 Squadron's history, although several stories of 605 Squadron activities were recounted in books published after the war, without identifying the New Zealand aircrew. Of the aircrew, Eddie Kuhn's story in particular has never been told publicly before. He steadfastly refused to speak of his ordeals and told his good friend, Don Layton (who served with distinction in No. 34 Blenheim Squadron in Singapore at the same time), that as long as he was alive he would not like his story told. Sadly, Eddie passed away in 2000. Don Layton put me in touch with Eddie Kuhn's widow, Barbara, and she kindly gave me access to Eddie's notes. They made chilling reading. Among Eddie's papers was a copy of Jim MacIntosh's war diary, published in May 2000 by Jim's widow, Joan. Coincidentally, my contact with an RNZAF historian, Bee Dawson, brought more information in the form of diary notes and photographs compiled by Bunt Pettit. This sudden stream of information was sufficient to compile this separate chapter on the trials and tribulations of those aircrew left behind when the rest of 488 Squadron were evacuated from Batavia. The diary notes of these three airmen set out clearly and graphically the events that happened to the six 'stay behinds' after the rest of the squadron was evacuated to Australia. It is important to their memories that this story be told.

Despite being posted to the new squadron, all six still considered themselves 488 Squadron with 'temporary' posting to 605 Squadron. They used Hurricane aircraft, some of which had been flown out from Singapore, but most were aircraft assembled after being found crated on the wharves at Tanjong Priok in Batavia and put together by the 488 groundcrew before they departed for Australia.

The squadron's orders were to hold up the Japanese advance for as long as possible to give the Allies time to bolster the defences of Australia and New Zealand. The shock of being left behind when the rest of the squadron departed for Australia would have been tempered by the feeling that they were to be involved in something worthwhile, even if the wider picture meant them facing the very real possibility that they would be overrun by the Japanese forces. Diary notes from these men do show that clearly they were given a lifeline, as they claim they were told that they were to make their way to the south coast of Java, to the port of Tjilatjap, to be picked up and transported to safety when the inevitable happened and they were overtaken.

The six were heavily involved in defence work out of Tjililitan airfield, which was close to the main port of Tanjong Priok. Jim MacIntosh's diary in particular shows mostly patrol work from 15 February until their first contact with Japanese bombers on 22 February. Jim notes in his diary that this day was the last operational day of 488 Squadron. He was not particularly thrilled with having to stay behind and the expression 'God, what a bastard' appears handwritten in his notes. Red Nelson, one of the 488 groundcrew, remembers speaking with one of the stay-behind pilots in the doorway of the dispersal hut at Tjililitan on the day the rest of the squadron was due to depart. He remembers them being quite despondent about being left behind and the prospect of capture by the Japanese.

The entry for 24 February sums up perfectly the odds these young men faced and gives a very clear indication of their bravery. On this day they attacked a flight of 42 Zero fighters, just the six of them! According to Jim, it was a 'hell of a dogfight' and Noel Sharp was forced to bale out after being shot down.

Jim MacIntosh complained of not sleeping too well at that time despite having a couple of days of quiet patrolling with no action reported. The six provided 'top' cover for HMAS *Perth* and USS *Houston* on 28 February while those naval ships made their escape from the Battle of the Java Sea. Tragically, both ships were sunk later that night after trying to attack the Japanese invasion fleet making a night landing on the northwest coast of Java.

Apart from patrol flying, there was little action reported other than sporadic attacks by bomber and fighter formations until the morning of 1 March. Before dawn on that day, the OC of 605 Squadron, Squadron Leader Wright, woke the members of his squadron and informed them that the Japanese had landed on the coast just 100 km away. They were instructed to get airborne at first light and carry out strafing operations against the invading forces. This they did. The transports were just 5 km off the coast protected by a line of cruisers that directed heavy anti-aircraft fire towards the Hurricanes. There was no air cover by the Japanese so the Hurricanes kept low over the beaches and shot the landing barges to pieces, causing fearful casualites among the troops approaching or landing. The covering fire from the offshore cruisers was negated as the Japanese could not lower their fire for fear of hitting their own troops. However, the ground fire from inland was heavy, indicating that the Japanese had landed virtually unopposed. The casualties that the Japanese suffered here at Cheribon and in other squadron attacks on the Moesi River in Sumatra were tremendous, so much so that when eventually the airmen were taken prisoner they never revealed their part in these attacks for fear of retribution.

It was on the first attack of the day that Noel Sharp received a direct hit on his engine. Trailing black smoke, he was forced to make a crash landing in an open area only a couple of kilometres inland from the beach. Grahame White had followed Noel's crippled aircraft inland and saw him crash. He circled around and saw him clamber out of the aircraft and wave to indicate he was okay. He ran, revolver in hand, towards nearby bush. He was at that time at least a kilometre behind the Japanese lines. Noel was never seen or heard from again, and it was feared that he was summarily executed by the Japanese, as he never showed up in any of the POW camps that were formed in the area after the capitulation. Noel had barely escaped with his life after being shot down just a few days earlier, but bravely made his way back to the squadron, battered and bruised ready to fly again. He had at that time baled out of his burning aircraft, landing in a canal. Unfortunately for him, his parachute came down over the top of him, and he very nearly drowned. He only just managed to reach the safety of the bank of the canal and took three days to find his way back to his squadron. It was a tragedy that the day Noel disappeared, the squadron flew their last operational flight.

Jim MacIntosh landed safely back at Tjililitan with a badly damaged aircraft while Bunt Pettit, Eddie Kuhn and Grahame White, with undamaged planes, carried on with strafing attacks for the rest of the day, causing huge casualties. This was to be the last day of operations for these men, as while they were away late in the afternoon, all the rest of 605 Squadron evacuated the airfield, leaving the five New Zealanders and the three remaining serviceable aircraft behind. On their return to base at the end of the day they were ordered to report to the CO of 242 Squadron, where they were told that there were now more pilots left than aircraft and consequently little use in carrying on. (Jim MacIntosh's diary notes indicate patrol work continuing until 6 March but his accompanying narrative indicates their final operational flight taking place on 1 March 1942, the day Noel Sharp disappeared. Bunt Pettit's diary notes confirm the 1 March date.) They handed over their three aircraft and headed back to their billets to wait for the hopeful return of Noel Sharp. They were eventually told to make a move as the Japanese were encircling Batavia, so after waiting until midnight, with no sign of Noel returning, they headed off in an old Chev Blitz Buggy truck to a prearranged meeting point at Bandoeng in central Java. They arrived at Bandoeng around nine o'clock next morning and were told to make their way to the southern port of Tjilatjap.

Later that night they caught up with the rest of 605 Squadron in a sugar factory at a place called Poernwerkerta, about 50 km inland from the port, where they found they had to scrounge for food. The factory seemed to have been a collection point for military stragglers from all over Java, all making their way to the south coast. On the following morning, 3 March, Bunt Pettit, Grahame White and Eddie Kuhn set off in their Chevy truck to have a look at the port. There were only a few small ships in the harbour and there were no signs of Japanese activity at all. They returned to the sugar factory to stay overnight. The next morning, 4 March, they were all transported by train to the port and set up camp in jungle areas just out of the small town. There were by now two larger ships in the port and one of them was clearly intended to be the means of their escape off the island and back to Australia.

Unfortunately, the Japanese had other ideas. As with the final days of Singapore, the Japanese were determined to cut off any means of escape from the island of Java. At around 10am, large numbers of bomber aircraft arrived and the port area and the small town were blasted out of existence. The men watched on, horrified, as all the shipping was systematically destroyed.

The raid was carrier launched and 180 aircraft took part. Five merchant ships were destroyed and a further eight vessels badly damaged. About 200 buildings were demolished or gutted by fire in the sustained attack. Any chance of evacuation was now gone. The death toll among the local population was enormous. Eddie Kuhn recounts helping to search for survivors but few were found. Many of those killed, despite getting to air raid shelters, had been blown to bits. It was a sickening experience for these young men and all they could really do was simply fill in the obliterated bomb shelters as ready-made burial pits. Bunt Pettit wrote of the anti-aircraft fire from all around them as they watched. Many Japanese aircraft were shot down and he remembers the shrapnel from the expended anti-aircraft shells falling like hailstones all around them. Many of the Javanese locals caught in the open and running to escape the bombing were hit with the expended shrapnel and suffered terrible injuries. Bunt and his mates were hiding less than 200 m from one of the many oil storage tanks scattered around the port. It took a direct hit and it was clear to them that it was time to move. The only option left was to travel inland, back the way they had come.

The trapped squadron members wandered around the area totally leaderless and looked for opportunities to escape from what they knew was clearly coming. They were left to their own resources. The war in Java was a lost cause, so they were determined to make the most of their situation and try to escape from the beleaguered island. The five of 488 Squadron were staying together but separate from fellow 605 Squadron members, as their diaries talk about meeting up with other members of the 605 group in different places. That night they slept in the local railway station.

On Friday, 6 March the port was attacked again,

eliminating any chance of evacuation from the area. A train showed up at 2am on the morning of 7 March to return them to the interior. They travelled to Tjiamis where they again met up with the 605 group sleeping at the rear of the local Dutch Resident's house. There was talk of taking a final stand against the Japanese but news of the Dutch capitulation reached them on the morning of 8 March. Both Bunt Pettit and Jim MacIntosh were scathing of the Dutch decision to surrender as both felt that the island had been given up without much of a fight. The Javanese seemed totally indifferent to their fate and were almost unconcerned that their new masters would be Japanese.

It appears that Eddie Kuhn and Jim MacIntosh decided to separate from the others. The rest of the group that they had been travelling with decided to remain in the Tjiamis area. Eddie and Jim found a motorbike, and after scrounging around for petrol headed back to the coast once more to try to find a boat to escape back to the Australian coast. This was not to be. In the end they camped out in various places, shifting from place to place, in fact, living a reasonably good life, eating well and living in relative comfort until orders came through for them to hand themselves in to the Japanese. They made the most of their time over the next two weeks until they were ordered to entrain for Batavia at 1.30 on the morning of 24 March.

We know that Jack Oakden, Graham White and Bunt Pettit were together at this stage as Bunt records both Jack and Grahame being stricken with both malaria and dysentery on 21 March 1942. They arrived at Batavia by train at 6pm on 24 March and were marched to the civilian prison at Boie Glodok and locked up for the start of their sojourn as prisoners of war. Eddie Kuhn and Jim MacIntosh were already in Japanese custody after being rounded up by the Japanese Army at Garoet on 21 March. They were initially locked up in a local school under armed guard, being kept there for nearly a week before being entrained to the same civilian jail in Batavia.

In all, 5100 air force personnel of various nationalities were left behind to be imprisoned by the Japanese. Apart from some naval personnel, survivors of sinkings off the coast, and some artillery units, they were the only Allied combatants on the island. There were no British Army troops in any numbers on Sumatra and Java. The defence of the islands was left entirely to the Dutch Army and local native troops, both of whom made dismal attempts to repel the invaders. In fact, they surrendered to the Japanese advance party who were so small in number that, at the time of the Dutch capitulation, they had not even captured a large port or town.

It would not be difficult to imagine the Japanese being quite bemused by the events of those weeks after the Dutch capitulation. The Japanese Army was by this stage severely depleted and their supply lines must have been badly stretched. The opposition to their invasion was token only. After the surrender, large groups of Allied servicemen wandered around the countryside, leaderless and fending for themselves. These servicemen all record living well, relaxing in sometimes hotel accommodation, feeding, drinking and generally having a good time. The Japanese seemed to have no contingency plans for the early finish of hostilities. Terence Kelly, an English author, who served in 605 Squadron, commented on the bizarre situation where many towns had accumulated large groups of Allied servicemen with nowhere to go, who carried on living the good life, co-existing with Japanese troops but both groups really having very little to do with one another. However, once the Japanese were organised and systems were set in place things changed very quickly.

The 'good life' vanished and the harsh reality of being rounded up and imprisoned was just a precursor of the nightmare that eventually came.

Jim MacIntosh's diary has a gap between 21 March when imprisoned at Boie Glodok and his later internment in the notorious POW camp known as the 'Bicycle Camp'. On 8 June he was shifted to Makasura, near Batavia, after seven weeks in the Bicycle Camp, where he said the food was okay but the treatment by the guards was very bad. He comments that he and Eddie Kuhn were still together. They did not meet up again with Jack Oakden until 24 July 1943, when several groups of prisoners were brought together at Tjililitan after being shoved around an assortment of POW camps. On 15 September the group, or 'draft' as they were known, was transported to Singapore. Jim was excited to hear the news on reaching Singapore that Deryck Charters, who had earlier been shot down over Malaya, was still alive. Sadly, Deryck never returned home, dying of dysentery on Christmas Day, 1943 in a POW camp in Thailand. The draft that included Eddie Kuhn and Jim MacIntosh left Singapore Harbour on 24 September 1943 for a horrific journey by sea to Japan, arriving on the southern coast of Kyushu on 12 October for them to begin life as slave labour in the factories, mines and shipyards of Fukuoka. Jim's diary account of life in these camps reveals incredible fortitude in the face of starvation, deprivation, brutality and slavery, such that the world never hopes to see again.

Eddie Kuhn told graphically of his treatment by the Japanese. He had earlier suffered ear damage after being caught in the open during one of the bombing raids on Kallang and forced to use a makeshift air raid shelter. The resulting blast from an anti-personnel bomb that exploded on the side of the shelter knocked him and his four fellow pilots unconscious and caused him hearing problems for the rest of his life. He commented that repeated blows to the side of his head by Japanese guards during his time in captivity did nothing to improve the state of his hearing.

Eddie had been locked in overcrowded conditions in the local civilian jail for about a week before being transferred to the notorious Bicycle Camp where the conditions were better but the ill-treatment from the Japanese and Korean guards was barbaric. Torture and beatings were daily occurrences. He was to be transferred to Surabaya with about a hundred other prisoners to supposedly work on airfields in the area. He was fortunate in a sense that he came down with a bad bout of dengue fever on top of the beriberi he was already suffering badly from and, consequently, could not travel. He found out after the war that not one of those that left without him to go to Surabaya survived. He was next sent back by ship to Singapore, spending time in Changi Prison, missing the draft to work on the Burma–Siam railway by a small margin. His good luck finally ran out, however, and his experiences from this point deteriorated to something from hell as he and many hundreds of others were jammed into the holds of floating hulks known as 'Hell Ships' and convoyed to Japan. He stated that he was never, ever able to erase the memories of that journey from his mind. He barely survived the appalling situation he endured over the coming years.

Eddie Kuhn recalled working the early shift on the wharves across the bay from the Japanese city of Nagasaki in August 1945, when, on a cloudless clear morning, he and his fellow workers noticed a small white cloud appear, gaining quickly in size until it filled the sky with flashes of light, but strangely no sound. He was not to know it then but he had witnessed the dropping of the atomic bomb on Nagasaki and, just two days afterwards, the war was over. Eddie returned to New Zealand two months later, spending nearly 12 months on sick leave to recuperate from his ordeal before taking up an invitation to travel to the UK for the Victory Parade. Eddie did fly again for a short while but finally failed a medical check due to his wartime suffering and never flew again.

Harry Bunt Pettit told a similar story to that of Eddie Kuhn and Jim MacIntosh. They separated after their last means of escape was destroyed by the Japanese bombing at the port of Tjilatjap. Bunt headed inland after the debacle at the port and was eventually caught by the Japanese at Bandoeng in central Java. The Japanese had no facilities to deal with thousands of prisoners, so they were ordered to proceed by train via Surabaya to Batavia. It would appear that they all were eventually imprisoned in the same civilian jail. Then followed stays in a series of camps, before Bunt was finally interned on the island of Ambon until the end of the war. They travelled there by ship — a voyage that took the best part of a month for a journey of 2400 km. Bunt recounts that of the 1000 men transported to Ambon Camp only 200 were alive at the end of the war. Some were transported to work as slaves on the Burma–Siam railway and many more were lost at sea while being transported around the Pacific.

Bunt in fact narrowly missed being decapitated by a very irate Japanese guard. The guard had been with a working party that Bunt was in charge of and he bent his sword trying to cut some palm fronds. Most of the working party laughed uproariously at this and the guard went berserk, making Bunt, as the senior officer, go down on his knees. Bunt remembers not being that scared and deciding to remain quiet, knowing that any show of fear on his part would give the guard an excuse to strike off his head. Eventually, sanity prevailed and the guard calmed down. The worst he suffered that day was a couple of blows to the back of his neck with the back side of the blade, but it was a near thing. Bunt Pettit was released when the Japanese capitulated in August 1945, and before leaving for the return to New Zealand was chosen to broadcast a summary of his experiences over the radio. Bunt stayed on a little later than the repatriated men from the camps to help retrieve documents and diaries that had been buried by himself and other officer prisoners in the Ambon Camp. His notes and documents relating to his time as a prisoner make chilling reading and reveal the depth of character that this officer had. He was well respected by fellow prisoners, and the commanding officers of two camps in which he was imprisoned wrote letters at the end of the war praising his discipline and effectiveness in dealing with the terrible situation he was placed in by the Japanese Army.

Pilot Officer Grahame White, the fifth member of the stay-behind group, fell victim to the draft used by the Japanese. All the Allied prisoners on Java were designated alphabetical classification depending on their camp of origin. These drafts were used by the Japanese to construct airfields on the various islands in the region, to be used as part of the master plan to provide air cover and bomber bases for future attacks. Prison labour soon became slave labour in clear contravention of the rules of war. The draft appeared to have forcibly separated the five ex-488 boys as they would have tried to stay together. They were separated when drafts were sent out from Boie Glodok civilian prison.

The Japanese had by early 1943 closed down the camps in the Surabaya area and shipped the prisoners to camps in Bandoeng and Tjimahi. Jim MacIntosh's diary records Eddie Kuhn being with him at Tjimahi Camp and both of them meeting up with Jack Oakden on 24 July 1943 when he arrived at Tjimahi as part of a draft from Bandoeng. Jim recorded that 'Oakie' had lost a lot of weight and was sporting a monster of a moustache. They spent some time catching up on old times as they would not have met for some while. Eddie Kuhn and Jim MacIntosh were eventually drafted to Japan, leaving from Singapore on 22 September 1943 via Tanjong Priok. The next mention of Jack Oakden is in a letter dated 17 September 1945, from Wing Commander T Hugh Nichols of the RAF, writing as officer commanding what appears to be the Officers POW Camp at Bandoeng, to Squadron Leader VB de la Perrelle. He thanks the New Zealand officers for their support during the time of their imprisonment. Both Bunt Pettit and Jack Oakden are mentioned by name in the same letter.[1]

The main groups of prisoners (about 6500 men) had been systematically shipped to the islands of Ambon, Haruku and Flores for airfield reconstruction. Late in November of 1943, the airfield work was completed and the by now starved and disease-ridden surviving prisoners were to be returned in batches to Batavia, supposedly for recuperation. Most were living skeletons. Some drafts, or the survivors of those drafts, were butchered by the Japanese when their allotted tasks were completed. (There are many documented cases of groups of 200 or 300 prisoners being executed with all traces of their demise and camp sites being obliterated by the Japanese.)

One of the lucky groups (if barely alive counts as being lucky) of POWs from the Palao Camp on the island of Haruku were forced onto a coal barge to travel to Ambon to meet up with another draft of POWs from Ambon's Liang Camp. We know Grahame White was in Liang Camp as he is mentioned after the war ended, in a letter from the officer commanding POW Camp Liang. He is thanked, with three other officers, for his efforts in the organisation of the camp until, as the letter says, 'the time they left Ambon for Java Nov. 1943 on which trip they are believed to have been drowned'.² The trip to Ambon takes less than a day but conditions in the packed holds were dreadful. Dysentery and sickness were rife. The holds were coated in black coal dust and air was virtually non-existent. Men died in just a few short hours and the bodies were bagged and thrown over the side without ceremony.³

The human cargo, including those from the Liang Camp draft, was transferred to the holds of a 6400-ton army cargo ship, the *Suez Maru*. Halfway through the loading, barges full of wounded Japanese arrived and these too were packed into the holds of the ship. The worst of the sick prisoners and the already dying were placed out on the deck so they did not have to be hauled out of holds when their end came. Their bodies were just wrapped in sacking and thrown overboard. There was no accounting for the efficiency of the Japanese!

On the afternoon of 26 November the *Suez Maru* cleared port and headed out due west into the Banda Sea accompanied by two Japanese Navy minesweepers, *W11* and *W12*, and set a course for Surabaya. During the next two days the minesweepers left the *Suez Maru* and headed off on differing courses. In the early daylight hours of 29 November, minesweeper *W12* caught up with the *Suez Maru* again, overtaking the ship and settling down to sail in front at the same speed.

Unbeknown to both of the Japanese vessels, the American submarine USS *Bonefish* was already tracking the pair and, at a range of just 2000 m, fired the first of four torpedoes at the two targets at 8am, followed closely by three more. There was no warning from the minesweeper, but the tracking torpedoes were spotted by a lookout on the *Suez Maru* and the ship made a violent turn. Three missed but the fourth caught the ship on the stern under the No. 4 hold. All of the prisoners were in

No. 3 and 4 holds, and many in the rear hold were killed on impact. Prisoners poured out of the No. 3 hold only to be told to get back down into No. 4 hold and rescue any survivors. There were very few. The hold rapidly filled with water and the ship slowly settled down by the stern. The Korean guards threw liferafts into the sea and everybody who was able to leapt into the water. Many were simply too weak and debilitated and remained where they lay in the hold and on the decks. By 9.40am the *Suez Maru* had gone to the bottom.

What followed was one of the very worst atrocities carried out on Allied servicemen by the Japanese in the Second World War. The minesweeper *W12* spent the next two hours cruising around picking up only the Japanese and Korean survivors. The captain of the *W12* was concerned for the stability of his small vessel, now crowded with the rescued. He was ordered by the senior Japanese officer to shoot the prisoners in the water. The prisoners had no chance. They were, by this time, in a long line, clinging to anything that would float. There was thought to be between 200 and 300 of them. They were machine-gunned and shot by rifle fire as they floated defencelessly in the water. Any lifeboats or rafts still afloat were rammed by the minesweeper. This atrocity took over two hours and the minesweeper did not leave the scene of the ghastly deed until it was certain that every last one was dead.[4]

Thousands of these pamphlets were air dropped over Asia by the Japanese.
*Collection of Bob Wright*

One British soldier, however, apparently did survive to tell the tale, being picked up by an Australian minesweeper, HMAS *Ballarat*, 24 hours later. The story of the *Suez Maru* remained untold until 1949, when one of the Japanese officer crew on the *W12* went public about the atrocity and the world found out about this dreadful episode. The final number who died that day cannot be accurately determined but 548 British and Dutch prisoners were known to have been counted onto the ship and it appears that there was only the one survivor.

During my research I found the name of Flight Lieutenant Grahame Prebble White, 411484, Royal New Zealand Air Force, on the list of known dead on the *Suez Maru*. He was just 24 years old and the only New Zealander listed. Confirmation of this was given to me by Allan Jones, author of *The Suez Maru Atrocity*. The atrocity was further compounded when the Allied War Criminal Inquiry in 1949 foreclosed the proceedings and released the perpetrators as free men.

The four survivors remaining from the original six 'stay behinds' were repatriated from the death camps of Japan and the Far East when Japan capitulated in August 1945. The trauma that they suffered stayed with them for the rest of their lives. The deprivation that they endured is beyond comprehension in this day and age.

Thus the chapter on 488 Squadron's time in the Far East was finally closed.

Leaving Tanjong Priok and travelling through the Sunda Straits on 23 February 1942.

ten

# Into calmer waters

ESCAPE AGAIN, REACHING THE RELATIVE SAFETY OF AUSTRALIA

No. 488 Squadron's groundcrew was ordered to leave the island of Java on the morning of 23 February 1942. They boarded the MV *Deucalion* and set sail for Australia in heavy rain later that afternoon. The captain of the ship had agreed to take them on condition that they provided their own food. Flight Sergeants Chandler and Guiniven organised supplies but as food was very scarce they only managed to obtain a limited amount. For the second time in his young life Bert was to be given a break. They had effectively escaped Singapore by the skin of their teeth; now, as they headed off through the Sunda Straits, they found out that the *Deucalion* had left Batavia two days earlier but had been forced to return to port after striking a reef and damaging hull plates. So for the second time Bert effectively left on the last ship out. They sailed out, fully expecting to be targeted by aircraft or submarine — the previous seven ships that had escaped on the same route had all been sunk by Japanese submarines. During the early evening they passed an Allied battle flotilla heading north, with the cruiser HMS *Exeter* and several others, one being the USS *Houston*. The sight of the *Exeter* silhouetted against the setting sun on a by now very calm sea was one that many squadron members recalled. All of that flotilla were sunk by

Meal break on the MV *Deucalion*.

the Japanese a few days later during the Battle of the Java Sea.

The *Deucalion* carried about 450 RAF, RNZAF and RAAF personnel. There were some stowaways on board who were rounded up and put under guard. They were three Australians and four English, but one further Australian somehow escaped detection and was not apprehended during the voyage. Again the sleeping quarters for most of the groundcrew were out in the open on the deck.

Some hours after the *Deucalion* left Tanjong Priok the

488 maintenance fitters group: (back row) Wilf Pentecost, Stu Smart, Ray Stephenson; (centre row) Johnny Helmore, Col Cameron, Geoff Hocken, Ted West; (front row) George Clancy, Nobby Hall, Errol Law.
*Collection of Stu Smart*

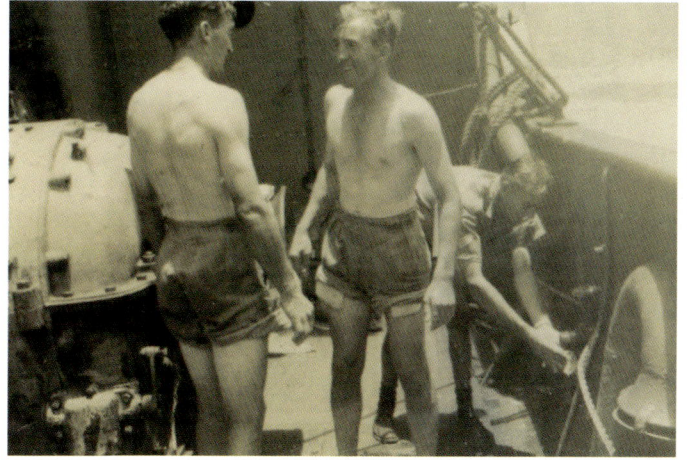

Stan Guiniven and Andy Chandler.
*Collection of Jim Cromie*

port was heavily bombed by over 60 Japanese bombers; as a result the port was closed and all shipping operations transferred to Tjilatjap on the south coast of Java.

As the *Deucalion* rounded the northwestern corner of Java down the Sunda Straits HMS *Exeter* again passed by them, heading northwards, but turned and circled them.

During the voyage a number of 488 Squadron maintenance fitters assisted the ship's crew with engine-room repairs. The engine pumps clogged up several times and had to be stripped and cleaned, so some at least felt they were earning their passage.

The 488 maintenance group on MV *Deucalion*: Bert Clayton is third from left in back row.
*Collection of Stu Smart*

A light-hearted moment when out of range of the Japanese bombers: Bert Clayton centre, Johnny Helmore on the right.
*Collection of Stu Smart*

Again luck was on Bert's side. Not too many of the other ships that passed through the Sunda Straits survived. Mines or torpedoes had claimed most of the ships that sailed from Tanjong Priok the previous night and the *Deucalion* was the only ship out of 12 which left Batavia that night that made it through, all the others being sunk.

It was a 10-day trip to Fremantle in Australia and the closer they got to the Australian shore the more they relaxed. As it turned out, they needed to be more vigilant as just 160 km off Fremantle the ship made a sudden and savage lurch to avoid what turned out to be a torpedo. The captain steered in the direction of the submarine, hoping that the homing-type torpedo which was seen by many on the *Deucalion* would make the sub its target instead of his ship. Seconds later there was a huge explosion about a kilometre away, shooting water hundreds of metres in the air. There was considerable confusion on board as to the actual sequence of events but the certainty was that the submarine had been hit, as the explosion was far greater than that expected from a torpedo. RAAF reconnaissance aircraft searched the area the following day and reported a large oil slick and wreckage. Max Boyd researched the story later and established that they were about 160 km out from Fremantle when the incident took place. Red Nelson was clear in his mind what had happened. He had been on deck with others on what was a beautiful moonlit night with calm seas. He was standing leaning over the port-side railing admiring the peaceful scene and no doubt feeling thankful that their ordeal of the past few months was almost over:

> *Suddenly, there was a huge explosion and for a split second I thought we'd been hit, but in the next split second there was a huge amount of water going skywards. The water reached a fair height and was lit up by a vivid red flame. After a few moments when everything settled down we were left wondering what had happened.*

At a 488 Squadron reunion in 1962 he remembers someone producing a Japanese naval document which confirmed that they had lost a submarine in the area on that particular date. So, again, 488 Squadron had cheated death and destruction by the slimmest of margins.

Later that afternoon, on Monday, 2 March, they reached the port at Fremantle and disembarked to stand on the safety of the Australian mainland. Six days later, on 8 March, the Dutch Government surrendered Java and Sumatra to the Japanese.

A smoko break on the way to Australia: Ray Stephenson's on the left.
*Collection of Stu Smart*

488 Squadron boarding the *Esperance Bay* at Adelaide on the final leg of their escape back to New Zealand.
*Collection of Jim Cromie*

*eleven*

# Safe but still far from home

### A JOURNEY ACROSS THE OUTBACK

The relief must have been immense as the survivors of 488 Squadron lined the ship's rails and looked out over the port of Fremantle. The submarine scare of just a few hours ago would have been very much on the minds of those young men as they contemplated what was still in store for them. Good food and comfortable beds would have occupied most thoughts at that time. The *Deucalion* had carried them into the port, passing Rottnest Light just after midnight, anchoring at 4am in the outer harbour, before berthing at Fremantle at 4pm.

The squadron was officially disbanded on 2 March 1942, the day they arrived in Australia. No. 488 (NZ) Squadron of the Royal Air Force effectively died on that day. The squadron disembarked and were trucked to Claremont Army Camp about 16 km from Perth. There they had what was described as the best feed served up during their entire sojourn in the East. They found out much later that at that time there was a serious food shortage in Perth, so the gesture by the Australian Army was appreciated that much more. Food had been a big problem for them during the latter days of their stay in Singapore and worsened during the time in Java.

The following day they were transported to Northam Military Camp 100 km north of Perth so missed seeing the city. It was a very large camp, as big as a small town, covering thousands of acres and capable of holding 10,000 men. On the morning of 4 March they were officially welcomed in a manner that just emphasised the difference in military cultures that they had experienced over the past few months. They were paraded and spoken to by the highest ranking RAF officer, a wing commander. He gave them a run-down on what was expected of them in this camp, and imposed tough rules in a manner that suggested they were being confined to camp. The Australian camp commandant then stood up and said while they were in 'his' camp they were under his rules and that they could come and go as they pleased. However, if they came home late at night they were not to come in through the guardhouse entry but were to return by the AWOL gate at the rear of the camp. He further advised them that the Western Australian beer was stronger than most, to take care and treat the local womenfolk with respect. The RAF wing commander was reported to be greatly angered at the 'Aussie' attitude, but there was at least some recognition of the suffering and deprivation that the young men of 488 Squadron had undergone.

Over the next few days there was time given for relaxation and the luxury of fresh fruit and vegetables, much sleeping and swimming in the local swimming hole. A number of the men were receiving hospital treatment, including John Hutcheson who was suffering from recurring bouts of malaria. Leading Aircraftman Leo Arden had developed a huge tropical ulcer which improved markedly with the onset of good food supplies. Gradually, most men put on weight and at least revived physically as the days went by. Bert well recalls the feelings he had at the time, which never quite left him for many years. These were of apprehension and of constantly being on guard, waiting for something traumatic to take place.

Meal break aboard the *Deucalion*.

Not surprisingly, clothes and footwear were a problem with many having no shoes; in fact, Max Boyd was trudging around in a pair of battered bedroom slippers until scoring a pair of shoes on 13 March. The clothing, if some of the photographs of the time are any indication, looked like it had been salvaged from a scrapheap. Bert Clayton remembered the then senior officer, Flying Officer De Suza, trying a 'get fit' and morale-boosting programme by parading the men for drill and marching them all over the place. They were, as he recalled, 'too physically weak and emotionally drained' to respond, and the reaction of the men to such well-intentioned initiatives convinced those in charge that there would be little use in continuing.

Boredom was a big issue at the time and one of the Australian staff sergeants organised work parties shifting fuel drums to dispersal points, and this helped to a degree with morale. The other overriding question concerned the squadron's immediate future. There was still a war

## 488's 'arsenal'

*One of the interesting stories that came out of this period in the life of 488 Squadron was the great variety of weapons still carried by the men. Most of these were found in the holds of the* Empire Star *when the men were left on board overnight on their arrival at Tanjong Priok. Bert scored a Thompson sub-machine-gun, while Herb Fenwick sported a magnificent pair of automatic pistols. Others had Tommy guns in their possession and Bert was asked by the Australian Army for a loan of his for instruction of their troops. They had never seen one before and Bert recalls showing one of their instructors how to assemble and disassemble the weapon. (Somehow Bert managed to return to New Zealand with his Tommy gun, in fact taking it along to his old school, Otahuhu College, after they requested him to speak to the school cadets. He must have carried ammunition back with him also as the cadets were allowed to fire several bursts from the weapon. Later, Bert was to swap the gun for a pair of wool-lined flying boots with George Clancy who had plans to shoot wild pigs on the family farm near Cambridge.)*

on and for some time rumours persisted that they were going to regroup and move up to the northern coast to help defend against what was thought to be the inevitable Japanese invasion. It was seemingly more than a rumour as it was known that Squadron Leader Manhire, the commanding officer of the RNZAF Technical Training School, was said to have travelled to Australia to head off the squadron to stop them being dispersed to other combat areas overseas rather than being returned to New Zealand and have the country lose all those well-trained technicians.

On 17 March they entrained and travelled eastwards across central Australia. They still had no idea of their end destination and seemed to be still far from home. Spirits, however, were good and the recuperation at Northam went a long way to restoring the men to better health both physically and mentally. The first call on the way was at Coolgardie, a brief stop for water before the journey continued to Kalgoorlie. The interior of Australia was desolate, with scattered scrub, very few trees and sand everywhere. Many of the small townships they passed through were run down and decrepit but the boys were by this time beyond caring. The carriages were hard riding and very uncomfortable. Where possible they all slept and hoped that they were heading towards home and not on to Darwin or some other defensive position.

Water for drinking and bathing was in short supply and some of the stops were made in areas where the temperature dropped considerably. The cold caused problems with a great many of them as clothing was still scant. Most squadron members were still in tropical kit with some lucky ones wearing jerseys or topcoats scavenged during their stay in Northam.

Slowly and gradually the countryside changed and by the time they reached Mallala they knew that their final destination was looking like Adelaide. Sand and sparse scrub was changing to rolling hills and green grass.

They stayed in two different areas when they finally reached the outskirts of Adelaide. Accommodation was very basic with most in tents with timber floors. The food was plentiful and they were free to travel into the city. Four days later, on Tuesday, 24 March, they took the train for Port Augusta and boarded the *Esperance Bay* bound for Auckland. They sailed for home late in the afternoon, not without some drama, as just off the Three Kings Islands they felt and heard a very loud thud and a change in the pitch of the engines. Later that day they noticed the mine-cutter frame on the bow of the *Esperance Bay* was bent and twisted. It had, fortunately for them, cut a mine cable and saved them from possible disaster.

Auckland Harbour was a wonderful sight. At the wharfside the wharfies were kept busy relaying messages by phone to relatives as the 488 men were kept on board for several hours before disembarking and being transported up to the Rutland Street Drill Hall for a final muster and parade. The Auckland boys were allowed to return to their homes but had to report back to Whenuapai air base by nine o'clock next morning. Bert walked up to the Otahuhu bus stop in Wyndham Street to face the humiliation by the bus driver who would not accept his Australian 10-shilling note. It was, as he said much later, a small price to pay to stand again on New Zealand soil. He would have walked to Otahuhu from the city had it been necessary.

twelve

# The aftermath

QUESTIONS NEEDING ANSWERS

During our family's stay in Singapore, Bert was chosen from his squadron to represent the Royal New Zealand Air Force at the opening of the Kranji War Memorial in 1957. Kranji is on the northern slopes of Singapore Island and contains marked graves of 4000 war dead. Another 24,000 names of military personnel who died but whose bodies were never recovered are inscribed on 12 columns. The site was well chosen as it was the arrival point of the Japanese attack on 8 February 1942. It is elevated and looks northwards over the Johore Straits towards the mainland of Malaya. I revisited the site in 2000 and found the memorial and the surrounding gardens and grave sites absolutely immaculate. Teams of gardeners were on their knees trimming the berms by hand. It was clear that even now, after all these years, the sacrifices made by countless thousands of young servicemen from all corners of the then 'Empire' would never be forgotten. Standing in front of the memorial and looking towards Malaya and the Johore Straits, you are confronted with the sight of the thousands of white crosses. It is a sobering and very emotional scene. Bert felt very honoured to be picked for the ceremony and I still recall with great pride the sight of him, at the appointed time, unfurling the New Zealand flag.

The efforts of 488 Squadron against all the odds at a crucial time in the history of the British Empire have gone largely unrecognised. I have a copy of the Official Report commissioned by the British Government, of Air Operations in the Far East from 8 December 1941 to 12 March 1942. The report was compiled by Air Vice Marshal Sir Paul Maltby, Assistant Air Officer Commanding, Royal Air Force, and presented to Parliament in London. Incredibly, 488 Squadron were not mentioned at all in the 68-page report, other than being in an index of squadrons shown to be on the respective airfields of Malaya and Singapore. Not a single mention.

The aircrews of the squadrons in Singapore formed the front line and took the brunt of the casualties. The groundcrew were an integral part of this work. In fact, the groundcrew of 488 Squadron were, in the last days, the only air force maintenance personnel left on Singapore Island, servicing a mixed bunch of pilots. Their aircraft were cobbled together from several squadrons and the aircrew that were left used any aircraft that could be patched up and put in the air. When the odds finally became impossible, the remaining aircraft were flown away and the groundcrew abandoned to their fate.

My research showed systemic failure of the defence system in Malaya and Singapore. Given better planning, foresight and execution, Singapore would never have fallen. The loss of Malaya and Singapore was the single greatest Allied catastrophe of the Second World War. The loss and subsequent surrender meant the imprisonment of over 100,000 military personnel. We were overcome by a foe that logistically should never have beaten us. We had both numerical and logistical advantages that were very poorly handled. (General Yamashita forced the surrender of Singapore with under 30,000 troops. The Japanese Army was desperately short of supplies and munitions and in the end was outnumbered three to one by the Allied armies.)

On the very first day of the Japanese invasion, 8 December 1941, the Japanese landings at Kota Bharu on the Malayan coast were well defended. Hudson bombers of the RAAF caused huge casualties off the coast and for a time held back the planned invasion. It was the failure of the combined operations room in Singapore to recognise and evaluate the situation, and their inability to provide more air support to prevent the landings and, on the following day, to give air support to the naval fleet that set in motion the rot that followed. Every available aircraft was sent north to attack these landings, but the Japanese gained an early foothold and continued to launch attacks further south. The quality of many of the staff officers was at best questionable. The pukka sahib syndrome mentioned earlier could be best summed up by the following example of the madness of the situation in Singapore. An Air Commodore from Air Operations arrived unannounced at Kallang in the final days. He asked why men were standing around at the time. He suggested that they be put to work picking up paper and debris that was blowing around in the light breeze. All about him were smashed aircraft, vehicles and buildings still burning as the airfield had been bombed and shelled nearly out of existence. Needless to say, he was given a short and unequivocal response.

Another incident reported by Max Boyd concerned a directive issued that ordered a stop to the practice of the groundcrew urinating against the wheels of their aircraft 'as it would cause corrosion of said wheels'. Of more concern should have been the obvious extensive damage all over the aircraft due to cannon fire in the air, bomb and shrapnel damage. The same mentality late in the campaign replaced our weary pilots with newly arrived but battle-hardened veterans and new Hurricanes from

Britain. These men, despite a total lack of experience with local conditions, were put in the air almost on their first day in Singapore. They struck mass formations of bombers shooting them down in numbers. The next day was a totally different story, as the bombers this time were escorted by Zeros, or Navy O's as they were known then. We lost 17 Hurricanes and had six pilots killed on the second day. The simple fact was the Japanese had aircraft that were way superior to ours, piloted by airmen who were better trained and had more experience, and more importantly they were able to have more aircraft in the air at any one time.

While the aircrews did hold the line for a time in northern Malaya despite terrible losses, the groundcrew of crucial airfields at Kota Bharu, Sungei Patani, Alor Star, Butterworth and Kuantan packed up and fled south. Some were not even under any attack at that time. They left countless quantities of armaments and fuel supplies which the Japanese used to great effect. The airfields were left intact, allowing comfort and shelter to Japanese bombers and fighters low on fuel from their bases in Saigon. The Japanese rather sarcastically referred to their gains as 'Churchill's supplies'. The amount of material left behind was a big contributor to the rapid advance by the Japanese Army as there was no chance that they would ever outstrip their supply line.

The loss of the battleships *Prince of Wales* and the *Repulse* was a disaster for the defence of Singapore. The High Command simply underestimated the capabilities of the Japanese, and by sending out the main defensive fleet to its destruction in the Far East — without air cover — the invaders were assured unfettered access to the coasts of Malaya and Thailand. The bomber aircraft that sank the Allied capital ships had flown all the way from bases in Indo-China without fighter escort, and even a half-dozen lumbering Buffaloes from the Singapore bases could just possibly have limited the damage done to the British fleet. The Navy contributed in no small way by refusing air cover for their operations and maintaining radio silence for a full hour after the first attack. While the capital ships of the Royal Navy were under attack, aircraft from 488 Squadron and all the other squadrons on the island sat waiting for the order that would have put them in the air.

Just why 488 Squadron groundcrew were left behind to fend for themselves in those last days is open to speculation. One possibility is that they were by far the most experienced maintenance group in the Far East. Most were handpicked for their work skills and experience and this was acknowledged by many officers, both from the RAF and the RAAF, who came in contact with them. The fact still remains that they had no aircraft to service so should have been evacuated sooner to help with the second line of defence in Sumatra and Java.

Even after all other air force squadrons had been evacuated, and right until the last possible minute, the groundcrew of 488 Squadron were told to hold their ground, at one time being issued with arms to try to hold back the Japanese advance. They had nowhere to retreat to and were reconciled to being overrun, and at best made prisoners of war. They were effectively in no-man's-land in the final days, caught between the British Army and the approaching Japanese. Somehow a miracle occurred and they took the very last chance they were offered to escape. That opportunity may well have been due to their previous commanding officer, Wilf Clouston.

The significance of Clouston's input cannot be understated. His control of 488 Squadron was taken away from him by RAF Operations, when he was seconded to their headquarters on 23 January 1942, and Flight

Lieutenant John Mackenzie was promoted to Squadron Leader. The British needed Clouston's knowledge of air fighting and fighter control, and it must have been a big wrench for him to leave the squadron that he had basically built from scratch. He is quoted publicly on several occasions speaking very highly of the men under him, and it is evident from anecdotal information and interviews with surviving members of the squadron that he too was highly regarded. John Mackenzie made a very effective and worthy replacement. In any event, it was the shifting of Clouston to headquarters that, in the end, probably saved many of the lives of the groundcrew members who were at that stage being left on the island to face capture by the enemy.

The shift to RAF Operations Headquarters would have given Clouston a clear overview of the situation and it would have been patently obvious that Singapore was doomed. His natural instinct would have been to plan to escape the debacle but that would have been tempered by his desire to do the best he could for his former squadron. It has been recorded by several sources that Clouston approached his now stranded groundcrew to try to broker a deal. All the serviceable aircraft that could be flown were now off the island, having been flown to Palembang in Sumatra by surviving aircrew members with the idea of regrouping to form a second line of defence. As outlined earlier, Clouston's deal was to have them get one more Hurricane into a flyable condition for him to fly to Palembang to join his old aircrew; in return, he would try to get all his groundcrew off the island and away to a safe haven. By the time this was arranged on 10 February 1942, there were only a few select groups given permission to board the few remaining ships in the port of Singapore.

We can only surmise that Clouston had sufficient

influence to allow this to happen and that the escape the 488 groundcrew were finally able to make was a direct result of his input. An aircraft was actually made available for Clouston but he never arrived to take it. He escaped instead on an air-sea rescue launch, *HSL105*, on 15 February 1942, with other members of RAF Operations Headquarters including Group Captain EB Rice, Wing Commander Robert Chignell (former OC of Kallang) and Squadron Leader Frank Howell, former commander of 243 Squadron. The vessel was sunk in the Banka Straits after a bombing attack lasting 20 minutes. Chignell was killed after the vessel was hit by a single bomb. The launch was sunk and the survivors picked up by two small steamers, the *Rentau* and the *Relau*, both of which were intercepted by the Japanese the next day. Clouston survived the sinking but was captured by the Japanese and spent the rest of the war incarcerated in the Selarang Garrison Prison at Changi. Group Captain Rice died as a prisoner of war in 1943 but Clouston did survive to return to New Zealand.

During the research phase of this narrative I heard and documented many accounts of individual bravery among both aircrew and groundcrew, too numerous to retell. There were outstanding acts of bravery among the aircrew and these are well documented in various publications. Simple acts by others in the squadron, such as the day that Murray Foster, the squadron accounts officer, arrived during an air raid with everyone's pay packets. He sheltered in a hole in the ground until the bombs had stopped dropping and carried on calmly handing out pay packets as if nothing had ever happened. It may not have been a particularly notable act, but it was brave all the same, and well-remembered by all those who witnessed it.

Despite the bravery shown by all members of 488

Squadron, decorations were few and far between. Noel Sharp was awarded a Distinguished Flying Cross after going missing in Batavia, John Hutcheson also a DFC, Eddie Kuhn a Distinguished Flying Medal, Cecil Franks, the squadron equipment officer, a Member of the Order of the British Empire (MBE), Wally Chandler and John Rees both received the British Empire Medal.

Jack Oakden, Harry Pettit, Noel Sharp and Grahame White, Jim MacIntosh and Eddie Kuhn were ordered to stay behind at Tjililitan in Batavia when the rest of the squadron were evacuated, as they were deemed to be the most experienced due to having done the most operational flying of all the aircrew of 488 Squadron. All were taken prisoner by the Japanese. Grahame White died on 29 November 1943 when the prisoner of war ship *Suez Maru* he was travelling on, heading back to Java from Ambon, was sunk by the US Navy submarine *Bonefish* northeast of Kangean Island in the Java Sea. Grahame's death was particularly tragic as the *Suez Maru* incident in the aftermath of the sinking was the scene of one of the worst atrocities carried out by the Japanese in the Second World War.

In all, 5102 air force personnel from several nations were captured and imprisoned by the Japanese on the islands of Sumatra and Java. Of those, 3462 survived to be liberated by the end of the war. Had Bert and his mates been captured the chances of them surviving the death camps would not have been good.

When war broke out in the Far East, the British had four Buffalo squadrons in Singapore and Malaya. They were No. 243 RAF, Nos. 21 and 453 Squadrons RAAF and No. 488 Squadron RNZAF. No. 67 Squadron RAF was based in Burma, having left from Singapore before the outbreak of hostilities. In all these squadrons only 15 aircrew were serving members of the Royal Air Force.

The rest were from Australia and New Zealand, the so-called 'Commonwealth Squadrons'. They numbered 118 aircrew. Twenty-eight of those were killed or captured by the Japanese.

Any written accounts of the fall of Singapore almost invariably mention the saga of the MV *Empire Star*. The ship featured in two of the most publicised controversies that occurred during the evacuation of Singapore. These were the supposed shooting and murder by Australian deserters of the Singapore harbour master, Captain TKW Atkinson RN, on the gangway of the ship, and the forced boarding of the *Empire Star* by armed Australian deserters. Both subjects appear in even recently published accounts of the last days of Singapore. Despite a very public denial by Jeremy Atkinson, the son of Captain Atkinson, the myth surrounding his death is still perpetuated in recent studies. All the documentary evidence points to Captain Atkinson dying during shelling by a Japanese destroyer, while he was escaping from Singapore in the harbour board tug *Yin-Ping*. I have a recent copy of Jeremy Atkinson's memorandum detailing the affair.

The story of the deserters has a ring of truth about it. Clearly, from eyewitness accounts by surviving members of 488 Squadron, there were Australian troops on board, they were armed, and they were arrested and taken away when the ship arrived in the port of Tanjong Priok in Batavia. There is ample documentary evidence on the deserters but very little evidence of shots being fired other than a brief burst of machine-gun fire from troops on the wharfside as the *Empire Star* left its berth in Keppel Harbour.

Statistically, the *Empire Star* should never have made it to safety. The Japanese lay in wait to the south of Singapore with aircraft, patrol boats, submarines and warships to apprehend any vessel which survived the bombing attacks from land-based aircraft. The *Empire Star* was one of the very few that escaped destruction of the scores of vessels of all shapes and sizes that left Singapore in the days prior to the island's surrender.

Sixteen vessels left Keppel Harbour on the morning of 12 February 1942. The *Empire Star*, at over 10,000 tonnes, was by far the largest ship to escape and carried the largest number of passengers. Only one other ship beside, the *Empire Star* and its escorting destroyers escaped that day and made it to the relative safety of Batavia. This was the SS *Gorgon* carrying 358 passengers.

Those passengers and crew that survived being attacked and sunk by bombs, torpedoes or gunfire on the other ships were either machine-gunned in the water, massacred on the beaches they struggled to reach after having their ships sunk from under them, or died in captivity in the death camps run by the Japanese.

The true number of the ships that carried escapees from the shambles in the days before the surrender to the Japanese on 15 February will probably never be really known. Most contemporary estimates do give the figure as nearly 50, but if the smaller vessels such as private yachts and small motor boats are taken into consideration the number is much greater. Richard Gough, who wrote the definitive work *The Escape from Singapore*, lists 156 vessels that are known to have left the harbour from 10 February to the capitulation day, 15 February. Of that number, most were recorded to have been sunk by torpedo, bombing, or capture by the Japanese fleet. Admiral Ozawa had his fleet in place from 10 February in the narrows of the Banka Straits off Batavia, so how the *Empire Star* escaped is nothing short of a miracle. The fact that they entered and travelled through the Banka Straits at night probably saved them. Fortune smiled again upon the New Zealanders when the ship carrying them from Batavia, in similar circumstances as the Singapore escape, defied the odds and delivered its cargo of young men to the safety of the shores of Australia.

Bert is very clear in his mind that they all owed their lives to the master of the *Empire Star*, Captain Selwyn Capon CBE. He has a picture in his mind after all these years of the captain on the bridge, standing out in the open, with just his head and shoulders above the bridge rails, scanning the sky with his binoculars and quietly giving orders to his helmsman as the bombs fell all around them. The gratitude felt by his many passengers is well recorded. When the ship finally docked in Batavia the nurses on board took up a collection for the captain and crew.

The Australian Navy, through its acting naval control officer, Lieutenant-Commander Geoffrey Lawson, wrote a letter to Captain Selwyn Capon personally congratulating him for his seamanship and bravery and advising him they were forwarding a report to the British Admiralty.

When 488 Squadron returned to the safety of New Zealand, Aircraftman George Cottrill, now posted to the newly formed No. 15 Fighter Squadron, which had a good number of the former 488 Squadron allocated to it, called on Captain Capon, with others, with gifts expressing the gratitude of those he took to safety. The response from Captain Capon is given below:

*6th August 1942*

*A/C. G.A. Cottrill MM*      *C/O Blue Star Line*
*R.A.F. 654223*              *P.O. Box 1222*
*15th (F) Squadron*          **WELLINGTON NZ.**

*R.N.Z.A.F. Station*
**WHENUAPAI N.Z.**

*Dear Cottrill,*
*I feel I cannot leave these waters, homeward bound on*

the present occasion, without sending you these few lines to express my sincere and unbounded appreciation of the tokens of gratitude which you lads so generously brought along to give to me just before leaving Auckland the latter part of last month. Actually, in addressing my letter to your own self, I am, as I feel sure you will readily understand, writing to all of you concerned, and therefore, I must ask you to be good enough to pass on to the others what I have to say.

What, of course, in such instances, is to be taken most into consideration is not so much the value of the gift of gifts as the kindly thought which proves beyond question how genuine is the sense of gratitude thereby betokened. I know full well that much careful consideration has been given to the carrying out of the idea, once conceived, and, what is more, no small amount of trouble also taken in the choosing of the gifts themselves. It all speaks for itself, summing up in that one word which is so eloquently expressive of the sentiment intended — GRATITUDE. As long as I am spared, these tokens will, I can assure you, be indeed prized and greatly treasured, and as a sailor man, what will naturally ever have its special appeal, it is the little greenstone anchor which I am inclined to think must have been specially carved unless by some chance it happened to be a unique find.

I cannot adequately express my feelings, because, strange as it may perhaps seem, nevertheless perfectly true, there are times when, deep down, I'm apt to be somewhat emotional. Suffice it then for me to say that I've now got a VERY soft spot in my heart for all the Officers and lads of the R.A.F. and R.N.Z.A.F. for whom my ship was privileged to afford a timely 'let out' in their hour of desperate need. For the miraculous survival from the sustained ordeal to which we were subjected that never-to-be-forgotten morning of 12th February we, each and every one of us on board at *the time, have every reason for the rest of our lives to be thankful to a merciful providence, of whom, as I afterwards pointed out and can but here repeat, I myself was but the very humble agent.*

*In conclusion I want you to know that, all being well, anytime I happen to be out here in these waters again I shall be greatly pleased to see any of you who are able to get the time off to come along.*

*With the kindest of thoughts and best wishes ever, and a big THANK YOU,*
*Yours cordially and in all Sincerity.*

*Selwyn N. Capon. O.B.E.*
**COMMANDER**

Selwyn Capon had also earlier taken the time to write to the father of Aircraftman Donald Stringer, an armourer of 488 Squadron, to advise him of Donald's safe landing in Batavia. He expressed the hope that Donald had since survived to return to his family. In the letter he describes the events that took place on the *Empire Star* but asks that the contents of his letter be kept confidential as he had yet to submit his official report to the authorities. He requested that the family contact him before he sailed from New Zealand to let him know that Donald had survived and returned safely. It says something about the compassion of the man. With George Cottrill, Donald Stringer helped man the machine-gun that downed one of the Japanese aircraft, and it would have been this action that brought him to the captain's attention.

Captain Capon, while praising the actions of his crew, significantly downplayed and understated his own part in the saga in his report to the ship's owners, the Blue Star Line. He stated, very matter of factly, the sequence of events during their run from Singapore followed by a statement on the actions of his crew. Although the crew behaved 'in a manner and to an extent unquestionably deserving of the highest commendation', Capon did not consider that this justified or merited any special recognition, and therefore he did not

> *advocate it, actually we, each one of us on board at that time, simply did our duty what, under circumstances of any such emergency did what was commonly expected and required of us. In those circumstances, as I feel sure you will understand and appreciate, it is team work which so materially counts that, in a great measure, accrues from example and leadership born of a high sense of duty.*

Sadly, Selwyn Capon never got to return to New Zealand after the war. His ship, the *Empire Star*, resumed its cross-Atlantic run carrying munitions and supplies. On 23 October 1942, just three months after his last visit to Auckland, while carrying general cargo and government stores from Liverpool to East London, South Africa, disaster struck. Just off the Azores, the German U-boat *U615* surfaced in the path of the *Empire Star* and its torpedoes sent it to the bottom. Being a comparatively fast ship the *Empire Star* was sailing unescorted and unencumbered by the limitations of a convoy as was its usual way. It was late in the afternoon, with clear skies and good visibility. The ship was almost in mid-Atlantic about 570 miles from the Azores, steaming southwards at 14 knots. It was blowing hard from the northwest with a heavy swell and breaking sea and to prevent damage to the valuable cargo Captain Capon had decided to stop zigzagging. At 3.43pm a torpedo from *U615* hit the ship amidships on the starboard side. The engine room was immediately flooded and all power failed, which stopped the ship. Four of the engine-room crew died in the blast. The ship listed heavily over to starboard. Captain Capon gave the order to abandon ship. After the crew had taken to the boats the ship appeared to stabilise, although sitting low in the water. Half an hour after the first explosion, the crew were contemplating reboarding when the ship was struck by two further torpedoes. The *Empire Star* sank almost immediately stern first, leaving the crew in three lifeboats in the heavy seas. Captain Capon ordered the boats to stay together overnight and planned to set sail for the Azores at first light the next morning. Dawn found the lifeboats separated in the heavy seas and although a second lifeboat was sighted later in the morning, containing Captain Capon, it was never seen again. The two remaining lifeboats were eventually picked up by the destroyer HMS *Black Swan*. It was the normal custom for German U-boat commanders to surface after sinking British shipping and check on the ship's name, destination and so on, but strangely this was not done. It was not uncommon for survivors to be taken on board the submarines and, later, loaded onto fuel supply tankers following the submarines, to be taken into eventual imprisonment.

Thus died a truly brave man. Selwyn Capon was born in Norfolk, England of Irish parentage in 1890. His name, along with those of the other 29 crew members lost with him, is inscribed on the Merchant Navy War Memorial, Tower Hill, London.

## Awards to crew of the Empire Star

*Captain Capon did single out several members of his crew in his report but the authorities extended his recommendations much further. The London Gazette of 15 September 1942 listed the following awards. Their number is still the highest given to any single crew of a merchant ship during the Second World War:*

> Captain Selwyn Capon CBE
> Chief Officer, Mr Joseph Lindon Dawson
>    OBE
> Chief Engineer, Mr Richard Frederick Francis
>    OBE
> Second Officer, Mr James Duncan Golightly
>    MBE
> Senior Second Engineer, Herbert Gordon
>    Charles Weller MBE
> Third Officer, James Peter Smith MBE
> Boatswain, W Power BEM
> Carpenter, S Milne BEM

*Official Commendations were given to the following crew:*

*Junior Second Engineer, JJ Johnson*
*Senior Third Engineer, J Middleton*
*Junior Third Engineer, JR Mitchell*
*Chief Steward, CE Ribbons*
*Second Steward, TS Hughes*
*Cadet, R Foulkner*
*Cadet, R Perry*
*Able Seaman, CP Barber*
*Donkeyman, HE Heaver*

*The Official Citation read:*

*The Master's coolness, leadership and skill were outstanding, and it was mainly due to his handling of the ship that the vessel reached safety. The Chief Officer showed great organising ability and tireless leadership throughout. Under the direction of the Chief Engineer, the Engineer Officers remained at their posts and kept the engine and also the fire service pumps working thus releasing all others of the engine-room staff to help the fire parties. The Second Officer was in charge of the guns and fought them with gallantry throughout the attacks. The Boatswain and Carpenter behaved magnificently throughout. They led the crew and worked tirelessly during the attacks. They were always present, leading fire parties, dealing efficiently with the fires and led parties that carried the wounded to safety.*

488 Aircrew: Tony Cox and Jack Godsiff in doorway at rear; (standing left to right) Noel Sharp, Deryck Charters, Jack Burton, Frank Johnstone, Alex Craig, Don Clow, Rod McMillan, Len Farr, Perce Killick, Wally Greenhalgh, Jim MacIntosh, John Hutcheson, John Mackenzie and Wilf Clouston; (squatting left to right) Jack McAneny, Harry Pettit, Vern Meaclem, Bunny de Maus, Terry Honan, Peter Gifford; (crouching left to right) Eddie Kuhn (behind Pettit), Bob Greening (behind Gifford).
*Collection of Bunt Pettit*

# Appendix 1

### 488 Squadron Personnel, Singapore and Batavia 1941–42

**Commanding Officer**
Clouston, Squadron Leader WG DFC (Wilf): captured by Japanese

**Flight Commanders**
Hutcheson, Flight Lieutenant JR DFC (John)
Mackenzie, Flight Lieutenant JN DFC (John)

**Administration**
De Suza, Flying Officer EW (Ernie), Squadron Adjutant
Foster, Flying Officer M (Murray), Accounts Officer
Franks, Flying Officer CW (Cecil), Equipment Officer

**Aircrew**

| | | |
|---|---|---|
| Burton, Sergeant JF (Jack) | Killed in action | 1 July 1943 |
| Charters, Sergeant CD (Deryck) | Died in POW camp | 25 Dec 1943 |
| Clow, Sergeant DL (Don) | | |
| Cox, Pilot Officer EW (Tony) | Killed in action | 18 Jan 1942 |
| Craig, Sergeant AG (Alex) | Killed aircraft accident | 18 Dec 1941 |
| de Maus, Sergeant WR (Bunny) | Killed aircraft accident | 16 May 1944 |
| Farr, Pilot Officer LR (Len) | Died of injuries | 25 Jan 1942 |

Gifford, Pilot Officer PD (Peter)
Godsiff, Pilot Officer JC (Jack)
Greenhalgh, Pilot Officer WJ (Wally)
Greening, Sergeant RS (Bob)
Hesketh, Pilot Officer GL (Butch) — Killed in action — 15 Jan 1942
Honan, Sergeant TW (Terry)
Johnstone, Pilot Officer FS (Frank)
Killick, Sergeant PEE (Perce)
Kuhn, Sergeant EG DFM (Eddie) — POW
MacMillan, Sergeant R W (Rod)
McAneny, Pilot Officer KJ (Jack) — Killed in action — 19 Jan 1942
MacIntosh, Sergeant WJ (Jim) — POW 3 years
Meaclem, Sergeant VE (Vern)
Meharry, Sergeant HJ (Jack) — Killed in action — 5 Aug 1944
Oakden, Pilot Officer FWJ (Jack)
Pettit, Pilot Officer HS (Harry) — POW 3 years
Sharp, Pilot Officer NC DFC (Noel) — Killed in action — 1 Mar 1942
White, Pilot Officer GP (Snow) — Died POW (ship sinking) — 29 Nov 1943

**Groundcrew**

| Name | Number | Trade |
|---|---|---|
| Adcock, Corporal JR (Johnny) | 39192 | Arm |
| Alexander, Corporal RA (Robert) | 39126 | Fit 2A |
| Anderson, Aircraftman First Class DT (David) | RAF 1000921 | F/Mech |
| Anderson, Aircraftman First Class IVS (Andy) | 391391 | F/Rig (Killed in action) |
| Ansdell, Aircraftman Second Class EW (Ernest) | RAF 1081085 | Elect |
| Anstis, Sergeant WG (Wilfred) | 39127 | Fit 2A |
| Appleby, Leading Aircraftman WG (Barker) | 391776 | Fit 2E |
| Arden, Leading Aircraftman LE (Leo) | 392005 | F/Mech |
| Ashley-Jones, Leading Aircraftman. HO (Herb) | 391888 | Arm |
| Barrie, Leading Aircraftman A (Archibald) | 40785 | W/T |
| Bennett, Corporal LIS (Louis) | 401319 | Elect |
| Binns, Leading Aircraftman OS (Sel) | 404778 | F/Rig |
| Black, Leading Aircraftman L (Lawrence) | 409023 | ACH/GD |
| Boddy, Leading Aircraftman JR (Jim) | 39187 | Fit 11A |
| Boyd, Leading Aircraftman TM (Tiny) | 401572 | F/Rigg |
| Briers, Aircraftman Second Class F (Frank) | RAF1199151 | F/Mech |
| Buie, Aircraftman Second Class JA (John) | RAF1111481 | F/Mech |
| Burgess, Leading Aircraftman RE (Raymond) | 404267 | Arm |
| Burnell, Leading Aircraftman KF (Ken) | 391033 | ACH |
| Callender, Leading Aircraftman WR (William) | 404018 | CLK/GD |
| Cameron, Leading Aircraftman CG (Colin) | 63096 | Fit 11E |
| Chadwick, Leading Aircraftman HW (Hugh) | 391911 | Fit 11A |
| Chandler, Flight Sergeant WA (Andy) | 36112 | Fit 2A |
| Chittock, Leading Aircraftman AW (Alexander) | 39087 | ACH/GD |
| Clancy, Leading Aircraftman GWE (George) | 40464 | Fit 11E |
| Clayton, Aircraftman First Class ALM (Bert) | 39367 | Fit 11A |
| Cleaver, Leading Aircraftman DOR (Darcy) | 391737 | F/Rigg |

| | | |
|---|---|---|
| Copeland, Leading Aircraftman LG (Leslie) | 391095 | F/Rigg |
| Cottrill, Aircraftman First Class GA (George) | RAF 654123 | I/REPR |
| Cox, Corporal CR (Clifford) | 402718 | F/Mech |
| Craighead, Corporal BG (Bruce) | 391639 | Fit 11A |
| Cromie, Aircraftman Second Class JA (Paddy) | RAF1061360 | F/Mech |
| Croskery, Aircraftman First Class JC (Jake) | 411553 | ACH/GD |
| Delap, Aircraftman Second Class JH (James) | RAF1077368 | F/Mech |
| Denham, Aircraftman First Class DJ (Douglas) | RAF933579 | F/Mech |
| Duffin, Leading Aircraftman PEH (Patrick) | 39092 | ACH/GD |
| Dunn, Aircraftman First Class AJ (Bert) | 39783 | Fit 11A |
| Edlin, Leading Aircraftman RH (Ronald) | 391533 | ACH/GD |
| Elliot, Leading Aircraftman SMcF (Sydney) | 391523 | CLK/PA |
| Ewart, Leading Aircraftman J (James) | 391400 | ACH/GD |
| Fenwick, Aircraftman First Class GH (Gordon) | 391097 | Fit 11E |
| Fitzgerald, Aircraftman Second Class JL (Fitz) | 401352 | F/Mech |
| Flynn, Aircraftman First Class LVA (Leslie) | 401851 | F/Mech |
| Friend, Aircraftman First Class R (Bob) | 391133 | F/Arm |
| Gardiner, Aircraftman First Class HF (Herbert) | 401321 | Elect |
| Gibbins, Leading Aircraftman T (Thomas) | 391100 | F/Mech |
| Gilfillan, Aircraftman Second Class KN (Ken) | 639105 | Arm |
| Gillatt, Leading Aircraftman R W (Ray) | 391004 | ACH/GD |
| Gouley, Leading Aircraftman RE (Robert) | 391894 | Arm |
| Grindrod, Leading Aircraftman B (Bernard) | 40905 | Arm |
| Guiniven, Flight Sergeant N (Stan) | 36512 | Fit 11A |
| Guthrie, Aircraftman First Class MW (Bill) | 411634 | R/Mech |
| Hair, Aircraftman First Class DW (Douglas) | 39231 | Arm |
| Halkett, Sergeant CF (Claude) | 37194 | Fit 11E |
| Hall, Aircraftman First Class FK (Frederick) | 404126 | F/Mech |
| Hall, Leading Aircraftman FT (Frank) | 401022 | Fit 11E |
| Hall, Aircraftman First Class RL (Reginald) | 401124 | Fit 11A |
| Hallins, Aircraftman First Class WJ (William) | 412066 | ACH/GD |
| Hargreaves, Leading Aircraftman WD (Des) | 402768 | F/Mech |
| Hart, Leading Aircraftman FE (Frank) | 40387 | ACH/GD |
| Hawtin, Leading Aircraftman AE (Alfred) | 37153 | Fit 11A |
| Helmore, Leading Aircraftman JO (Johnny) | 402640 | Fit 11E |
| Herbert, Corporal BR (Bruce) | 438015 | Fit 11E |
| Hill, Aircraftman First Class CG (Claude) | 40390 | ACH/GD |
| Hocken, Leading Aircraftman GK (Geoff) | 401001 | Fit 11E |
| Hooper, Aircraftman First Class EC (Eric) | 391458 | ACH/GD |
| Howard-Taylor, Sergeant W (Bill) | 39850 | Fit 11E |
| Howell, Aircraftman Second Class FA (Frank) | RAF1130716 | F/M(A) |
| Hutchens, Cyril | [No info available] | |
| Innes-Jones, Leading Aircraftman EA (Eric) | 391611 | F/Rig |
| Jackson, Aircraftman First Class A (Arthur) | 403207 | R/Mech |
| Jackson, Leading Aircraftman LJ (Lloyd) | 391995 | Arm |
| Jamieson, Aircraftman First Class R (Robert) | 403698 | F/M |

| Name | Service No. | Trade |
|---|---|---|
| Johnston, Leading Aircraftman RB (Robert) | 401697 | E/A |
| Lang, Aircraftman First Class RJ (Reginald) | 39618 | F/M |
| Law, Leading Aircraftman EH (Errol) | 401650 | Fit 11E |
| Lee, Aircraftman First Class MK (Maurice) | 40830 | Arm |
| Linton, Sergeant JB (Jack) | 40367 | R/Mech |
| McGill-Nutt, Leading Aircraftman GN (Grantham) | 39486 | F/Rig |
| McKay, Leading Aircraftman WNA (William) | 39249 | E/A |
| McKenna, Corporal EF (Edward) | 391057 | ACH/GD |
| Mackie, Leading Aircraftman GM (Gordon) | 39375 | Fit 11E |
| Maher, Corporal S (Stanley) | 391788 | Fit 11A |
| Mahoney, Aircraftman First Class DW (Dennis) | 403185 | F/Rig |
| Maloney, Leading Aircraftman WB (William) | 40796 | W/Opr |
| Mant, Leading Aircraftman JB (Jack) | 40521 | F/Rig |
| Montgomerie, Sergeant IH (Ian) | 36149 | Fit 11A |
| Morgan, Sergeant FJC (Frederick) | 39170 | Fit 11A |
| Moulynox, Sergeant JA (James) | 39257 | Fit 11A |
| Murray, Leading Aircraftman WN (Wally) | 402321 | F/Rig |
| Myers, Aircraftman First Class MR (Maxwell) | 437034 | F/Mech |
| Nelson, Leading Aircraftman HF (Red) | 401892 | F/Mech |
| Newcombe, Corporal RK (Roydon) | 39261 | Arm |
| Newton, Aircraftman First Class MT (Maxwell) | 39404 | Arm |
| Nixon, Leading Aircraftman RER (Robert) | 403400 | F/Mech |
| Norman, Aircraftman First Class AF (Arthur) | 403722 | F/Mech |
| Oakey, Aircraftman First Class VAB (Vernon) | 40835 | Arm |
| O'Connell, Corporal TMA (Thomas) | 38105 | CLK/GD |
| O'May, Aircraftman First Class HM (Harry) | RAF1101285 | F/Mech |
| Ogilvie, Aircraftman First Class RN (Roderick) | 391629 | Fit 11E |
| Palmer, Aircraftman First Class EFJ (Edward) | RAF1199069 | I/Rpr |
| Patterson, Flight Sergeant EH (Eric) | 39193 | F/Arm |
| Patterson, Aircraftman First Class JES (James) | 40580 | F/Rig |
| Payne, Sergeant HA (Herman) | 37215 | F/Arm |
| Payne, Leading Aircraftman SA (Stuart) | 392065 | ACH/GD |
| Pentecost, Leading Aircraftman WR (Wilfred) | 401535 | Fit 11E |
| Pharazyn, Sergeant DH (Dennis) | 39837 | R/Mech |
| Pritchard, Aircraftman First Class GR (George) | RAF1125911 | I/Rpr |
| Ragg, Sergeant EL (Elliot) | 39644 | Eng/Ass |
| Randall, Corporal WA (Clem) | 39853 | Fit 11E |
| Ranson, Aircraftman First Class FG (Frederick) | 391116 | F/Rig |
| Rees, Flight Sergeant J (John) | 37218 | Fit 11E |
| Rhodes, Aircraftman First Class SW (Stanley) | 401024 | F/Rig |
| Robins, Leading Aircraftman JT (John) | 402490 | F/Rig |
| Robinson, Aircraftman Second Class CK (Charles) | RAF1185350 | F/Mech |
| Rough, Aircraftman First Class JL (Len) | 391977 | W/T |
| Rowe, Aircraftman First Class JB (James) | 403238 | W/T |
| Russell, Corporal HC (Henry) | 391586 | Eng/Ass |
| Sager, Leading Aircraftman JH (James) | 401878 | R/Mech |

| | | |
|---|---|---|
| Schultz, Corporal JW (Joseph) | 40440 | ACH/GD |
| Service, Aircraftman Second Class AS (Archie) | RAF1054724 | F/Mech (Killed in action) |
| Sigley, Leading Aircraftman LG (Gordon) | 391142 | R/Mech |
| Smart, Leading Aircraftman S (Stu) | 39386 | Fit 11E |
| Snook, Leading Aircraftman R (Ronald) | 391474 | ACH/GD |
| Southwood, Leading Aircraftman C (Cyril) | RAF614706 | F/Mech |
| St George, Leading Aircraftman RS (Sandy) | 403883 | F/Rig |
| Stoodley, Leading Aircraftman LJ (Leonard) | 401192 | F/Mech |
| Stephenson, Corporal RN (Raymond) | 391119 | Fit 11E |
| Stevenson, Flight Sergeant F (Fred) | 638055 | ACH/GD |
| Stevenson, Aircraftman First Class WE (Walter) | 39282 | Arm |
| Stewart, Aircraftman First Class HC (Hugh) | RAF1076933 | I/Rpr |
| Stringer, Aircraftman First Class DH (Donald) | 40841 | Arm |
| Swallow, Leading Aircraftman FH (Frank) | 39390 | Fit 11A |
| Thompson, Corporal DF (Donald) | 402629 | CLK/GD |
| Thompson, Leading Aircraftman HG (Harry) | 411659 | R/Mech |
| Thompson, Leading Aircraftman LD (Lindsay) | 391026 | ACH/GD |
| Treanor, Leading Aircraftman DA (Douglas) | 401530 | F/Mech |
| Tutty, Leading Aircraftman CH (Cuthbert) | 40450 | ACH/GD |
| Underwood, Leading Aircraftman VM (Vernon) | 404286 | F/Arm |
| Vyle, Leading Aircraftman AL (Albert) | 391909 | Arm |
| Wahlberg, Leading Aircraftman NP (Norman) | 391256 | Fit 11A |
| Weckesser, Aircraftman First Class DW (Daniel) | 403748 | F/Rig |
| Welch, Leading Aircraftman WD (William) | 392081 | ACH/GD |
| Wells, Leading Aircraftman SW (Sydney) | 405726 | F/Rig |
| Welsh, Corporal TL (Thomas) | 391647 | Fit 11A |
| West, Leading Aircraftman EJ (Ted) | 39329 | Fit 11E |
| White, Leading Aircraftman AE (Albert) | 40212 | ACH/GD |
| Whitehouse, Leading Aircraftman BG (Brian) | 391080 | ACH/GD |
| Wilson, Aircraftman First Class DE (Douglas) | 40456 | ACH/GD |
| Wright, Aircraftman First Class RJ (Robert) | 40456 | Elect |
| Yanovich, Sergeant IT (Ivan) | 39301 | Arm (Killed in action) |

Note: There was considerable crossing over of groundcrew from and to other squadrons based at Kallang. The lack of aircraft in the final days meant redistribution of personnel to assist where they could to keep the remaining aircraft fit for action. Hence some of the above personnel may not have been part of the original complement of 488 Squadron that arrived from New Zealand and some that may have been seconded to the squadron may not show on the list at all.

# Notes

**Introduction**
1   From the memoirs of Bert Clayton.

**Chapter 2: An introduction to the East**
1   From account by ex-488 Squadron member Bernard Grindrod (Australian National Archives).

**Chapter 3: The struggle to become operational**
1   Although it is still common practice to use the identification of Japanese aircraft as made by the RAF at the time, it has become apparent that there were never any true Zero fighters over Malay or Singapore at the time of the campaign. Practically all the fighters who met over the Malay/Singapore area during the December 1941/February 1942 period were the Army Type 97 or Type 1 Fighters, later given the Allied codenames 'Nate' and 'Oscar', respectively. They are also referred to as Nakajima Ki-27 and Ki-43, although these 'Ki-number' names were not known by Allied intelligence until much later in the war. Japanese Navy bombers were sometimes seen over Malaya/Singapore during the campaign, in addition to Japanese Army types such as the Type 99 Light Bomber (later known as 'Lily'), and the Type 97 Heavy Bomber ('Sally'), also known as Kawasaki Ki-48 and Mitsubishi Ki-21. No Navy fighters were ever present. This has come as a major shock to many who served with the Allies, as they were told at the time that the single-engined Japanese fighters with retractable undercarriages were Zeros, or 'Navy noughts', and that was that. It was not until decades after the war had ended that the RAF came to accept that this was so.

**Chapter 4: The arrival of the storm**
1   See Masanobu Tsuji, *Singapore: The Japanese Version*.
2   See Peter Elphick and Michael Smith, *Odd Man Out*.
3   Information gained from several sources including JD Balfe, *War Without Glory* and Peter Elphick, *Singapore: The Pregnable Fortress*.
4   A copy of the ditty was kindly given to me by Barbara Kuhn.

**Chapter 6: The end draws near**
1   Comment made by Bunt Pettit during the course of an interview given to Mary Lambie, Researcher for the New Zealand Defence Force.
2   Comment taken from Arthur Donahue, *Last Flight From Singapore*.
3   Comment taken from Terence Kelly, *Hurricane Over the Jungle*.

**Chapter 9: Of those that were left behind**
1   Letter from Wing Commander T Hugh Nichols, dated 17 September 1945, from archives written in Batavia.
2   Letter from Officer Commanding Liang POW Camp on the island of Ambon from Archives.
3   This account is from the COFEPOW website (Children of Far East Prisoners of War: www.cofepow.org.uk) as compiled by Dennis Couran.
4   From Allan Jones, *The Suez Maru Atrocity: Justice Denied*.

# Bibliography

**Manuscripts and archives**

'488 Squadron Official History 19/09/41 to 02/03/42', author unknown, typed version of handwritten diary, Air Force Museum, Christchurch, File No. 88/271.1.

Annabell, Ross, 'The Death of a Squadron', newspaper article, Air Force Museum, Christchurch, Archives.

Gifford, Peter, 'History of 488 Squadron', article, Air Force Museum, Christchurch, Archives.

Grindrod, Bernard, 'The Singapore Debacle: a personal account', Department of Premier & Cabinet, Australian Government Archives.

**Newspapers and periodicals**

Hutcheson, John, 'The fall of Singapore', *Sport Flying*. (Extract from personal diary notes published in serial form.)

Maas, Jim, 'Fall From Grace: the Brewster Aeronautical Corporation 1932–42', *American Aviation Historical Society Journal*, Summer 1985, p. 118.

**Reports**

Capon, Captain Selwyn, *The Escape of S.S. Empire Star from Singapore*. Official Report to the Blue Star Line, 7 March 1942.

Maltby, Air Vice Marshall Sir Paul, *Report on Air Operations during the Malayan Campaign*, British Government Official Report, February 1948.

**Unpublished material**

Atkinson, Jeremy, Notes regarding the demise of his father.

Boyd, Max, Diary notes.

Clayton, Albert Lionel Mark, Personal memoirs.

Cromie, James Alfred, 'Diary of an Ulsterman in the Pacific'.

Hargreaves, Woolford Desmond (Des), Extract from handwritten diary notes sent by Jack Mant to Max Boyd (1988).

Hutcheson, John, Personal diary notes.

Pettit, Harold S, Personal papers and memoirs.

**Books**

Angelucci, Enzo and Peter Bowers, *The American Fighter*, Orion 1985.

Balfe, JD, *War Without Glory*, Macmillan, Melbourne, 1984.

Barber, Noel, *Sinister Twilight: The Fall of Singapore*, Cassel, 2002.

—— *The Singapore Story*, Fontana, 1978.

Bentley, Geoffrey, *RNZAF: A Short History*, AH & AW Reed, 1969.

Brooke, Geoffrey, *Singapore's Dunkirk*, Leo Cooper, London, 1989.

Chapman, Spencer, *The Jungle is Neutral*, Times Books International, 1948.

Clisby, Mark, *Guilty or Innocent: The Gordon Bennett Case*, Allen & Unwin, 1992.

Cull, Brian, *Buffaloes Over Singapore*, Grub Street, London, 2003.

—— *Hurricanes Over Singapore*, Grub Street, London, 2004.

Donahue, Arthur, *Last Flight From Singapore*, Macmillan, New York, 1943.

Elphick, Peter, *Singapore: The Pregnable Fortress*, Hodder & Stoughton, 1995.

Elphick, Peter and Michael Smith, *Odd Man Out*, Hodder & Stoughton, London, 1993.

Falk, Stanley L, *Seventy Days to Singapore*, GP Putnam & Sons, New York, 1975.
Field, SE, *Singapore Tragedy*, Oswald–Sealy, Auckland, 1944.
Gough, Richard, *The Escape from Singapore*, William Kimber & Co., London, 1987.
Jones, Allan, *The Suez Maru Atrocity: Justice Denied*, Allan D Jones, Essex, 2002.
Kelly, Terence, *Hurricane over the Jungle*, William Kimber, London, 1977.
—— *Living With Japanese*, Kellan Press, Kent, 1997.
MacIntosh, Jim *The War Diary of a POW*, Mansell Publishing, California, 2000.
Maas, Jim, *F2A Buffalo in Action*, Squadron/Signal Publications, 1987.
Moffatt, Jonathan, *Moon Over Malaya: The Argyll & Sutherland Highlanders*, Tempus Publishing, Gloucestershire, 2002.
Montgomery, Brian, *Shenton of Singapore*, Secker & Warburg, London, 1984.
Morrison, Ian, *Malayan Postscript*, Angus & Robertson Ltd, Sydney, 1943.
Owen, Frank, *The Fall of Singapore*, Penguin, London, 1960.
Rocker, George, *Escaped Singapore Heading Homewards*, Graham Brash, Singapore, 1990.
Ross, Squadron Leader JMS, *Royal New Zealand Air Force, Official History*, Government Printer, Wellington, 1955.
Rudge, Chris, *Air-To-Air*, Adventure Air, 2003.
Shores, Christopher, Brian Cull and Yasuho Izawa, *Bloody Shambles Vol. 1*, Grub Street, London, 1992.
—— *Bloody Shambles Vol. 2*, Grub Street, London, 1993.
Simpson, Ivan, *Singapore: Too Little Too Late*, Leo Cooper, London, 1970.
Smith, Colin, *Singapore Burning*, Penguin, London, 2005.
Taffrail (Captain Taprell Dorling DSO, FRHistS, RN), *Blue Star Line at War, 1939–1945*, W Foulsham, London, 1973.
Thompson, Peter, *The Battle for Singapore*, Portrait, London, 2005.
Tsuji, Masanobu, *Singapore: The Japanese Version*, Ure Smith Pty Ltd, Sydney, 1960.

# Index

Numbers in **bold** refer to photograph pages.

## A

'A' Flight   **72**, 93, 96, **101**, 102, 107, 214, 219
accommodation   25
    Batavia   207–208, 214
    Kallang   **38**, **39**, 39, 124, 134
    Perth   243–47
    Telok Kurau English School   **125**, 125–27, 130
Adcock, 'Johnny', Corporal   12
Adelaide   248
aircraft (see also under aircraft type)   38, 272
    accidents/near misses   37, 64–69, 96, 98, 99, **99**, 135, 158
    fuel   **165**, 165
    in action   96, 97–98, 102–106, 110
    losses   64, 66, 67, 69, 80, 88, 98, **99**, 106, 108, 110, 114, 115, 118,140, 158, 211, 213, 223, 252
    recovery   150–52, 157
    spare parts   51, 62, 63–64, 136, 139, 167, 209
    work on   **57**, **58**, 61–62, 84 86, **100**, 108–9, 136, 138–39
aircrew 488 Squadron   21, **266**
    training (lack of)   8, 25
    withdrawal to Batavia   21, 156–58, 167–69, 178
Airmen's Mess   90
air raid shelters   52, 60, 140–41
    Foxholes   **59**, 60–61, **60**, **61**, 74, 85, 86, 87, 117, 119–23, 128, 132, 150
    Gammons Shelter   120–21, 159
    slit trenches   8, 60, 138
Alor Star   78, 82
Anderson, Andy, Aircraftman   118
Anderson, Margaret, Sister   198
anti-aircraft guns   **60**, 61, 67, 74, 89, 91, 97, 179

ANZAC Club   47, **48**, **49**, 117
Appleby, 'Spike', Leading Aircraftman   **57**
Arden, Leo, Leading Aircraftman   244
Argyll and Sutherland Highlanders   164, 176–8, 187, 191
armaments/ammunition   52
      coastal defence guns   149
      faults/failures   113
arrival in Singapore   29, 35–38
Ashley-Jones, Herb, Leading Aircraftman   150
Atkinson, Captain TKW RN   13, 257
*Atlantis*   74–77
attitude towards those who escaped   15, 20–21, 200, 201
Australia, threat to   9, 11, 17, 157, 209, 221
Australian troops   80, 162, 166, 251
      deserters   177, 185–86, 188–90, 204, 257
      groundcrew walk-out   81–82
*Automedon* SS   76–77

# B

'B' Flight   6, 95, 215
Batavia, defence of   208–224
blame for defeat   6–8, 11, 149, 185, 250–52
Boddy, Jim, Leading Aircraftman   **43**, 45, **147**, **217**
*Boutkae*, SS   38
Boyd, Max   13, 52, 84, 97, 107, 117, 124, 128, 132, 134, 159, 161, 165–66, 191, 214, 215, 240, 245, 251
Brewster Buffaloes   7, 8, 28, **36**, 36–37, 38, 51–57, **52**, **56–57**, **58**, **59**, **62**, **63**, 65, **75**, **78**, **84**, **96**, **100**, **101**, **106**, **107**, 114, 143, **217**
      and altitude   54, 86, 87, 106
      in dives   110
      interrupter gear   55, 103
      shortcomings   54–56, 100, 105–106, 108, 109–110
      spare parts   51, 58, 62, 63–64, 130, 136, 150
British officers, attitude to 'colonials'   109–110, 133, 139, 165, 207, 215, 244, 251

Brooke-Popham, Sir Robert  8, 68
Brooker, Richard  **167**
Buitenzorg  208, 210, 213, 215
Bukit Timah  31
Burnell, Ken, Aircraftman  37
Burton, Jack, Sergeant  **37**, **102**, **266**

C

Cameron, Col, Leading Aircraftman  **61**, **238**
Capon, Captain Selwyn N. OBE  173, **175**, 187, 189, 195–9, 204, 259–63, 265
Carpentier Oleting school  208, 215
Carter, Flight Lieutenant  182
Chadwick, Pat, Leading Aircraftman  184
Chandler, Andy, Flight Sergeant  **62**, 62–64, 91, 92, 137, 151, 161, 180, 237, **239**, 256
Changi Prison  18, 229
Charters, Deryck, Sergeant  **37**, **115**, 115, 228, **266**
Chignell, Wing Commander  90, 255
Christmas 1941  90–1, **92–93**, **94–95**
'Churchill Supplies'  79–80, 252
Churchill, Winston  71, 74, 144, 185
civilians
    casualties  78, 103, 117, 127, 133, 134
    Javanese, death of  225
    massacre of Chinese civilians  181–82
    workers  31, **43**, **44**, 139, 157
Clancy, George  **43**, **49**, **57**, **110**, **156**, **238**, 246
class distinctions  8, 11, 33, 47–49, 58, 151
Clayton, Bert  15–20, **16**, 22, **23**, **27**, 44, **49**, **60**, 61, 70, 87, 88–89, 98, 110–11, 115, 123, **125**, 139, 151, 164, **179**, 179–84, **202**, **239**, **240**, 245, 246, 249, 259
climate  28, 31–32, **34**, 40–41, 46, 62, 66, 110, 152, 216
Clouston, Wilf, Squadron Leader DFC  35–36, **36**, 43, 57, 58, 63, 83, 88, 90, 91, 92, 98, 114, 127, 129, 135, 150, 161, 178–79, 184, 201, 252–54, **266**

Clow, Don, Sergeant   **37**, **109**, 118, 132, **266**
communications (equipment)   53, 62, 69, 98, 211
Cottrill, George, Aircraftman   196, 259, 261
Cox, Tony, Pilot Officer   **37**, 67, 94, 102, 114, **266**
Craig, Alexander, Sergeant   88–9, **266**
Cromie, Jim 'Paddy', Aircraftman   12, 82, 117, 119, 128, 132, 138, 195, 219

**D**
'Daisy Cutter' bombs   133
*Danae*, HMS   157
Dawson, Joseph Lindon   195, 264
Delap, Jim   119, 219
de Maus, 'Bunny', Sergeant   95, **96**, 150, **266**
Denham, Douglas, Aircraftman   219–20
de Suza, Ernie, Flying Officer   27, **201**, **202**, 215, 245
*Deucalion*, MV   237–41, **238**, 243, **245**
Dodd, John   190
Donahue, Art   154–55, 158, 167–71
dispersal areas   60, 69, **70**, 77, 97, **112**, 151, **206**, **216**
Dunkirk   6, 178
Dunn, Bert, Aircraftman   **43**, **49**, **87**, 87–88
*Durban*, HMS   193
Dutch aircraft/crew   52, 64–65, 90, 91, 95, 96, 108, 112, 116, 227

**E**
Elliot, Paul Lester 'Shorty' Sergeant   100
*Empire Star*, MV   21, **172**, **198**, **202**, 246, 257–58
    arrival in Singapore   173–74
    Australian deserters   177, 185, 204, 257
    Australian nurses   **186**, 187, 192, 194, 198–200, 259
    awards to crew   204, 264–65
    embarkation   184–89
    journey to Java   191–205, **200–202**
    loss   262–63
*Empress of Asia*, MV   144, 176, 192

Esperance Bay  **243**, 248
*Exeter*, HMS  237, 239

**F**
Farr, Len, Pilot Officer  65, 66, **100**, **102**, 118, **128**, 128, 129, **266**
Felton, Pilot Officer WWG  96
Fenwick, Herb, Aircraftman  246
Fisken, Geoff  111
Fitzgerald, 'Fitz' Aircraftman  **43**, 151
food
      Batavia  214, 215, 224, 226–67
      *Empire Star*  175, 187, 189, 199, 201–202, **202**
      Kallang  39–42, 46, 84, 147
      Perth  243, 244
      *Tasman*  26, 28
Force Z  82–84
Foreman, 'Judge'  91
Foster, Murray, Flying Officer  255
Franks, Cecil, Flying Officer  64, 91, 93, 94, 256
Friend, Bob, Aircraftman  **49**

**G**
'Galloping Gertie'  90
Geylang  69, 124, 138
Gifford, Pete, Pilot Officer  **37**, 65, 66, 102, 110, **112**, 113, **140**, 150, 151, 152, **266**
Gillatt, Ray, Aircraftman  37
Godsiff, Jack, Pilot Officer  **37**, 67, **70**, 98, 102, **266**
Green, Eddie  187
Greening, Bob  **266**
Greenhalgh, Wally  **102**, 148, **150**, **266**
Grindrod, Bernard  41, 43–44, 136, 150, 197
groundcrew 488 Squadron  21, 250
      Australia  241–48
      Batavia  207–217
      deal with Wilf Clouston  161, 178, 252–55

escape from Singapore   180–205
escape from Batavia   **236**, 237–41, **238–39**, **240**, **241**
Japanese approaching   150, 165–71, 253
left behind   21, 145–47, **156**, 161, 170–71, 178, 250, 252
praise for   8, 58, 93, 132, 164, 168, 252
relationship with aircrew   48, 106–107, 116, 137, 157
return to New Zealand   15–16, 248
weapons   166, 183, 184, 207, 246
Guiniven, Stan, Sergeant   62–63, 120–21, 132, 165, **201**, 237, **239**
Gurkha Guard Company   61

# H

Halkett, Sergeant Claude   152
Hall, Nobby, Aircraftman   **49**, **61**, **238**
Hall, F, Aircraftman   217
Hall, Reg, Aircraftman   **49**, **63**, **147**
Hamilton, Margaret   199
Happy World   42, 97, 124–25, **126**
Hargreaves, Des, Leading Aircraftman   **59**, **60**, 89, 110, 134, 166, 214
Harvards   38, 56
health problems   27, 41, 226, 228, 244
Helmore, Johnny, Leading Aircraftman   **238**, **240**
Herbert, Bruce, Corporal   **43**, **102**
Hesketh, GL 'Butch', Pilot Officer   **70**, 70, 90, 101, 107, 110
Hocken, Geoff, Leading Aircraftman   **165**, **238**
Honan, Terry, Sergeant   **37**, 65, 66, 67, 90, 105, **106**, **266**
Hooper Eric, Aircraftman   37
Howard-Taylor, Bill, Sergeant   **165**, **171**
Howell, Frank, Aircraftman   119, 255
Hudsons   80–81, 116, 251
Hurricanes   107, 116, 127–29, 130–31, **130**, **134**, **137**, 140, **141**, 143, 148, 152, 164, **167**, 208, 220
Hutcheson, John R ('Hutch'), Flight Lieutenant   6–8, **7**, 12, 35–37, **37**, 38, **50**, 56, 67–68, 69, 74, 82, 90, 91, 92, 98, 102, 105–106, 114, 117, 128, 132, 139, 140, 143, 155, 156, 157, 210–13, 215, 244, 256, **266**
Hutcheson, Mike   6, 12

Index   279

## I

Insects, snakes and creepy-crawlies   39, 43, 46, **110**, 110

## J

Japanese   **163**
    artillery   143, 151, 160, 169
    bombing attacks   74–75, 77, 84, 86, 96, 97, 111, 112, 117, 118, 119–25, 128–29, 130–31, **130–31**, 143–44, 146, 150, 156, 159, 160, 174, 194–98, 211, 253
    entry into war   73–74, 76–77
    'recco' plane   86–87, 89, 91, 135, 165, 168
    reconnaissance   68–69, 78, 154, 168–69, 194
Johnstone, Frank, Pilot Officer   37, **102**, 112, 151, **155**, 156, **266**
Julian, Flight Lieutenant   164

## K

Kallang Airfield   **7**, **29**, 42, 45, 52, 58, **60**, 66, 83, 84–85, 88, **104**, 128–29, 135
    destruction   120–25, **122**, 124, 130–31, **130–31**, 132, 134, 137, 139, 143, 147, **147**, 148, **148**, **150**, 154, 159–60, 163, **171**
Katong   117, 137, **138**, 138
Kawashima, Staff Officer   144
*Kedah*, HMS   193–94
Kelly, Sergeant Terence   168, 227
Keppel Harbour   **24**, 29, 35, 173–74, **184**, 258
Kigensetsu   164, 166
Killick, Perce, Sergeant   37, **102**, 105, **106**, **266**
Kiwi resourcefulness   51, 52, 58, 64, 136
Kluang Aerodrome   37, 38
Kranji War Memorial   129, 249
Kuhn, Eddie   13, **37**, 45, 65, 69, **70**, 93, **102**, 111, **111**, 118, 132, 148, **218**, 219–20, 223, 224–25, 226, 228–30, 231, 256, **266**

## L

Law, Errol, Leading Aircraftman   **238**
Layton, Don   220

leisure activities   29, 42, **45**, 45, 47, 90–91, 97, 117, 158
Llewellyn, Squadron Leader   **137**, 158

## M

Malaya (map)   **79**
Maltby, Air Vice Marshal   164, 250
McAneny, Jack, Pilot Officer   45, 52, 65, 105, **115**, 115, **266**
MacIntosh, Jim, Sergeant   13, 38, 52, 75, **75**, 78, 89, **102**, 105, 140, **218**, 219, 220–23, 226, 228, 231, 256, **266**
Mackenzie, John N 'Mac' DFC, Flight Lieutenant   35–37, 38, 56, 64, 69, **72**, 75, 82, 84, 87, **87**, 88, 90, 92, 101, **101**, 102, 105, 108, 116, 117, 127, 145, 158–59, 208–210, 214, 254, **266**
MacMillan, Rod, Sergeant   105, **266**
mail from home   45–46, **60**
Malayan airfields, fall of   80–82
Maloney, 'Red', Leading Aircraftman   117
Manhire, Squadron Leader   247
Mant, Jack 'Hopper', Leading Aircraftman   **58**, 118, 134, 166, **217**
massacre of Chinese civilians   18, 181–82
Meaclem, Vern, Sergeant   **37**, 106, **266**
Meharry, Jack, Sergeant   **37**, 45, 65, **66**, 66, 90, 116, 140, 210, 213
Montgomerie, Ian, Sergeant   45, **201**
Moss, Eric, Captain   177, 187
Murray, Wally, Leading Aircraftman   165–66, 183

## N

NAAFI   41–42, 46, 90, 124, 134
Nelson, Hugh 'Red', Leading Aircraftman   12, 169, 191, 205, 221, 240
Netherlands East Indies forces – *see* Dutch
Newcombe, Squib, Corporal   117
New Zealand, threat to   9, 11, 17, 20, 157, 209, 221
Nixon, Robbie, Leading Aircraftman   **59**, 60, **144**

## O

Oakden, Jack, Pilot Officer   70, **70**, 108, 156, 157, **218**, 219, 226, 228, 231–32, 256

Oakey, Vern, Aircraftman   151
O'May, Harry, Aircraftman   **60**, 119, 134, 137–38, 166
Ozawa, Admiral   200–201, 258

**P**

Palembang   116, 145–46, 148, 164, 167, 210, 254
Patterson, Eric, Flight Sergeant   91, 134, 166
Pentecost, Wilf, Leading Aircraftman   **238**
*Perak*   145–46
Perth   213, 243–47
Pettit, Harry 'Bunt', Pilot Officer   13, **37**, 91, 94, **102**, **104**, 105, 132, 157, 209, **218**, 219, 220, 223, 224–25, 226, 230–31, 232, 256, **266**
Pharazyn, Dennis, Sergeant   70
Phillips, Admiral Sir Tom   82–84
*Prince of Wales*, HMS   82–84, 88, 149, 177, 252
prisoners of war   10, 13, 18, 146, 204, 226–35, 256
Pritchard, George, Aircraftman   119
Pukka sahib (attitude)   9, 32, 42, 44, 251
Pulford, Air Vice Marshal   164

**R**

RAF No. 67 Squadron   36–37, 51, 256
RAF No. 232 Squadron   107, 115, 128, 140, 145, 151–52, 154, 156, 158, 161, 164, 167, 168, 197, 209, 210, 214, 219
RAF No. 243 Squadron   52, 67, 68, 69, 70, 93, 99, 100, 111, 116, 119, 125, 127, 131, 152, 256
RAF No. 605 Squadron   209–210, 219–20, 222–27
RAF No. 488 Squadron   **27**
   disbanded   19, 20, 243
   formed   21, 38
Randall, Clem, Corporal   12, 39, **60**, 65, 67, 97, 119, 120–21, 124, 132, **134**, 137, **144**, 152, 180
Rees, John, Flight Sergeant   45, 93, 151, 152, 256
*Repulse*, HMS   82–84, 88, 96, 149, 177, 252
return to base after incidents   108, 113, 114, 115, 151, 212–13, 223

Rhodes, Stan 'Dusty', Aircraftman   166
Rongotai Aerodrome 2   2, 25

**S**
Selarang Barracks   18
Seletar airfield   31, 45, 51, 64, 67, 103, 113, 118, 128, 135, 137, 143, 150, 152, 154, 157, 167, 189
Sembawang airfield   31, 113, 143, 151
    Naval base   31, 71, 82, **143**, 144, 147–48, 175
Service, Archie, Aircraftman   **60**, 118–9
Sharp, Noel, Pilot Officer   45, 65, 69, 78, **78**, **84**, 90, 91, 113, 148, 210, 212, **218**, 219, 221, 222–23, 256, **266**
Siglap   18, 182
Sigley, Gordon, Leading Aircraftman   **63**
Sikh Indian army troops   44, **44**, 61, 139
Singapore   **24**, **30**, 47
    pre–invasion   9, 31–33
    1950s   10, 18–19
    surrender to the Japanese   9, 17, 208
Singora   83
Smart, Stu, Leading Aircraftman   12, **57**, 113–14, 123, 147, 169, 195, **238**
St George Sandy, Leading Aircraftman   119, 121
'Stay behinds'   **218**, 218–35
Stephenson, Ray, Corporal   **39**, **156**, **165**, **238**, **241**
Stewart, Hugh   119
Stewart, Second Lieutenant   197
Stringer, Donald, Aircraftman   261
*Suez Maru*   13, 233–35, 256

**T**
Tanjong Priok   202, 238, 257
*Tasman*, SS   25–29, **26**, **27**, 35, 37
Telok Kurau English School   125, 126–27, 181–82
Tengah airfield   31, 139, 143, 152
Tjilatjap   221, 234

Tjililitan  **206**, 208, **216**, 221, 256
Torney, Sister Veronica  198
training (and lack of)  53, 62, 64–65, 69, 70, 128, 146, 166, 252
Tsuji, Masanobu  68, 78, 143
Type 97 aircraft  111, 116
Type 100 aircraft  91

## U
uniform, clothing  28, 43–44, **43**, 245, 247

## W
Watts, Group Captain  156–57
Wavell, General  162
Weckesser, Don. Aircraftman  **58**
West, Ted, Leading Aircraftman  12, 126, 180, **238**
White, Grahame 'Snow', Pilot Officer  37, 65, 67, **102**, 105, 148, **218**, 219, 223, 224, 226, 231, 232–35, 256
Wirraways  65
Woolridge, Captain  189, 191
work ethic  42, 51, 58, 62, 87
working conditions  39, 70, 84, 86
Wright, Squadron Leader  222

## Y
Yamashita, General Tomoyuki  17, 68, 162, 164, 250–51
Yanovich, Sergeant  123, 166

## Z
Zero aircraft  61, 105, 106, 114, 221, 252, 272

Hobsonville Air Force Station holds a unique place in RNZAF history as the only station to have been built primarily for seaplanes. From the early days of aviation, it served the Air Force well in times of both war and peace. This is a lively social history of the station and its people — from commanding officers and their wives to the gardeners and aircraftmen.

Bee Dawson is a social historian who delights in bringing Air Force history to life. She has a firm belief that 'it's not just about the aircraft'. This is her third book on RNZAF history.